Grow
It
Indoors

Illustrations by Susan McNeill

New York

GROW IT INDOORS

A Practical, Personal How-to and Why Guide
to Growing Successful Houseplants

Richard W. Langer

Saturday Review Press/E. P. Dutton & Co., Inc.

Portions of "Bottling Your Plants" originally appeared in *Family Circle* under the title "Great Idea: Gardening in a Bottle," copyright © 1973 by Richard W. Langer.

Library of Congress Cataloging in Publication Data

Langer, Richard W
Grow it indoors.

Bibliography: p.
1. House plants. I. Title.
SB419.L35 1975   635.9'65   74–17261

Published simultaneously in Canada by Clarke, Irwin & Company Limited, Toronto and Vancouver
ISBN: 0-8415-0357-5
Designed by The Etheredges

For Tant Astrid, whose acres of wild flowers I roamed, and Tant Gunhild, in whose splendid gardens I played hide-and-seek, and in memory of Tant Elin, whose regal manners during afternoon tea in the greenhouse well suited her patent Florist by Appointment to the King of Sweden—and awed my young child's mind. All of them taught me to appreciate plants in different ways.

Contents

CONTENTS

HOW TO USE THIS BOOK

Growing houseplants is for me one of the most pleasant diversions there is. It's a relaxing form of puttering, neither strenuous nor stultifying, that has all but disappeared from twentieth-century life. As the fingers play, the mind wanders on, problems are solved, dreams are spun, minor worries and cares seem somehow to become buried. And that's the reason for this book. Just remember as you read it—diversity is the way of things in horticulture. Rarely is there only one right way to make a plant thrive. That's part of the fun of growing things.

If you're just starting out with plants, you'll find the most common ones are usually so because they are the easiest to grow. But I've put the chapter covering most of them, "Easier Than Plastic," in the middle of the book in the hope that you'll be tempted by all the other green and flowering wonders as you thumb your way through. Should there already be plants gracing your windowsill, perhaps you'll decide to broaden your pastures after reading the chapter on palms, which are really rather trouble-free, or indoor roses, or the fragrant plants.

The plants in this book are listed by their Latin names for the sake of clarity. I have also included as many popular names as I can find, and by using the index you should be able to locate the plant you want under any of its everyday names. The reason for consistently adhering to the plants' formal names is that the popular ones can be very confusing. Sansevieria, for instance, is known as mother-in-law's tongue, supposedly because it is just as sharp. Dieffenbachia is known as mother-in-law's tongue, too, because the poisonous crystals from its sap will, quite literally, temporarily paralyze any tongue to which they are applied. If you ask a grower for mother-in-law's tongue, you may get a sansevieria or you may get a dieffenbachia. If you ask for sansevieria, that's the plant you'll get. Of course you should specify the species as well, but more of that in the back of the book, where there is a brief nomenclature section for the curious.

If you look up a plant in the index and turn to the corresponding page, scanning the few words under the heading "microclimate" for that plant will tell you exactly what general growing conditions are necessary for it to thrive. Any special pamperings and/or potential problems are covered in the paragraph beneath.

For instance, concerning temperature requirements (given throughout the book in degrees Fahrenheit), plants fall into one of three categories, as follows:

WARM	60°–65° F at night
TEMPERATE	50°–55° F at night
COOL	40°–45° F at night

Note that the range is given in average night temperatures. These are the temperatures recommended for the plant for most nights of the year, say from fall through late spring. Obviously there will be deviations from week to week. Daytime temperature can go as much as thirty degrees higher. Night temperature is traditionally used as the base line in horticulture, because this is the time the plants are at rest and also when they are most likely to become cold damaged. Additionally, it's usually a more constant factor. If you're not normally up at 2:00 A.M. with a thermometer in hand, you can buy an inexpensive maximum-minimum thermometer. Hang it by the window, and it will automatically record the lowest night temperature for that location. Or you can settle for something much less exact: a good guess. Most homes fall into the warm or temperate range. Plants listed for these categories should do well as long as they have the right amount of light.

The energizer of all plant life is sunlight. Within limits, the more of it the better. The limits are delineated by the three categories of light listed under "microclimate" for each plant.

The amount of sunlight from any of the four exposures varies tremendously, not only because of obstructions like trees or adjacent buildings, which can make a southern window darker than most northern ones, but also through the physical location of your home. A house or apartment in southern California, for instance, may well get more sunlight through its northern windows in any given month than similar windows with southern exposure in a Vermont house. For this reason the microclimate descriptions that follow are based on the number of hours of sunlight during the summer. That is, any area in your home that receives two to three hours of sunlight in summer is suitable for the group of plants demanding partial sun, even if the area gets no direct sunlight during the winter. The plants will adjust automatically to the reduced light intensity and rest in that season, becoming healthier and stronger for the next year's burst of growth and bloom—another way in which plants bring pleasure to your home, their cyclical growth brings the cycle of the seasons indoors.

SUN	A sunny south window, but the plants will also do well in an unobstructed east or west window. Essentially these plants need *a minimum of five hours of direct sunlight a day during the summer.* For the most part they are not at their best under artificial light unless it is both intense and on for sixteen hours or more each day.
PARTIAL SUN	An east or west window, or a north window that gets some direct sun during part of the year. Essentially these plants need *a minimum of two to three hours of somewhat diffused sunlight a day during the summer.* Most grow well under artificial light.
SHADE	A north window, or away from the windowsill at another window, where the light is bright but direct sunlight is almost nonexistent. The plants will also do well under artificial light of not particularly great intensity such as that often found in offices.

The other two factors affecting your houseplants' well-being are the type of soil they are grown in and the way the soil is watered. Traditionally, potting soil is broken down into three categories: loamy, humusy, and sandy. Making the right one is easy; recipes are given later in the book.

Watering, that most inexact of all horticultural sciences, is usually done by feel. Most plants either like their soil constantly moist (but not wet) or prefer soil allowed to dry out (but not to go really bone dry) between waterings. Under the "microclimate" heading for each plant, you'll find the notation "kept constantly moist" or "left to dry between waterings." The key in watering is good drainage. With it you'll be hard pressed to overwater a plant that needs constant moisture, for the excess will drain out. Even so, remember moist is not wet.

This book is arranged with a listing of the plants first to help you make your selection, followed by a second section on their care to assure that they remain healthy and happy. Although the book can easily be read from beginning to end, it isn't necessary to do that. Read it in the order that suits you best. Did someone give you a palm tree for your birthday? Then start with "Palms in the Parlor." Are you considering buying that gorgeous flowering bromeliad in the plant store window? Then peruse "Carl Olaf Bromel's Bounty" first. Do you already have some plants, and do they in turn have little fuzzy white things all over them? Turn straight to the back of the book and check "Pets, Pests, and Other Problems." Or perhaps you never realized how fascinating cacti can be and how relatively easy some orchids are to tame. Whichever plant grabs your fancy, try not to buy a lot of specimens from one group when you're just starting out. Get one of the easy cacti, a palm, a fern, a begonia. . . . See how you and they get along. If it turns out you're absolute death on ferns, stay away from them awhile and concentrate on other plants.

Wherever you start, remember growing plants is an art, not a science; pleasure, not work. There are no such things as hard-and-fast rules, only general ideas that you can take, modify, and build on. Above all, get to know your plants. It not only makes growing them easy, but also because there's so much variety in plant life, familiarity with their individual ways makes for more fun.

The Plants

Palms
in the Parlor

Would you believe an eight-hundred-year-old palm tree some hundred-odd feet tall, whose pelvis-shaped nuts, weighing over forty pounds each, sell for ten thousand dollars—and the whole botanical Rube Goldberg growing underwater? The coco de mer has had at one time or another all these attributes except the last, and even its underwater habitat was sincerely believed in for decades.

The proper name of the coco de mer is *Lodoicea maldivica*, although, consistent with its other quirks, the palm does not grow on the Maldive islands after which it was named. The nomenclature came about because a seventeenth-century botanical explorer by the name of Rumphius kept bumping into floating coco de mer in the currents coming from the Maldives and made the simple assumption, later proved rash, that they grew where they appeared to be coming from.

The propensity for floating around was responsible for the coco de mer's reputation as a submersible palm. For centuries half-empty nuts had drifted up on the shores of the Indian Ocean. (Unlike the common coconut, a coco de mer is too heavy to float until most of it has rotted out.) Since no one had actually glimpsed the trees from which the nuts

came, the conclusion was obvious: they must grow under the sea somewhere. Supposedly on a clear day they could be seen distinctly—until
you dove in after them, at which point they vanished.

As with so many botanical oddities, people were convinced that the
mysterious coco de mer nut was an aphrodisiac. Its shape, remarkably
like that of a female pelvis, did little to dispel the idea. Along with the
other exotic novelties brought home by sixteenth-century European explorers, it became a prized possession of royalty. The Hapsburg ruler
Rudolf II offered four thousand gold florins for one, back in the days
when a florin was worth a florin. The particular nut in question, which
incidentally Rudolf II did not acquire, belonged to Admiral Wolfert
Hermanssen of the Royal Dutch Navy, who received it from the Sultan
of Bantam in Java as a token of thanks for helping to stave off the Por-
tuguese.

Then in 1768 the bottom fell out of the coco de mer market. A
French engineer by the name of Barré was surveying the island of
Praslin in the Seychelles and came across a whole valley filled with the
palms. Shortly thereafter coco de mer nuts flooded India and began to
make their way to Europe with some frequency. Still a bit dear, but not
something you'd give your kingdom for anymore.

Although a few stands have been planted in other parts of the world,
L. maldivica is endemic only to its native Seychelles. Guesswork has it
that the palm's very limited distribution is a product of its not exactly
manageably sized seed. Sometime back in geologic history when the
granitic Seychelles were left stranded in mid-ocean as the continents
drifted apart, the coco de mer was left isolated on the islands. Many
species of plants became extinct at that time, and it was probably only
a fluke that these palms continued to thrive where they did. The date
palm was equally isolated in its origins somewhere in India before man
disseminated its more easily transported seeds into almost every corner
of the world where it could survive.

Of course, germination can also be a problem for the coco de mer.
Not only is germination sporadic away from the native islands, but once
a nut does sprout, after nine months or so, it needs lots of room. So
that the new palm doesn't grow directly under the mother tree, and because even the marvelous Seychelles don't have six-foot squirrels to carry
the heavy nut around, it sends out a long ropelike projection that worms
along underground six to twelve feet before surfacing to form a new tree.
The seedling remains attached to the seed by this lifeline for several
years before it is able to grow on its own.

Of the few remaining stands of coco de mer, most are still to be found on the island of Praslin, where the Seychelles government in 1948 wisely created a sanctuary. Despite the reserve set aside for them, the question remains, What will be lost to future mankind if this palm becomes extinct? Perhaps nothing. Perhaps as much as a cancer cure. In terms of world agriculture, the palm family as a whole is second in importance only to the grasses, yielding, besides the edible seeds and fruits, sugar, oils, waxes, and fibers. The coco de mer, as a unique plant, represents a genetic and biosystematic bank that could, just possibly could, become an amazing biologic resource.

After all that, sad to say, while I'm convinced the coco de mer could be grown successfully in any thirteen-by-thirteen-foot granite-lined living room—for coconuts, which are similar in their horticultural requirements, do very well in our New York City apartment with little care—the real problem is getting those big pelvis-shaped seeds. Oh well, a palm in the parlor is worth two on the beach.

UP UP AND AWAY

Palms are unusual trees. Morphologically they are related to lilies by their flower structure. As monocots—that is, plants having a single seed leaf—they are in a sense giant-sized grass. Their flowering habits are not particularly important to the indoor grower, since the chance of bringing a potted house palm into bloom is slim indeed. But the fact that they are monocots has a direct bearing on how you treat them. As much as you may have heard about pinching back or trimming off the growing tip of a plant to make it lush and bushy, you can't try it with a palm or you'll have no palm left.

Unlike temperate trees, whose trunks grow simultaneously in thickness and height, most palms grow at a single aboveground point, the terminal bud. If you've ever eaten palm cabbage, it was this tender young bud you tasted. You also in effect devoured a whole tree, since once the terminal bud is removed the tree is dead.

Because they usually have only one growing point, palms have a strange way of reaching maturity that helps make them almost ideal houseplants. Imagine if you can an oak tree sitting more or less at ground level like a stump, growing thicker and thicker, never becoming more than four or five feet tall until the trunk itself has a diameter of three or four feet. Well, a palm never becomes quite as thick as an oak, but that's mainly how it grows—sideways—until the trunk has almost reached its maximum diameter. Then it begins slowly raising its head. Which means you should be able to keep a palm happy in your parlor for thirty years or so before you have to knock a hole in the ceiling.

Below ground, supporting a palm's slowly rising superstructure, is a relatively fine root web, usually with the large taproot associated with other monocots such as grass. But unlike, say, the crabgrass that refuses to be excised from the lawn no matter how roughly and fervently you yank it out, palm roots are very susceptible to damage. Rarely should a palm be repotted. It likes tight shoes.

My coconuts, provided they are well watered and fed, seem to be happiest uprooted only once every four or five years. When repotting them, I've found it better to split their pots in half—or more likely in several pieces, I not being the best pot splitter around—than to try to knock the plants out in the customary fashion. Try turning a five-foot palm upside down and knocking it out of its pot gently sometime. The pot-splitting method means acquiring another pile of shards during the operation, and may not be really necessary, as coconuts are one of the more readily transplantable palms. The occasion is so infrequent that I find the extra care well worthwhile. It does keep root damage to a minimum. And as with the green growing tip, if the palm's sensitive and brittle roots are damaged, it will die. Summer, when root growth is at its height, is the best time to transplant because new roots are assured to replace those inevitably injured, no matter how careful you are.

TWO BRANCHES IN THE FAMILY

Palms fall neatly into two categories, defined by their leaf structure: the fan palms, most commonly seen in use, as their name suggests, by slaves in Biblical movie spectaculars, and feather palms. The feather palm leaf is called pinnate; the fan-shaped, palmate.

The largest pinnate palm leaves are found on *Raphia ruffia*. A single leaf may measure sixty-five by twelve feet. To match, the flower raceme, the stalk on which the numerous blossoms are borne, may be eleven feet long. So, all in all, this tree seems rather unsuitable for home cultivation. However, the *Caryota mitis*, another feather palm—one of particular horticultural interest because the genus to which it belongs is the only one of bipinnate palms, that is, plants whose main leaflets are divided a second time into smaller leaflets—is a great houseplant. In general, with the exception of *Livistona chinensis*, the Chinese fan palm, and unless you're

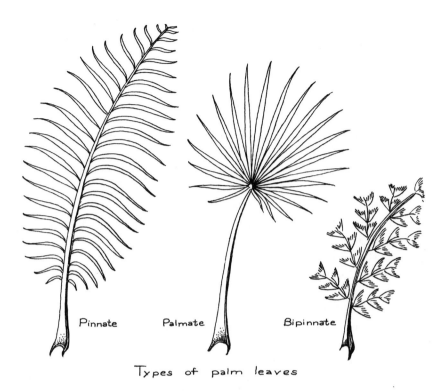

Pinnate   Palmate   Bipinnate

Types of palm leaves

in the movie business, the feather palms are a better bet than the fans in that they usually grow a little more quickly.

CREEPING TRUNKS AS WELL

There are over four hundred species of climbing palms. Except for their leaves, they bear little resemblance to the customary image of a palm. They creep and crawl like lianas up other trees, sometimes reaching a height of a hundred feet. If you have a rattan chair, it's made from the long canes of these palms.

As yet almost no climbing palms are available for home growing. However, since they are easy-to-grow exotics with, for palms, an unusual ability to withstand cold—specimens of daemonorops survived the Florida deep freeze of 1958, when so many other species were decimated—I'm sure one of these days we'll be seeing small or dwarf varieties at the local houseplant center. Most likely they will be the desmoncus, or hook, palms. If you get one, grow it as you grow your other palms, but look out for the clawed leaves groping around for something to hang onto as they climb. The single-trunked *Chamaedorea elatior*, or Mexican rattan palm, is a less insistent climber than the hook palms, just as curious, and already to be found at some nurseries.

THINK DESERTED BEACHES

Although they are the second most valuable family of plants, very little is known about the soil needs of palms. This is probably because they have been grown mostly in their wild state rather than under intensive cultivation. Except for the date and the coconut, it is only recently that palms have been planted in intensively cultivated commercial groves. In their native areas the palms grow like weeds, and true cultivation has rarely been necessary. This easy-grow quality, of course, is what endears the plants to indoor growers.

The one soil requirement that has been ascertained beyond a doubt is good drainage. When you think of those south sea island beaches studded with swaying coconut palms, drainage may not be part of the daydream. But that's why those palms are there. Tidal shifts cause a constant fluctuation in the water table, supplying the palm roots with good aeration as well as moisture. At the same time, the soil is loaded with nutrients washed down from the highlands. Date palms surround oases for a similar reason. Although desert soil may seem hard packed and firm, it is open enough for water and nutrients to be constantly available.

A good potting mixture for most palms can be made up from equal parts of heavy loam, coarse sand, and peat moss, with a cupful or two of dried cow manure. The manure is not absolutely necessary, but it will give the plant a healthy start in its new home.

While on the subject of soil and potting, let me add that, unlike the procedure for most houseplants, you should not remove any of the old soil from the root ball of a palm when repotting it. Since it is so sensitive, leave the root system as undisturbed as possible. If the old soil is really packed, try to match the firm quality in the new potting mix. Otherwise the roots will tend to remain where they are rather than growing into the fresh soil. It's as if they refuse to take the easy way out.

THIRSTY AND HUNGRY

There's another thing about those sensitive palm roots. *As long as drainage is good*, it is better to err in the direction of overwatering than underwatering. For palms, dry roots mean dead roots.

If by this time palms are beginning to sound too fussy for you, please reconsider, because they are very easy to care for. Take fertilizing, for instance. Palms are heavy feeders, and it's a good idea to give them some water-soluble fertilizer, particularly one high in nitrogen, every three to four weeks during the growing seasons of spring, summer, and fall. But should you forget to feed them for a while—two or three years, say—the palms, if a bit slower growing, will usually remain quite content.

LEISURE LIVING

Speaking of slow growth, palms are rather snaillike in their development, even given the full sunlight throughout the morning that the majority naturally prefer. Yet, indoors, it's a good idea to slow their growth still more by cutting the amount of light to a bright but dappled shade. Palms not only tolerate shade, they do quite well in it, thriving on anything from less than an hour or so of direct sunlight to nothing but office fluorescents. And by limiting the direct sunlight to which they are exposed you get smaller, but more fully developed and richer green plants.

NOT PARTICULARLY TASTY

The palm family supplies man with numerous comestibles ranging from coconuts and dates to betel nuts and palm toddy. Pests, on the other hand, don't find the plants much to their liking, which makes things easy for the home grower. Red spider mites, mealybugs, and scale may on occasion attack a weakened plant. But they are easily eradicated from the palm's stiff and tolerant leaves. Aphids don't even attempt to dine on any but the youngest, most tender leaves.

Coconut palms do come down with *Chitinoaphelenchus cocophilus*, a bacterial infection as hard to cure as to pronounce. Rusts also cause considerable damage, and I remember vividly large tracts of Fiji's once magnificent coconut groves standing topless and bare as a result of this plague. But these diseases are endemic only to regions of massive species growth. The chance of your isolated coconut palm at home coming down with one of them is very unlikely, unless it was already infected when you got it. In that case there's no real remedy.

THIRTEEN TO MAKE YOUR GROVE

Palm nomenclature is a bit confused, still in the process of being straightened out. Quite often you'll find nurseries or plant stores selling plants that no longer exist—under the name by which they're sold, that is.

Caryota mitis (Fishtail Palm, Tufted Fishtail Palm)
> MIRCOCLIMATE: Warm partial sun
> Sandy soil kept constantly moist

This is the lush, multiple-trunked, cluster-forming palm of bygone years' hotel lobbies. The bipinnate foliage, unique among palms, helps accent its jungly appearance. A close relative, *Caryota urens*, is one of the best producers of jaggery, or palm sugar, giving up to twelve gallons or more of high-quality sugar a day. But it's rarely available as a houseplant. *C. mitis* won't satisfy your sweet tooth; nevertheless, this green beauty will certainly soothe your eyes. The leaves are naturally soft colored, without luster, so don't buy specimens with spray-waxed shiny leaves. Likes humidity. Hates air conditioning, but will probably tolerate it if placed well away from vents.

Chamaedorea costaricana (Bamboo Palm)
> MICROCLIMATE: Warm partial sun
> Sandy soil kept constantly moist

Guess where this one originates? Like all *Chamaedorea*, *C. costaricana* is a shade lover. The deep green foliage will bleach out in prolonged direct sun. It is a small palm, as implied by its liking for shade, and thus ideal for a houseplant. It is also ideal for overly air-conditioned office buildings, not minding the unseasonal cold. Reaches fifteen to eighteen feet in the wilds, but the bamboolike canes will remain manageable if the plant is kept in a relatively small pot or tub, which it prefers anyway.

Chamaedorea erumpens (Bamboo Palm)
> MICROCLIMATE: Warm partial sun
> Sandy soil kept constantly moist

Another bamboolike palm with short pinnate leaves along the full length of the reeds. The suckering, or multiple, stems grow in clusters. The leaves droop more than on either *Chamaedorea costaricana* or *Collinea elegans*. The terminal, or last two, leaflets on each leaf are twice as wide as any of the others. Tolerant of abuse, including an air-conditioned environment, once well established and past the seedling stage.

Chamaerops humilis (European Fan Palm, Hair Palm, Mediterranean Palm)

    MICROCLIMATE: Temperate sun

                    Sandy soil kept constantly moist

This is the only palm native to Europe, originating in Spain and Morocco. There is only one species in the genus, but it is extremely variable in appearance, ranging in height from under four feet for dwarf specimens to over twenty for the giant models. Some grow multiple trunks; others remain solitary. Leaf color runs the gamut from green to almost dark blue. The leaves of all varieties are very stiff. While the tree needs good light, it is among the hardiest of all palms. Can be grown outside as far north as the Carolinas on the East Coast and most of California on the West. Remains low like a spreading bush when kept as a tub plant.

Chrysalidocarpus lutescens (Areca Palm, Yellow Butterfly Palm)

    MICROCLIMATE: Warm partial sun

                    Sandy soil kept constantly moist

Grows in dense clusters with heavy feathery foliage hiding most of the stems. The stalks are naturally yellowish, so when you catch sight of them, don't start worrying about their being sun bleached or rush for the fertilizer. The palm needs warmth and moisture. Throws out many suckers that can be divided off as new plants. The common name, areca palm, is not to be confused with the genus *Areca*, which is a palm of a different color entirely, including the species *A. cathecu*, the betel nut palm.

Cocos nucifera (Coconut)

    MICROCLIMATE: Warm partial sun

                    Sandy soil kept constantly moist

The common coconut palm is not usually thought of as a parlor palm. Nonetheless, I include it here because I happen to like growing coconut palms in my parlor. Also they are probably the best known of all the palms. Can be grown from seed, but you need the whole coconut, husk and all. I once saw a specimen grown from a nut that had been husked, but it seemed to be more a product of luck than of normal germination. Set the unhusked nut in soil so most of it is aboveground, with the stalk depression at an angle such that some water will tend to seep into it when you water the seed, which should be done daily. The coconut will take four or five months to germinate. The palms are very cold sensitive.

Cocos nucifera

Leaves tend to remain whole rather than separating into their full pinnate glory when the plants are grown indoors. From my own observations of young coconut palms on the lee side of Espírito Santo, I've come to the conclusion it's the lack of wind that keeps them this way, but it's only a hypothesis.

> *Collinea elegans* (Dwarf Mountain Palm, *Neanthe bella*, Parlor Palm)
> MICROCLIMATE: Warm partial sun
> Sandy soil kept constantly moist

Old Dependable, once known as *Chamaedorea elegans*, reaches up to eight feet in height and is a relatively fast-growing palm—please note the

Collinea elegans

word "relatively"—a new frond or three a year and you're doing well. Probably the most tolerant palm available to the home grower. Small seedlings are perfect for a prehistoric look in the terrarium and dish garden. Once they outgrow their miniature settings, they can be potted in the normal-sized containers without much difficulty. Tolerant of low-light conditions, air conditioning, and neglect to a degree that would destroy most other plants. Needless to say, they do better with good care. Easily grown from fresh seeds, if available, with germination time usually less than two months.

Howea forsteriana (Kentia Palm, Paradise Palm, Sentry Palm)
MICROCLIMATE: Temperate partial sun
Sandy soil kept constantly moist

A palm relatively new to the Western world, introduced to Europe from its native Lord Howe Island, east of Australia, as recently as 1871. With its lush tropical appearance, it became an instant houseplant hit during Victorian times and has been an increasing favorite ever since. Graceful, waxy, deep green fronds on arching slender stalks. Its jungly good looks

Howea forsteriani

are usually accented by keeping half a dozen or so plants in one tub. Does well in moderate temperatures a bit chilly for many of the other palms. Withstands considerable neglect if necessary, but soil kept either too dry or too wet, and temperatures too cold, will cause the leaf tips to turn brown. One of the easiest of palms to grow from seed. Even has a relatively short germination period, usually around two months.

Licuala grandis (Ruffled Fan Palm)
    MICROCLIMATE: Warm shade
                Sandy soil kept constantly moist

Because of its fascinating foliage—each leaf resembles an opened fan, pleated but dividing only slightly at the tip—the plant is a tempting one when available. However, though it does take to the shade, it is not really suitable for indoor cultivation unless you like keeping your home in the eighties with humidity to match.

Livistona chinensis (Chinese Fan Palm, *Latania borbonica*)
    MICROCLIMATE: Temperate partial sun
                Sandy soil kept constantly moist

Once the most popular of all palms for home growing, *Livistona chinensis* today is being rapidly replaced in favor by *Howea forsteriana*. Still, it's a

Livistona chinensis

tough plant that asks no more than lots of water and enough space to grow in. But buy a specimen only a little smaller than you want the tree eventually. It is a very slow grower, which is the main reason it's losing the popularity contest. Seeds germinate readily and quickly, taking only six weeks. Plant some when a child is born and you'll have an excellent-sized specimen—by the time he or she is in high school.

Phoenix roebelenii (Pygmy Date Palm)
MICROCLIMATE: Warm partial sun
Sandy soil kept constantly moist

You can grow the full-sized date palm *Phoenix dactylifera* from dates purchased at your local grocery store, but make sure they are unpasteurized, or the seeds will have been killed in the processing. Takes around two months to germinate and several years to develop into a showy plant.

Palms of the *Phoenix* genus are easy to recognize because they are the only palms with spikes instead of leaflets at the base end of the leaf. *P. roebelenii* is the pygmy species most often grown at home. Unlike *P. dactylifera*, it does not need full sun. Very tropical looking and likes it

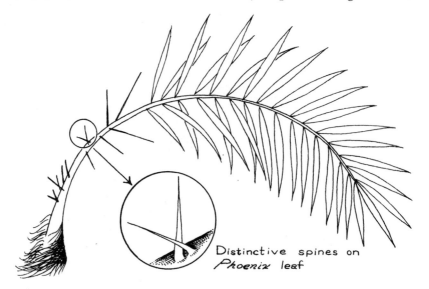

Distinctive spines on *Phoenix* leaf

warm, yet takes surprisingly well to air conditioning. For that matter, there are reports of groves of date palms in Iran remaining healthy and abundant fruit setters after being blanketed by snow. Also tolerant of dry atmosphere as long as the plant itself is well watered.

Rhapis excelsa or *R. humilis* (Broadleaf Lady Palm, Lady Palm, Slender Lady Palm)
MICROCLIMATE: Temperate partial sun
Humusy soil kept constantly moist

Whatever the label says, you won't know which of these two plants you're getting. No one is really sure which is which, or if there even is a which, since they may both be the same species. Nevertheless, it or they make very attractive houseplants with their fanlike leaves on slim bamboolike canes covered with brown fibers. Widely used in Japan and their native China as pot plants. Thrive in either a cool or a warm location. They are heavy feeders, but like the soil a bit drier than other palms do. This is particularly true following division, until the new roots get a firm hold on things.

Veitchia merrillii (Christmas Palm, Manila Palm)
MICROCLIMATE: Warm partial sun
Sandy soil kept constantly moist

Adding a proper formal look to any room, this single-trunked palm with pinnate leaves is another abuse-tolerant specimen. One of the easiest of palms to grow from seed, with germination usually occurring in a month or less.

AND AFTER MANY A SUMMER DIES THE PALM

Palms are one of the most durable plant families around, so much so that they fall into a botanical group known as pyrophytes, those that benefit from having the countryside burned over and destroyed. Because their trunks are not dependent on continuous external growth in the manner of our common bark-covered trees, palms often survive devastating fires. In fact, the landscape having been denuded of plant competition, the palms do better than ever.

On the other hand, although a palm may easily outlive its owner, once it starts to go, it's gone. There's no rescuing a palm with one foot in the grave—for, being a monocot, with a single growing point, it only has one foot. Throw it out and start again. Or at least put it in a corner till it's all over. I know how difficult it is to turn your back on a plant that still has a small spark of life in it. But sometimes it just has to be done.

SEE YOU NEXT YEAR

Along with the palm's other adaptations for survival, its seeds have a special characteristic that must be taken into account if you are trying to sprout your own. Even if you start with fresh, viable seeds, if they somehow become too dry, they may take an extra six months to germinate. Also seeds from the same fruit germinate over a peculiarly broad time range, like a time-release cold capsule. In this way, the palm makes sure that at least one group of seeds germinates when the weather's right. For example, August Braun of the Caracas Botanical Garden in Venezuela reports that 15 percent of the seeds of a specimen of *Roystonea venezuelana* germinated after sixty days, another 45 percent after a hundred and twenty days, 29 percent after a hundred and fifty days, and 11 percent after a hundred and sixty-five days. Fine, if yours happen to be from the first batch. But if they happen to be from the second, you will have an unexpectedly long wait ahead of you. So, while you're waiting, how about growing something that looks like a palm but puts out the green a bit more quickly—a fern?

Ferns and Cycads: Green Grow the Fossils All Sparkling and New

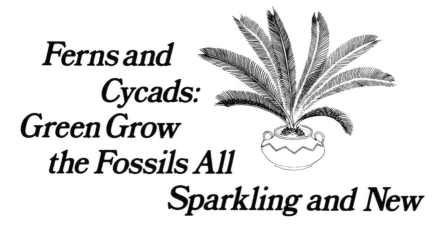

Ferns are the most primitive of all houseplants, and most of them really look as primordial as they are. I remember a hillside in Samoa, a steep precipice Susan and I stumbled on suddenly beyond the banyans of a mesa. At the far end of the gorge a narrow ribbonlike waterfall spilled into mist below. All around us, clinging to rock outcroppings, were huge tree ferns ten to twenty feet high. Susan and I looked at each other, both thinking the same thing: there had to be a pterodactyl around somewhere.

Ferns predate even the dinosaurs. Their heyday was the Carboniferous period of the Paleozoic era, three hundred million years ago, when they dominated the world. That's about a hundred thousand years before the first plant ever to have flowers evolved. In the warm moist climate of the time, the primal ferns thrived lushly beneath the shade of immense primitive trees. Today all that remains of their culture is billions of tons of coal, some ten thousand species of ferns, and sixty-odd cycads.

Yet those relatively few species of ferns that have survived to the twentieth century literally cover the globe from most northerly Alaska to the Antarctic. Species from either one of these extremes are, of course, unsuitable as houseplants unless you find a way to leave the light on after you close the refrigerator door and want to try raising them there. They need a cool to cold habitat year round. Still, 5 percent of all the known ferns grow in these outlands, and their adaptation, including, for instance, large paper-thin leaves capable of maximizing the brief available sunshine during summertime, is quite amazing. There are even a few species that remain green throughout the long, dark polar winters.

Another adaptive oddity among ferns is found in certain tropical water species. Some of these have leaves only a single cell thick. They can't even support themselves the way the leaves of a regular plant do, but must float on water, and a raindrop falling dead center will tear the tiny leaf to ribbons.

But these curiosities plus the desert species represent only 10 percent of the known ferns. That leaves plenty of variety to choose from in this ancient form of life. And ferns, all sizes and shapes of them, are great plants for those areas of limited light found in so many corners of our homes. There is, however, a slight problem of a different sort to be dealt with before furnishing your fernery.

PLANTS CAN'T READ A HYGROMETER

But you can. And, frankly, if you live in an area of the country that requires home heating in the wintertime, and you intend to raise a lot of plants, particularly ferns, it wouldn't be a bad idea to get one. A hygrometer to measure relative humidity costs less than a good dinner out, and it not only will keep those fronds waving happily, but will probably cut down both your heating and your medical bills as well.

The dry central heating that warms twentieth-century houses is extremely unhealthy for plants—and almost as unhealthy for human beings. In the wintertime, most homes are quite literally drier than the Sahara at high noon. The steam-heated cubbyhole in which I am writing this book on a cold January eve, for instance, is so dry it's really doubtful that it can support any life but bacteria and other microorganisms. Yes, that's right, I don't have any plants here—on purpose. With plants here I'd spend all my time puttering about with them rather than writing.

Winter morning sore throats, stuffy noses, itchy skin, headaches, and scores of other minor ailments can be attributed at least in part to the superdryness of our man-made environment. It also makes furniture, paintings, and almost all porous objects age more quickly.

A multitude of plants, their pots standing on pebble-and-water-filled dishes or trays, will help raise the humidity considerably, as will daily misting. Setting the pots in an indoor windowbox spread with damp sphagnum moss on top of a deep layer of pebbles supplies even more moisture in the localized area of the plants.

But the relative humidity in a heated home in winter is still often less than 20 percent, whereas the majority of plants and people are more comfortable at a humidity of 50 percent. And most ferns are coziest when it goes up to 70 percent. A general rule of thumb is that the finer the fronds, the higher the humidity should be. Of course you can grow ferns in the bathroom. But the best solution to the dryness problem is to humidify your abode. It's better for everybody.

So where does the saving in heating costs I mentioned come in? Remember the old cartoon of the desert rat sitting beneath a cactus on a scorching desert plain and wiping his brow? "Sure, it's hot, but at least the humidity is low." Well, it's true. When the humidity is high, you feel heat more. If you raise the relative humidity from 10 percent to 50 percent, you can usually lower the thermostat four to six degrees and still *feel* just as warm. If you've been heating your dry house at seventy-four degrees, you'll be as comfortable at sixty-eight degrees with the humidity increased to 50 percent or more. And your plants will love you for it.

OTHER HEALTH TIPS

Ferns for the most part, their popular image aside, are not true bog plants. Even when living in swamps, they do so on hummocks, and muddy feet will kill them. They like moist rough-textured soil and demand good drainage. So when you ready a pot for ferns, cover the bottom inch or two with shards. Then fill with a good topsoil, peat moss, and coarse sand mixture of equal parts. It must be porous and open to allow the necessary drainage and air circulation around the roots. A tablespoonful of bone meal for a pick-me-up and a couple of charcoal pieces for sweetening, that is, to keep the soil from becoming too acid, should be added to the mix if possible. As to the pot itself, use a squat one rather than the regular cone-shaped pot.

Ideally, a fern should not be potted on, or moved to a bigger pot, until the root ball is a fibrous mass. And when repotting, don't go from a four-inch pot to an eight-inch one. Like palms, ferns don't take well to all that new-found room. Step them up an inch at a time.

Another thing ferns don't take to is heavy fertilizing. Better to transplant to fresh soil when the old becomes exhausted, losing its texture and feeling dusty rather than crumbly when dry. And as for insecticides, most of them are sudden death to the touchy fronds as well as the bugs. Actually, ferns are relatively insect-free once past their youth and as long as the surrounding atmosphere is moist. In early stages of development they may be susceptible to the ever-present fungi. But these should not give you trouble unless you are raising ferns from spores, in which case everything has to be sterilized. Healthy, humid ferns are tough, so don't worry about all those brown scales that seem to take over your plant. Chances are they are only spore capsules, easy enough to distinguish from scales of the pest variety, since real scales never have become regi-

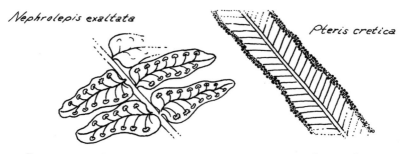

Examples of sori, or spore capsules, on fern fronds

mented enough to line up neatly in double rows the way spore capsules do. Isolated scales, brown or white, are possible intruders, of course. Pick them off before they get out of hand.

One more thing: ferns like company, but at a discreet distance. If you have more than a single fern, don't put them so close to each other that their leaves touch. The fronds will tangle and, being rather brittle, will soon look tattered, browned, and disheveled. Despite their lush appearance, most ferns are slow growing. Damaged ones take a long time to get back into shape; all you can do is cut back the tattered fronds and await the replacements.

ELEVEN FRIENDLY FRONDS

Asplenium bulbiferum (Hen-and-Chicken Fern, Mother Fern, Mother Spleenwort)
MICROCLIMATE: Warm shade
Humusy soil kept constantly moist

Here's a fern that could cause a real population problem. Scores of plant-lets develop in spring and summer along the tops and edges of the fronds.

These adventitious buds, as they are called, are easily rooted in sterilized soil. Some will just drop off to start their new life on their own in any handy surrounding pots. Remove the plantlets when they are about three-quarters of an inch tall. Take part of the old frond off with them and pin

A mothering *Asplenium bulbiferum* frond

this to the soil with a regular straight pin to keep it anchored while the roots grab hold. If all those extra plants from adventitious buds aren't enough for you, *Asplenium bulbiferum* can also be propagated by division. *A. viviparum* is a slightly hardier species with the same mothering quality. The fronds of a mature *A. bulbiferum* plant reach up to three feet in length and are composed of an arching wiry grooved black stalk bearing medium green leaflets. They will remain healthy and growing in an atmosphere of only 30 percent relative humidity. Really high humidity, say 70 percent or more, will cause browning. An average humidity of 50 percent is your best bet for *A. bulbiferum* and the other ferns included here.

Asplenium nidus (Bird's-Nest Fern)
> MICROCLIMATE: Warm shade
> Humusy soil kept constantly moist

Before opening up, the young coiled leaves of this plant lie at its heart, resembling—with a bit of applied imagination—bird's eggs. Unlike the ferny-looking ferns, *Asplenium nidus* has long oblate single leaves a pleasant green with black midribs and wavy margins. The leaves are tough and flexible despite their thinness, making the plant a hardier house fern

Asplenium nidus

than many. If new fronds seem stunted or deformed, the plant is either not warm enough or has been in a draft.

Cibotium chamissoi (Man Tree Fern)

MICROCLIMATE: Warm partial sun

Humusy soil kept constantly moist

Are you willing to spray a tree trunk after breakfast every morning? If not, don't add *Cibotium chamissoi* to your collection yet. While it keeps surprisingly well indoors, this "tree"—a four- or five-foot specimen is about par, although it measures thirty-five feet in its natural habitat—has a fibrous trunk that must be kept always moist. In fact, all tree fern trunks should be sprayed daily. Beneath the massive Nile green head of fronds is a shaggy mane of light brown to black hairs that are equally moisture loving. Quite often the section of trunk bearing the crown is sawed off and anchored in a shallow bowl of water or potted directly. It roots well, bringing the fern down to more manageable size. Sawed off or not, this fern makes a lush houseplant. But wait to get one until you've grown some easier ferns successfully first.

Cibotium schiedei (Mexican Tree Fern)
    MICROCLIMATE: Warm partial sun
                Humusy soil kept constantly moist

Much more abuse-tolerant than *Cibotium chamissoi, C. schiedei* still needs plenty of moisture. But should the soil for some reason dry out, this tree fern can usually be revived with a good solid dowsing. Its apple green fronds, two to four feet long, are often members of the wedding and other such receptions decorated by florists, who appreciate impressive appearance combined with durability. Grow it as a tub plant and keep it moist. Propagation is by spores, and growing a fern from spores is not recommended for the beginner. Besides, the plant is a very slow grower. That's why, although it's a tree fern, you usually see it without much of a trunk.

Cyrtomium falcatum 'Rochefordianum' (Holly Fern)
    MICROCLIMATE: Temperate shade
                Loamy soil kept constantly moist

One of the hardiest ferns for indoor growing, as you will no doubt ascertain yourself by observing the sturdy leathery texture of its large simple leaves. Makes an ideal pot fern, rarely growing higher than a foot. As for moisture, a cactus it's not, but *Cyrtomium falcatum* 'Rochefordianum' will withstand even occasional drying out of the roots. Preferring night temperatures in the fifties, it will settle, nevertheless, for warmer nocturnal weather.

Davallia bullata 'Mariesii' (Ball Fern, Squirrel's-Foot Fern)
    MICROCLIMATE: Warm partial sun
                Humusy soil kept constantly moist

The genus *Davallia* is a podiatrist's dream of popular names, with images shifting in size and shape from the squirrel's foot of *D. bullata* 'Mariesii' to the rabbit's foot of *D. fijiensis* to the deer's foot of *D. griffithiana*. The furry feet are actually rhizomes, stems of a special type that produce both roots and leafy shoots.

Because of their dual role, rhizomes don't seem to be able to make up their minds whether they should grow above or below the ground. In the case of a davallia they usually grow aboveground. Don't try to bury the rhizome; it not only would be a futile task, but might induce rot. For that matter, the feet will creep right out of the pot anyhow after a while. This cruising soon makes for a most attractive bushy plant, since leaves erupt all along the rhizome, rather than arising simply out of the crown as in most common ferns.

Davallia bullata 'Mariesii'

Should the creepers creep too far, train them up a piece of bark-board. Or simply break them off and lay them *on top* of the soil in another pot or two for new plants. Fasten each section lightly to the soil with copper wire bent into oversize staples, so the rhizome will be able to anchor itself. A plastic tent covering the pot for the first couple of weeks helps supply extra humidity. But make sure the pot is not exposed to direct sunlight while the lid is on. That would make things too steamy and warm even for ferns.

Dicksonia squarrosa (New Zealand Tree Fern)
    MICROCLIMATE: Temperate partial sun
                       Humusy soil kept constantly moist

Any small child lucky enough to have this fern around the house is probably convinced he has his own palm tree. Beneath a spreading crown of three- to five-foot-long fronds it has a black trunk studded with leaf bases that look eminently climbable. As with other tree ferns, the trunk must be kept moist with daily misting. On the whole, however, the specimen is surprisingly tough, adapting to much cooler climes than one would suppose from its jungly appearance. Its cousin, *Dicksonia antarctica*, can even survive some frost. Both are very slow growing, so if possible purchase them close to the size you want them to be when you retire.

Nephrolepis exaltata 'Bostoniensis' (Boston Fern)
MICROCLIMATE: Temperate partial sun
Loamy soil kept constantly moist

Yes, the Boston fern really comes from the city of the same name. At least that's where it was first discovered in 1894 as a cultivar, a plant with slight variations developed through cultivation rather than by nature. For

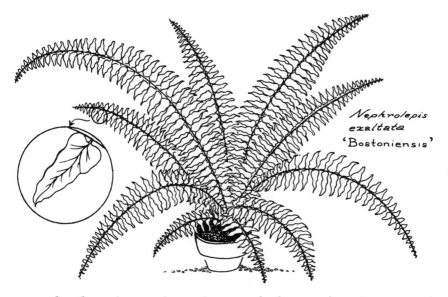

Nephrolepis exaltata 'Bostoniensis'

many decades a favorite houseplant, *Nephrolepis exaltata* 'Bostoniensis' went out of vogue as central heating came in. It's presently going through a revival along with the Tiffany lamps and Oriental rugs always conjured up in the same image, and happily so, for it is one of the easiest of all ferns to tend. As long as it has high humidity, at least 50 percent, and some light, it will thrive. Dry air, however, not only retards growth but invites white scale, brown scale, and mealybugs to dine. The fern spores are not viable, but plants will reproduce in spring by sending out runners. For best propagative results, hang the plant outside during spring and summer.

Platycerium bifurcatum (Common Staghorn Fern)
  MICROCLIMATE: Temperate partial sun
                Humusy soil kept constantly moist

Of the many species of staghorns, this is the easiest one to grow because of its acclimation to a wide range of temperatures. It has been known to survive ten degrees or more of frost. But its preference is for night temperatures in the more comfortable fifties. Being epiphytic, that is, a plant that normally grows with its roots dangling down from the treetops rather than buried in soil, the staghorn is best grown the way it's usually sold, mounted on barkboard or in a basket of sphagnum and osmunda. Hang it on the wall as you might a stuffed moose head—not above the mantel though, if you use the fireplace often. Leaves should be sprayed daily, and once a month dunk the plant gently in a pail of half-strength fish fertilizer solution. A bit of extra work, but well worth it for a really remarkable plant. Suckers for new plants will develop from the roots

Platycerium bifurcatum

hidden beneath the brown shield-shaped fronds. The brown fronds themselves have no reproductive value. They serve mainly to trap falling pieces of bark, dead insects, and other nutrients for the roots. The long antlerlike green fronds, on the other hand, bear spores. They also photosynthesize in the manner of a regular leaf. The brown and the green are two amazingly different specialized leaves on one plant.

Polypodium aureum (Golden Polypody, Rabbit's-Foot Fern)
    MICROCLIMATE: Warm partial sun
                    Humusy soil kept constantly moist

Another multifooted fern, this one among the easiest to grow of the tropical varieties of ferns. Does well in a shallow pot or a hanging basket, wherever the big, twisted, almost silvery blue fronds can best add their touch of contrast among your plants. Propagate by breaking the foot.

Pteris cretica (Brake Fern, Cretan Brake, Table Fern)
    MICROCLIMATE: Warm shade
                    Loamy soil kept constantly moist

Frequently raised in cozily humid terrariums because of its manageably sized fronds (less than two feet long) and lacy appearance. Sturdier than most as a live-in houseplant. There are numerous cultivars. Almost all are fairly undemanding as to soil and light. Propagated from spores.

THE DOPPELGÄNGER CYCLE

Medieval European tradition had it that anyone carrying fern seeds in his pocket would become invisible. It was a hard theory to dispute, since part of the myth was that fern seeds themselves are invisible. No one had ever seen a fern in flower, much less been able to gather seeds.

The reason was, of course, that ferns don't flower. They reproduce by means of a most intriguing two-phase cycle: one for growth of the regular plant species, and one for development of a miniplant designed solely for sex.

Starting with the familiar green frondy plant, we have a sporophyte, or spore-bearing generation. During this period, spore cases develop on the undersides of the fronds. When conditions are advantageous, these spores are dispersed, some landing close to home, right below the original plant, others being carried for miles by the wind. Happening to settle in a favorable spot, they develop into plants—not at all the ferns with which we are familiar, however. Instead they become tiny heart-shaped plantlets no larger than a quarter of an inch in diameter. This is the gametophyte, or sexual stage of the fern cycle.

But there is no flowering involved. There are no birds and bees for pollination. No seeds are formed. Sperm and egg cells develop on different parts of the plantlet's underleaf. Then all it takes is enough moisture for a droplet of water to condense. The sperm will float over to the egg and fertilize it. After that, the other side of the cycle resumes and the familiar fern begins to develop, croziers growing from right within the plantlet.

To boot, ferns can reproduce vegetatively by division or with runners. No wonder they've survived since the Paleozoic era.

CYCADS NEXT

The cycads, slightly further along on the evolutionary scale than the ferns, are the most primitive seed bearers. They are strikingly handsome, slow-growing palmlike plants. One six-foot specimen has been estimated to be over a thousand years old. Since cycads are on the verge of extinction, it's at least reassuring to think that the ones we still have around will last awhile—with care, which is easy enough, as they need little of it and are less fussy than ferns about humidity. And if you buy one for a houseplant, you should be getting your money's worth, because there's no reason the plant shouldn't be in the family for several generations.

Cycas circinalis (Crozier Cycad, Fern Palm)
MICROCLIMATE: Temperate partial sun
Humusy soil kept constantly moist

A typical crozier
(so named for
its resemblance to a
bishop's staff)

Cycas revoluta

One of the easiest cycads to care for, and a good, relatively fast grower, taking no more than a decade to grow a foot. It makes a choice, enduring indoor plant, its stiff glossy fronds above a heavy trunk adding exotic lushness to any room. Cats tend to use the trunk for sharpening their claws, but it usually manages to survive even such mistreatment.

> *Cycas revoluta* (Sago Palm)
> MICROCLIMATE: Temperate partial sun
> Loamy soil left to dry between waterings

The hardiest of cycads. Will do well on a sun porch up north even in winter as long as temperatures do not fall below freezing for prolonged periods. Down south, it makes an excellent plant to wheel out on the patio for the summer; in many areas it can be left there all year, since it likes cool winters.

Both *Cycas circinalis* and *C. revoluta* can be propagated by removing the suckers or bulbils at the base of the trunk during the parent plant's rest period. This stage is easily enough determined, for the leaves appear in flushes once every year or two. Set the bulbs in a loamy soil and sand mix and cover with plastic to retain moisture until they begin to grow.

Zamia furfuracea (Jamaica Sago Tree, Scurfy Zamia)
> MICROCLIMATE: Temperate partial sun
> Humusy soil kept constantly moist

The handy table-sized cycad. Its leathery green fronds don't exceed three feet and will usually remain smaller indoors. A tuberlike trunk adds interesting texture and a minipalm appearance. Overall, it's a distinctive decorator plant with a constitution of cast iron.

THE INSTANT COLLECTION

Welwitschia mirabilis (Mr. Big)
> MICROCLIMATE: Temperate sun
> Sandy soil left to dry between waterings

Here's a most curious and ancient plant. It's not a fern, and it's further along the evolutionary scale than cycads, since it bears true flowers, but I include it here because of the incredible age an individual specimen can achieve. Some have been reported to live two thousand years—although I'm not sure which observer was around that long.

Yet there is only one species known in the genus, which means that if you manage to get hold of a plant you'll have a complete representative collection. Most likely you won't get that specimen, though. The plant is not readily available. Also it really needs greenhouse conditions and three or four pots, one on top of another, in which to sink its deep taproot.

If you can't have one of your own, at least keep your eyes open for the plant when you go to the botanical gardens, for it's a most unusual curiosity. It is composed of only two slow-growing, monstrously long straplike leaves. But they grow and grow and grow. Unlike other plants, whose leaf growth comes at the tips, *Welwitschia mirabilis* leaves grow from the base of the plant itself. In the plant's native habitat of southwest Africa, before the leaves get to be more than twenty feet or so long the desert winds shred them into leathery thongs. But, technically, they never stop getting longer, are endless, and could keep growing forever.

Fragrant Favorites from the Fourth Dimension

A flower is beautiful, a fragrant flower is at least momentary ecstasy. For me there is little in the world as joyful and relaxing as lying beneath the pendulous boughs of an old lilac bush in spring. The surrounding fragrance transports me, half dozing in the speckled sunlight, into a childhood world without care. Even a whiff of the lilacs' sweet smell from a freshly cut bunch in the old silver pitcher on my desk triggers a host of old memories and future dreams for a moment as real as today itself. The sense of smell is funny that way. Less is known about it than about any of our other senses, and we rarely use it these days. But when we do, the effect of this fourth dimension can be overwhelming.

If little research has been done on our sense of smell, even less is known about the whys and wherefores of fragrances in flowers. Although scent glands have long been known to exist in such beings as butterflies, crocodiles, and, of course, skunks, it wasn't till the mid 1960s that osmophores, the perfume-producing glands in plants, were discovered. Yet along with shape and color, fragrance is aesthetically one of the most important aspects of a flower, not only for us human plant lovers, but for attracting insects as well. And these pollinators are what count as far as the plants are concerned, assuring their future generations.

The cultivation of flowers for fragrance, like most civilized amenities of Western man, goes back to the ancient Greeks. They laid out their gardens so that the most fragrant plants were placed near the windows of the house, where their salutary effects could be most appreciated by the occupants. Medieval monks also planted sweet-smelling herbs near windows, those of their infirmaries in this case, so that the patients might benefit.

The height of appreciation of floral fragrances was probably during England's Victorian age. Nosegays became an everyday accessory, and numerous small romantic works on the language of flowers circulated among the better classes—who never used the vulgar word "smell."

Speaking of smell, and quite apart from flowers, many plants exude a diffuse odorous substance from every leaf and pore, so to speak. Small oil cells are distributed throughout the epidermal tissue, or skin, of the leaves and stems. The aromatic oils dispersed through these are used by man for their medicinal qualities, in paints and waxes, and as basic specialty chemicals. Interestingly enough, the plants themselves seem to have no need of them. It's just another way of eliminating metabolic by-products and waste, like human perspiration.

The fragrance of flowers is much more specific. Not only is it produced solely by the specialized osmophores located in the flower itself, but, just as some men are drawn to women wearing Chanel No. 5 and others to those exuding Jolie Madame, a floral scent often attracts only one species of bee or fly or moth, the one species most efficient at pollinating that particular flower. Some plants, certain irises and delphiniums, for instance, have actual road maps of scent along their petals. When a bee lands on the flower, scented patches lead it, like Hansel and Gretel following their trail of crumbs, right to the center of things where all the sweets are located. In the process, the insect is carefully guided past the pistil and stamen to ensure pollination.

THE SCENT FACTORY

Osmophores are glandular cells in the flower usually located where they will be well exposed to the atmosphere. During their short existence they really work at making fragrance. So industrious are they in converting carbohydrates to something enticingly smelly that measurable quantities of heat and even electricity are produced—not enough to give you a shock when you stick your nose into the flower for a whiff, but I find the thought of a flower generating electricity when it yields its fragrance quite startling.

Although the scent organs create odors that on the whole man finds pleasant, some can be described as nice only by the particular insect for which they are intended. *Himantoglossum hircinum,* for instance, gives forth the odor of a goat badly in need of a bath. *Cirrhopetalum ornatissimum,* they tell me, smells like stale whale oil, although I haven't been close enough to whale or flower to verify this. There's a species of *Pleurothallis* that in flower attracts only a fly belonging to the order Diptera which happens to find its obnoxious odor of fermentation particularly appealing. On the somewhat more positive side, *Trigonidium obtusum* exudes the scent of the female *Trigona droryana* bee; all the male bees just love it to death.

SPECIAL BLEND

Women may douse themselves with perfume, and men with aftershave lotion, but they are almost alone in the animal kingdom when it comes to borrowing fragrances from flowers. Not entirely alone, however. Some male Euglossini bees visit orchids of the Catasetinae subtribe for the sole purpose of dabbing on perfume.

The Catasetinae produce aromatic oils in such profusion the oils actually lie on the flower petals like droplets of dew. The bees have thick tufts of fine hair on their front legs for gathering the oil. They smear it on their back legs, which contain a spongelike material encased in a hard shell almost like a bottle. Each bee's "bottles" can hold up to a sixteenth of an ounce of perfume.

For some time after the discovery of the bees' proclivity for perfume there remained the question, Was it just vanity? That seemed unlikely in such an industrious race of insects. Then again, if it wasn't, what did the bees do with the perfume? Most probably, according to recent observations in Brazil, the male bee when ready to mate forces an airstream over its rear legs with quick movements of its wings. The perfume evaporates rapidly, surrounding the bee in an odoriferous cloud. Other bees join it and form a lustful swarm. The limit of their mating area is defined by the smell. The ways of nature are truly incredible.

THE FRAGRANT ONES

Many indoor plants are fragrant to various degrees. The following, however, are particularly so, and are grown for their scent perhaps more than their visual effect. All are intense users of energy, particularly when producing their fragrant blossoms. They need several hours of direct sunlight daily to flower. If you can't provide it, settle for realizing your olfactory fantasies out of glass-stoppered bottles.

Amomum cardamon (Cardamon Ginger)
MICROCLIMATE: Warm partial sun
Loamy soil kept constantly moist

An excellent example of a plant that exudes fragrance from every pore. Pick a leaf and crush it between your fingers for a most refreshingly

Amomum cardamon

spicy aroma. Originating in Java, *Amomum cardamon* is the plant from which comes the spice of the same name, so popular in Scandinavian and Oriental cooking. Your chances of a home harvest of cardamon are slim, but with good care the plant will produce conelike spikes of yellow flowers subtly sheltered among the leaves. The plant itself is a perennial herb with creeping rootstock and dark green lance-shaped leaves on bamboolike canes reaching up to six feet indoors. Throughout its spring and summer growing period it needs heavy watering, but during its winter rest cut back the supply considerably.

> *Bouvardia longiflora* (Sweet Bouvardia)
> MICROCLIMATE: Temperate sun
> Loamy soil left to dry between waterings

Here's a small shrub from Mexico whose glistening snowy white trumpet-like blooms will fill an entire room with the scent of orange blossoms. Grows to three feet indoors, but can easily be kept more compact with pruning, which also prevents it from getting straggly. The pruning should be done *after* the May to June blooming period. If you prune it in mid-winter, there will be no flowers, since they develop almost exclusively on the shrub's tips. A postblooming trim, on the other hand, often results in a second aromatic yield in late fall, after a couple of weeks with fifty- to sixty-degree temperatures to reinitiate bud formation. Propagates easily from tip cuttings of the woody branches in January or February.

> *Brunfelsia calycina* (Brazil Raintree; Yesterday, Today, and Tomorrow)
> MICROCLIMATE: Temperate sun
> Loamy soil kept constantly moist

I don't know how *Brunfelsia calycina* acquired its popular name, but it is true that if this shrub-sized plant is not supplied with plenty of atmospheric moisture yesterday, today, and tomorrow, it will never bloom. In many ways, including its intense need for sun, *B. calycina* might best be classed a greenhouse plant. However, it can be grown indoors and is well worth a try if you can supply the required light and moisture. Richly fragrant white-centered lavender to white funnel-shaped flowers are brought forth in profuse showers for the first six months of every year. Needs a rest period after blooming, and watch how you prune, since next year's crop of blossoms will develop on this year's woody growth. The plant should not be moved around much or it won't flower.

Carissa grandiflora (Natal Plum)
> MICROCLIMATE: Temperate sun
> Loamy soil kept constantly moist

Ranges to seven feet tall, although dwarf varieties such as 'Boxwood Beauty' keep to a more manageable two or three feet in height. The closely set, leathery leaves are evergreen, but must be washed monthly to retain their richness. The white star-shaped flowers, borne in clusters, are very fragrant. Flowering can occur at any season and is followed by plumlike reddish fruit. The fruit tastes like sweet cranberries, although, from the size of the average harvest, you're probably better off leaving it on the plant for decoration. *Carissa grandiflora* is easily shaped by pruning and it lends itself well to the topiarist's art.

Cypripedium acaule (Pink Lady Slipper)
> MICROCLIMATE: Cool partial sun
> Humusy soil kept constantly moist

Don't try to grow this one unless you can give it a summer vacation out-of-doors and a winter rest on a cool sun porch. Still, there is something rather amusing about growing a flower that smells like a watermelon, though it's downright déclassé when you consider that cypripediums are members of the orchid family. Plant yours in a well-drained pot, using a soil mixture of equal parts leaf mold, sphagnum moss, and sharp sand. Water heavily while in growth and bloom. The solitary flower, greenish brown with crimson, rose-veined pouch, reaches up to five inches in diameter on particularly robust specimens. As the deciduous shoots begin to wither in fall, reduce liquids. The plant normally rests between November and March, with hibernation most comfortable in the forty- to fifty-degree range. At this stage its wilted appearance is rather unpresentable, and the plant is best kept in whatever out-of-the-way corner you reserve for your other sleepers.

Daphne odora (Winter Daphne)
> MICROCLIMATE: Temperate partial sun
> Loamy soil kept constantly moist

An easy-to-grow spreading evergreen up to four feet high that from January through March should supply you with a steady procession of fragrant waxy white to pink flower clusters. The sweet and intense perfume of a single thriving plant will fill a room. The variegated version is a bit slower growing, making it a better houseplant. It also blooms in profusion. Propagate by layers and cuttings.

Dendrobium moschatum
> MICROCLIMATE: Temperate partial sun
> Orchid mix left to dry between waterings

An orchid truly fit for the sultan's harem. The canelike pseudobulbs that store food for the resting season at their best will grow six feet tall and be covered from late winter through summer with clusters of three- to four-inch, heavily textured flowers just dripping with the aroma of musk. The flowers themselves have pale to orange yellow-tipped petals; the lip bears a large purple black blotch on either side. Dendrobiums as a whole are some of the easiest-to-grow orchids. Their essential requirements are good light, high humidity, and night temperatures that do not drop below fifty-five degrees. Summers spent outdoors in almost full sunlight help assure good flowering.

Dryopteris fragrans (Wood Fern)
> MICROCLIMATE: Temperate partial sun
> Humusy soil kept constantly moist

Here's a delicate little fern whose leaves, when bruised, are supposed to give off a most enduring fragrance of new-mown hay. It prefers a potting mix with lime in it. My pot sits prepared but sans plant, waiting for its first specimen. The plant is rarely sold by dealers and I haven't found one yet. If you do, let me know.

Epidendrum phoeniceum
> MICROCLIMATE: Temperate partial sun
> Orchid mix left to dry between waterings

Every kid's favorite. The blossoms of *Epidendrum phoeniceum* emit the fragrance of chocolate cake. A summer bloomer whose long-lasting flowers have brilliant reddish-purple lip and, appropriately enough, chocolate-colored sepals and petals. An easy-to-grow, appealing orchid for the beginner. Blooms well as long as it is given a rest period of reduced watering after the year's flush of green growth.

Exacum affine (Persian Violet)
MICROCLIMATE: Warm partial sun
Humusy soil left to dry between waterings

Looks about as much like a real violet as the so-called African one does. But unlike the African violet, *Exacum affine* is most delightfully fragrant.

Exacum affine

Although it is a profusely blooming tropical perennial, new plants are usually started from seed every March for June to October blooms. Takes poorly to drafts, but surprisingly well to a dry atmosphere.

Jasminum sambac (Arabian Jasmine)
MICROCLIMATE: Warm sun
Loamy soil kept constantly moist

Jasmine is one of the most fragrant of all floral perfumes. The aroma from a single small jasmine plant can fill a room with fragrance for the better part of a year. Unfortunately, most jasmines do not thrive as houseplants unless you can keep their room quite cool or have an unheated sun porch, so when you get your plant, make sure it isn't just any old jasmine, but *Jasminum sambac*.

J. sambac is one of the few species that like the indoors. It's the one whose flowers are used in making jasmine tea. Its essential oils are also commonly extracted for Oriental perfumes. The shrub grows to eight feet, but usually remains considerably smaller indoors, where it is best grown on a small trellis. Needs good humidity for the best show of flowers. These are small and white, turning purple as they fade. The plant blooms

Jasminum sambac

from February to November under ideal conditions. If you don't like blossoms in your tea, how about in a martini? *J. sambac* is from the same family that gives you olives.

Lycaste aromatica

> MICROCLIMATE: Temperate partial sun
> Orchid mix left to dry between waterings

Another of the fragrant Orchidaceae, this one is surrounded by a strong aroma of cinnamon and is excellent as a beginner's orchid. The plant is relatively small, with pseudobulbs to three inches and leaves rarely over a foot and a half long. Easy to grow and free flowering. The flowers, waxy, with greenish sepals, golden yellow petals, and red-dotted lip, are borne individually on slim stalks in winter and spring. Water well during April to October flowering, cut back after main growth. The key to success is good ventilation without drafts.

Lycaste aromatica

Mahernia verticillata (Honey Bells)
    microclimate: Temperate sun
                           Humusy soil kept constantly moist

This rambling, small-leaved, almost fernlike bush from South Africa is rather ungainly and not particularly attractive. But the tiny bell-shaped flowers with their cool lily-of-the-valley perfume transform the ugly duckling into something marvelous to behold for several months during late winter through spring. Grows nicely hanging at nose level. Although cuttings root easily, you'll probably have to grow your first specimens from seed, since the plants themselves can be hard to come by.

Maxillaria tenuifolia
    microclimate: Temperate partial sun
                           Orchid mix kept constantly moist

Orchids have the highest degree of pollinator specificity of any plant family. They are so choosy about who pollinates them that some species literally can set seed only if helped by a nectar-seeking moth with an eighteen-inch-long tongue. One of the results of this selectivity is that the insect-attracting quality of the plants is both unique and specific. Take *Maxillaria tenuifolia*: the rust red and yellow flowers smell like coconut. I can't help but wonder which escapee from the cookie factory does the pollinating of these.

Among the earliest cultivated orchids to be exported to the Continent from Central America, *M. tenuifolia* made its debut there in 1839. It is a small plant, usually around a foot high. The strongly scented flowers, heavy in texture and long lasting, are apt to be half hidden in a rat's nest of leaves and pseudobulbs when they bloom, summer, fall, and winter.

Neomarica gracilis (Apostle Plant, Slender False Flag)
    MICROCLIMATE: Temperate partial sun
                      Loamy soil kept constantly moist

The swordlike leaves of this member of the iris family are arranged in a flat fan. The two-inch white, blue, and brown flowers are showy but not long lasting. However, they keep coming.

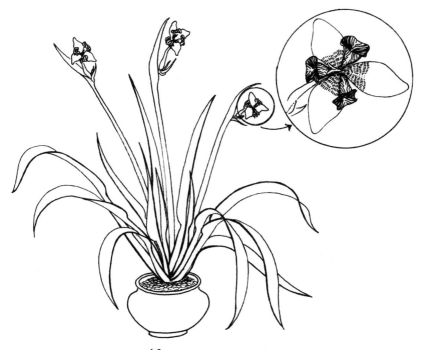

Neomarica gracilis

Neomarica northiana bears less fragrant but larger flowers, up to four inches, is just as easy to grow, and has the advantage of often producing postfloral adventitious plants at the flowering nodes. The stalks bend under the weight of the new plantlets, lowering them gently to the ground or an awaiting, freshly filled pot, where they will root readily. Both species can also be propagated by rhizome division.

Osmanthus fragrans (Fragrant Olive, Sweet Olive)
MICROCLIMATE: Temperate sun
Loamy soil kept constantly moist

It's hard to believe that such a heady jasminelike perfume can be produced by the tiny white flowers of *Osmanthus fragrans*. But it certainly is, and lavishly. The plant is easy to grow, if somewhat difficult to propagate from cuttings. The fine-toothed, holly-shaped leaves are a glossy olive green and up to four inches long. The clustering flowers prefer a cool, moist atmosphere.

Stapelia gigantea (Carrion Flower, Giant Toad Plant, Zulu Giant)
MICROCLIMATE: Warm sun
Sandy soil left to dry between waterings

Here's a giant flower, ten to fifteen inches across, with an intense smell. Unfortunately the plant is pollinated by carrion flies. Three guesses what the flower smells like. The odor can be overpowering; then again, sometimes it's not so bad. I'll leave it up to you whether you think the star-shaped yellow flower with crimson bands makes it worth putting up with the stench. The plant itself is a low-growing, leafless succulent with grooved four-sided fleshy stems. Keep it cool and almost dry in winter, and in full sun. In summer, shade it a little from the noonday sun and water it more. Propagates easily by division or cuttings if you're of a mind to do so. But if you'd rather add flowers intriguing for qualities other than an unpleasant odor, how about some that bloom only in time for the late night movie?

Plants for Night People

We all expect to see crocuses in spring, roses in summer, chrysanthemums in fall. But how do the plants know when to flower? And how do the crocuses in New Jersey know to bloom earlier than those in Minnesota, later than those in South Carolina? Better yet, how does the passion flower know when it's twelve noon, the hour it opens, or the evening primroses that it's 6:00 P.M. and time to greet the evening? Do flowers sense the seasons and the hours through external factors such as temperature and light? Is the timing coded into the seed itself, so the plant blooms a precise number of days after germination? Or perhaps, as absurd as it might seem at first thought, do the plants have a built-in sense of time, an internal clock?

LINNAEUS'S CLOCK OF FLOWERS

In the quiet of the 1700s, when the passing of time was measured in days rather than nanoseconds and Linnaeus was meticulously attemping to classify all the world's plants, he discovered one could tell what time of day it was by observing certain flowers opening or closing.

The spotted cat's ear uncurled its flowers at six in the morning, followed by the African marigold at seven, hawkweed at eight, and so on till the white water lilies shut their buds at five in the afternoon and evening primroses opened theirs at six. Obviously this was a seasonal clock at best, dependent on the plants' being in bloom, but the precision with which the flowers opened and closed unfurled a whole series of whys and wherefores that has kept the scientific community busy ever since it was noted.

The whole process of flowering is, in fact, an answer in search of questions. The flower is there. Its purpose in propagation is clear. Everything else about it is pretty unclear—including, for some researchers, whether a flower is really a flower or just a superspecialized leaf.

THE LONG AND THE SHORT OF IT

The questions what causes flowers to open at a given time during the year, and why, found a partial answer in a rather roundabout way. It all came about as a result of the general public's smoking habits and the world's preference for Virginian cigarettes. Shortly after World War II two research scientists at the United States Department of Agriculture, W. W. Garner and H. A. Allard, were busy with a new cultivar of tobacco, the Maryland Mammoth strain. It was a great plant for producing a profusion of tobacco leaves. But there was a serious drawback: the Maryland Mammoth bloomed in fall, too late to set seed before the frost in the Maryland-Virginia tobacco belt. And even the best of cultivars wasn't going to help the farmers if they didn't have seed for the following year's crop. Growing the plants in greenhouses, it was theoretically possible to vary all the environmental conditions in an attempt to force the Maryland Mammoth to bloom earlier. For over two years Garner and Allard worked at the problem. But no matter which factor they altered—more or less nutrition, more or less water, keeping the plants potbound, and so on—Maryland Mammoth stubbornly refused to bloom until fall. Then one day Garner and Allard shortened the day. They cut the plants' daily light exposure to what they would receive in fall, their natural flowering season. Shortly thereafter the plants stopped their vegetative growth and burst into bloom.

And so was made the initial discovery of photoperiodism, the growth response of a plant to the length of the daily light and dark periods. Since, to bloom, the Maryland Mammoth needed short days, with less than twelve to fourteen hours of light, they were categorized as short-day plants. Other plants, spinach and winter wheat, for instance, needed more than twelve to fourteen hours of light to flower, and were classed long-day plants. Those such as cucumbers and everbearing strawberries, to which the length of day didn't matter one way or the other, were called day-neutral.

Photoperiodism can be very important when you are growing house-plants under artificial lighting. Many specimens are long-day plants from the tropics. Give them ten hours of fluorescent light a day and you may end up with some really spectacular foliage. Give them two more hours of light a day and you may have a profusion of flowers as well.

Day length is not the sole controlling seasonal force in flowering. Vernalization, a product of plants' reaction to winter temperature declines, is also a factor. To a lesser degree, and on a daily basis, this is why it is important that night temperatures for your plants drop.

Other factors are known to be involved, but probably less is understood about them than about the moon—literally. Perhaps you'll make one of the key discoveries simply by watching your plants. After all, the long-day/short-day discovery was made only in the twentieth century and with no really specialized tools, merely observation and speculation.

TICKTOCK

Of course, by now you've realized that observing the twelve to fourteen hours upon which a plant bases its flowering or nonflowering doesn't really solve any riddles. Instead it presents new ones. For instance, just *how does the plant know when the day is twelve hours or longer?*

Although there is still more than a little debate on the subject, the most likely answer to the question is that the plant itself has a natural internal, or endogenous, rhythm. The rhythm is self-sustaining, is based on an approximately twenty-four-hour cycle, and controls not only the plant's flowering, but leaf movement and overall development as well. The most controversial part of this theory, known as the Bünning hypothesis after the German botanist who conceived it, is that the plant actually uses its internal rhythm to measure the passing of external time.

DRUNK PLANTS AND ANTARCTIC MIDSUMMERS

Many years will probably pass before the external/internal clock controversy is resolved. The behavior of inebriated bean plants seems to support Bünning's hypothesis. When bean plants, one of the most common for experimental purposes, are given excessive amounts of alcohol, like drunk people they lose their sense of time. In fact, they become totally time disoriented, exhibiting a much slower and more erratic leaf movement than sober beans. This almost certainly implies an internal time-telling mechanism.

Another thing supporting Bünning's hypothesis is the research of K. C. Hamner carried out in summertime at the South Pole. He found that fruit flies and hamsters, as well as plants, retained their normal internal clocks even when brought up entirely on platforms made to revolve counter to the earth's rotation right on its axis. His specimens were raised virtually without any external time clues whatsoever. Even the earth's magnetic field and the effects of the globe's spinning had been eliminated. And still the plants could tell time.

BUILD A BETTER FLOWER

So what has all this to do with the nocturnal gardener? Well, simply, as you may have noticed, certain plants fail to accommodate people who are away from the house all day. A friend of mine had been growing *Chlorophytum comosum* for years. It wasn't until one spring when he came down with a bad cold and stayed home from work for a few days, however, that he noticed the plant was in bloom. The small white flowers weren't spectacular. But that wasn't the reason he'd never seen them before. They were open only during the day.

This habit of some flowers—being very inconsiderate of the working individual—is actually tied to pollinator specificity rather than to any direct attempt to snub the plants' keeper. After all, the primary object of the flower is to be pollinated, so seeds will form. Some specific insect is better than another at pollinating that type of flower. Accordingly, through evolution, the flower has modified itself to suit this insect's shape and habits more precisely with each passing eon.

Take red clover, *Trifolium pratense*, for instance. The flower is so constituted as to need a rather large bee looking around for nectar in order to be pollinated. An ordinary-sized bee simply wouldn't be up to the job. Now all the bees in the area can smell the nectar. Since it's located at the bottom of a nine- to ten-millimeter-long tube, however, they can't all reach it. Bees incapable of pollinating the flower depart hungry. But bumblebees just happen to have ten-millimeter or longer tongues. . . . *

---

* This brings up the old Darwinian paradox that for a nation to successfully foster the growth of red clover it needs a large population of old maids. Old maids keep

Or how about *Thunbergia grandiflora*? Here's a flower plagued by insect petty larceny. The pollinator is one *Xylocopa latipes*, a small winged insect averse to work. It's drawn to the particular nectar of *T. grandiflora*. Since the flower has a very narrow throat, however, the insect has to expend quite a lot of energy wriggling its way down to the nectar lode. In doing so, of course, pollination is assured by the wriggling. But, as we've said, *X. latipes* is lazy. It's known as a habitual nectar thief in the trade. Rather than squirming its way down that narrow passage, it will settle down on the outside of the flower, chew its way through to the nectar, and eat its fill without having pollinated the flower. Since the flower lasts only a day, *T. grandiflora* hasn't got a chance.

But wait a minute. The plot thickens. Besides a free-flowing nectary inside the flower, *T. grandiflora* has a series of nectaries on the outside at the base of the flower. So why doesn't *X. latipes* dine on these? Well, under isolated greenhouse conditions, it will. At first. Then it will chew its way into the main nectary as usual. Out in the wilds, however, the exterior sweetshops attract a different clientele, namely, ants. Bellicose ants that tend to send *X. latipes* flying away for dear life if it so much as tries to land anywhere on the outside of the flower. The larcenist is foiled on all fronts.

The ants, however, because of yet another mechanism, never go inside the flower. The hungry *X. latipes* is left with no choice but to get his lunch the hard way—and pollinate the flower the way he's supposed to.

And then there are some plants best pollinated by bats and moths. These plants, naturally enough, bloom predominantly during the night, when their nocturnal nuzzlers are active. (Many flowers, of course, stay open twenty-four hours a day, but that's another story.) Others, although open all day, are fragrant only at night. But when your *Epiphyllum oxypetalum* is ready to bloom, you know it will wait till you come home in the evening before it opens. It simply isn't used to catering to a daytime audience.

---

cats. The more old maids, the more cats. Cats, of course, catch mice. Therefore, the more cats, the less mice. Since mice dig up bumblebee nests, the less mice, the more bumblebees. And since bumblebees are needed to set seed in red clover, the more bumblebees, the more seeds set. *Post hoc, ergo propter hoc,* etc.: the more old maids, the more clover.

TEN BY MOONLIGHT

Allophyton mexicanum (Mexican Foxglove, Mexican Violet)
MICROCLIMATE: Temperate partial sun
Humusy soil kept constantly moist

For night people, *Allophyton mexicanum* is the flower that ends the evening's fragrant concert. The lovely but minute, half-inch, violet to purple bell-shaped flowers are sweet smelling—for just a little while, right after sunrise, although the flowers themselves remain open for several days. Blooms almost all year round, but particularly profusely in summer, with the flowers rising on short purple stalks from the center of the rosette formed by long, leathery, dark green leaves. Propagated easily by division or from seeds.

Brassavola nodosa (Lady of the Night)
MICROCLIMATE: Temperate partial sun
Humusy soil left to dry between waterings

Brassavola nodosa in bloom is guaranteed to keep you awake at least part of the night, enjoying the flower's rich fragrance. The plant is quite compact, for an orchid, with stemlike pseudobulbs on the thin side bearing deeply channeled fleshy leaves. The flowers are yellowish green with

Brassavola nodosa

a broad white lip. They bloom usually from late fall to early winter, although in some cases new clusters of flowers appear almost year round. The flowers are very fragrant—but only at night. They are pollinated by moths, you see.

A bearded cousin, *B. digbyana*, is also moth pollinated. It, however, has not yet become so specific and remains fragrant during the day as well as at night.

Cestrum nocturnum (Night Jessamine)
MICROCLIMATE: Warm sun
Loamy soil kept constantly moist

Although the creamy white trumpetlike flowers are almost insignificant in size, their fragrance is phenomenally strong. One plant will easily saturate a whole sun porch. And a sun porch is one of the best places to grow this evergreen shrub, not only because of its size, since plants grow readily to eight feet in pots, but because even though the flowers are night-fragrant, the plant as a whole needs a lot of solar energy to produce them. It can be grown as a regular houseplant as long as conditions are sunny and the atmosphere moist. Easily propagated from half-hardened wood of the new growth, that is, new growth around six months of age.

Epiphyllum oxypetalum (Queen of the Night)
MICROCLIMATE: Warm partial sun
Humusy soil kept constantly moist

One of the night-blooming cacti, the easiest and best to grow as a houseplant. It is a jungle cactus and needs rich soil as well as good atmospheric humidity. Feed the plant well during the spring to summer growing season. Very fragrant, large, four- to six-inch-diameter white blossoms with reddish edging erupt directly from the soft, waxy, flattened stems. Mature plants may reach a height of six to eight feet, with countless four- to eight-inch stems all capable of bearing blooms. The keys to flowering are cool night temperatures, fifty to fifty-five degrees for most of the growing season, and reduced watering during the wintertime. Easily propagated by cuttings in spring and summer. However, flowers will not usually develop on branches less than two years old.

Numerous hybrids are available, with blossoms in every imaginable color except, for some strange reason, blue. Most of the hybrids, however, are day bloomers, so look out.

Ervatamia coronaria (Crape Jasmine, East Indian Rosebay)
MICROCLIMATE: Warm sun
Loamy soil kept constantly moist

Somewhat similar in appearance to the gardenia, but easier to grow, *Ervatamia coronaria* is a night-fragrant shrub. While the crisp waxy flowers rarely exceed two inches, the glossy green elliptical leaves are up to five inches long. Grown in a twelve- to fifteen-inch pot, the plant will usually remain manageable in size for indoor, if not exactly tabletop, cultivation. In areas where night temperatures seldom drop below sixty degrees, *E. coronaria* can be summered outdoors, where the fragrance from only one or two plants in bloom can saturate a whole moonlit patio.

Hylocereus undatus

Hylocereus undatus (Common Night-Blooming Cereus, Honolulu
Queen)
MICROCLIMATE: Warm partial sun
Humusy soil kept constantly moist

This tropical cactus originates in Brazil, not Hawaii as one might be led
to guess by its popular name. However, it is grown widely as hedging in
the islands, giving wind protection, fruit, and beautiful flowers. It is one
of the largest of the night-blooming cacti, with three-angled climbing
stalks sometimes two inches in diameter. The white flowers are huge, as
much as a foot across, even when the plant itself is only two feet tall.
Very fragrant and very impressive. But each flower is a single feature: it
blooms and fades away in the same night.

Nicotiana alata 'Grandiflora' (Jasmine Tobacco)
MICROCLIMATE: Temperate sun
Loamy soil kept constantly moist

Tobacco may be an evil weed, but the miniatures make attractive
floriferous houseplants. This two- to three-foot perennial herb is best
grown as an annual, fresh from seed each year. The old plants can be revived, come spring, but it's easier to dispose of them after flowering. The
usually yellow trumpetlike flowers emit a fragrant sugary perfume at
night. Although they are normally open round the clock, the flowers will
close on cloudy days. The fuzzy stalks bearing the flowers and the large
soft ovate leaves up to five inches long are sticky.

Nyctocereus serpentinus (Queen of the Night, Serpent Cactus, Snake
Cactus)
MICROCLIMATE: Warm sun
Sandy soil left to dry between waterings

Another night-blooming cactus, this one of the spiny, typically cactusy-
looking desert variety. Woolly areoles with white to brownish spines on a
cylindrical multiple-ribbed stem. The funnel-shaped flower is white and
sweetly scented. The fruit is red and sticks around during the day as
well as at night.

Pelargonium gibbosum (Gouty Geranium, Knotted Geranium)
MICROCLIMATE: Temperate sun
Loamy soil left to dry between waterings

With its swollen joints, this plant truly looks arthritic. The flowers, which form in June, are greenish yellow and rather unexceptional—except for the lovely fragrance they give forth at night.

Pelargonium gibbosum

Selenicereus grandiflorus (Night-Blooming Cereus, True Queen of the Night)
MICROCLIMATE: Warm partial sun
Humusy soil kept constantly moist

Another one-night stander, and again large, up to a foot or more across. The salmon-colored trumpetlike flower with a white interior spills over a most pervasive vanilla fragrance in the moonlight. The plant itself is composed of grayish green to purple angled clambering stems with aerial roots and insignificant spines. Keep drier in winter to initiate blooming. Once spring growth starts, water profusely, but make sure the pot has good drainage. Blooms in summer, the flower opening shortly after sunset and dropping off by morning.

AND SO TO SLEEP

The nocturnal clockwork in plants is not limited to their flowers. Numerous plants close up shop entirely for the evening. For instance, the various clovers or *Trifolium, Oxalis* species such as *O. carnosa* and *O. incarnata*, and the popular sensitive plant *Mimosa pudica* all fold up their leaves at night. They do this, as Darwin discusses in his *Power of Movement in Plants*, to keep warm by minimizing radiation loss. Which is fine for them.

But if you've bought a specimen of *M. pudica* and come home every evening only to find it already asleep, it can be somewhat frustrating. The plant will certainly be a pleasure on weekends, though. And if you have only Saturday mornings to play with your flowers, even in that short a period of time they can give you an amazing amount of pleasure. Why, with only an hour a week to spend on them, you can grow a windowful of orchids.

Orchids: The Ugliest Plants in the World

Orchids under cultivation have been described variously as pots of tangled gray green worms, dried onions, and whiskers. Not exactly a flattering description of the plants bearing perhaps the most beautiful flowers in the world. Still, looking at it realistically, the orchid as a foliage plant doesn't have much to offer. In fact, it's a pretty scruffy mess.

For a long time, even the flowers didn't really impress me much personally, my observance having been limited more or less to high-school days when corsages were in vogue and one would set me back a week's paper-route money. Then I visited the Singapore Botanical Gardens when orchids by the thousands were in bloom. It was an overwhelming, indescribable spectacle, not just the fragrance and dapplings of exotic color spread so lavishly across walls and fields of green, but the complex variety of species whose existence I had never suspected.

And with all this, I found out, the Singapore gardens grow a very limited range of plants, for one of their main emphases is raising and nurturing native Malaysian orchids that are in danger of extinction because of the inroads of civilization. The intricate beauty before me represented only a small segment of the Orchidaceae family. The world at large offered thousands and thousands more—species ranging from *Bulbophyllum minutissimum*, with blossoms so small one needs a magnifying glass to see them in detail, to others like *Grammatophyllum speciosum*, whose six- to eight-inch blooms are borne fifty or sixty at a time on lampostlike floral stalks ten feet high, to *Dendrobium appendiculatum*, which could really be called the lightning flower, since the blossoms remain open only five minutes. I became a convert.

WHAT IS AN ORCHID?

Orchids are thought to have originated in the warmer regions of Southeast Asia, spreading from there to most of the rest of the world. With migration to cooler areas, the plants lost their tropical evergrowing habit and joined the temperate zone plants in a cyclic growth pattern. But even some of the tropical varieties are seasonal, resting during the dry season.

The orchid plant itself, as mentioned before, is unimpressive. It is the flower that gives it distinction. One of the major differentiating characteristics of the orchid flower is that its stamens and pistils are welded

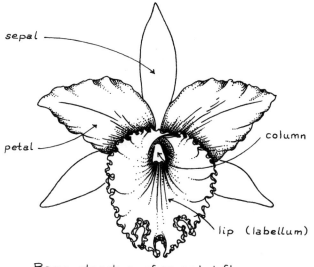

Basic structure of an orchid flower

together in a single reproductive structure called the column. The flower is also characterized by having three sepals, which protect the bud and become petallike in color and shape as the flower develops, as well as three petals, one of which is highly modified and called a lip.

The development of Orchidaceae flowers is intimately tied to the evolution of pollinating insects. In fact, one of the most remarkable systems of pollination in the whole plant world is that of the ophrys orchids. It is so remarkable that Darwin was driven to despair trying to unravel its mystery. Some of these orchids have neither nectar nor fragrance to attract insects. Yet they are not wind pollinated, and they are not self-pollinating. Their insect-attracting ability turns out to lie in their shape —and, as Julian Huxley remarked, considering the sensibilities of Victorian morals, perhaps it was better that Darwin failed to find the answer to the riddle. The central pollen- and ovule-bearing part is shaped like an insect, specifically, like a female wasp of a given associative species. These orchids have real sex appeal. The male wasp, attracted to the flowery mannequins, actually attempts copulation. Frustrated by one pseudocopulation, he flies on to another "female" and another, transferring the pollen from the anther of the first flower to the stamen of the next.

HARDIER THAN YOU MAY THINK

Orchids became a rich man's fancy in England and Europe during the middle of the nineteenth century. But not till the end of the 1800s did orchid growing really capture the imagination of Americans. Part of the reason was the difficulty of duplicating those dark, dank, stiflingly hot jungle conditions under which the flowers supposedly thrived. Even given the closest possible approximation to what was believed to be a jungle environment, most specimens under cultivation died. With a single choice plant going at five hundred to a thousand or more dollars—of the old, valuable kind—one can readily see the limitations of orchid raising as a hobby.

The problem lay in the artificial jungles created for the plants, which in no way truly simulated the real ones. When in later attempts at cultivation heat was reduced and fresh air circulated, the orchids began to thrive. With World War II and fuel rationing, however, all appeared lost. Thousands and thousands of plants were doomed to die for lack of heat. And yet they didn't. It was found that they could survive much cooler temperatures than previously believed. In fact, they did better given a cool climate, particularly at night.

Although you're not about to see tropical orchids growing wild in Alaska, they are much more tenacious than one might think, and they keep growing and blooming year after year. Orchids are designed for survival. They need lots of moisture, of that there's no doubt. But, surprisingly, some orchids are even easier to care for than that familiar houseplant standby, the begonia.

IT'S NOT HOW WARM YOU KEEP THEM, BUT WHEN YOU KEEP THEM WARM

Fluctuating temperatures from daytime to nighttime are essential for the blooming of orchids. Usually a ten-degree drop from the day's average is needed. With the lowered temperature the plant is able to conserve the energy it generated during the day by reducing its respiration rate. That is to say, it "sleeps," and thus uses up less energy, just the way you do. Under a constant temperature, the plant stays revved up all night, yet is unable to continue photosynthesis because there's no light. Eventually fatigue sets in.

Not only temperature, but the air itself, should change. Drafts are unpopular; stale air is just as much so. Fungi are attracted to orchids. Good air circulation keeps them from settling down.

Windowsill orchids usually get plenty of air circulation through the convections that develop from the cool of the windowpane. However, orchids grown under a light in some corner of the house that is normally without good airflow (the most extreme case I've seen was a butler's pantry filled with them) may need the addition of a small fan blowing *away* from the plants.

A NOTE ON THE NUMBER OF FEET

Orchids come in two basic varieties. There are the orchids with one "foot," the monopodials, and those with several "feet," the sympodials.

Monopodial orchids have one central stem, usually beneath the leaves, where it remains unobserved. Growth occurs at the tip. Lateral branches may develop and can be forced by cutting off the main growing stem below the leaves. Do it in such a manner as to include some new roots on the cutting while leaving the old roots and part of the stem growing; the cut-off head can be planted too. Meanwhile the old body should be sending out new shoots in several weeks to months. The new shoots emerging from the stump form plantlets. These side shoots are called keikis, a name adapted from the Hawaiian. Once the keikis have developed a good root system of their own, cut them free from the mother and pot separately.

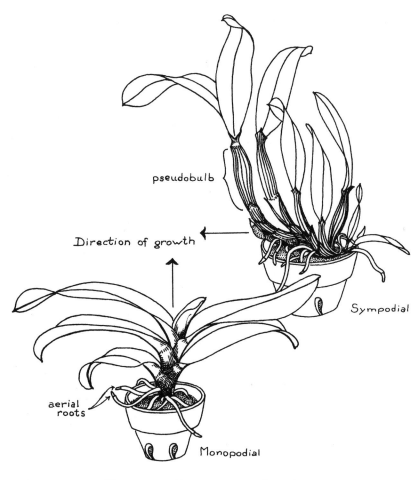

pseudobulb

Direction of growth

Sympodial

aerial roots

Monopodial

Basic growth patterns of orchids

The sympodial orchids keep growing through basal buds that develop into new stems with the same characteristics as the original. It's like an endless chain of Siamese twins, triplets, quadruplets, and so on, with each new bulb remaining attached to the old one by means of a rhizome, or rootlike stem. Often stems branch and rebranch, making a real rat's nest of the pot, not to mention "walking" right out of it.

In some species, the new stems swell with water and food storage cells as they mature. They are then referred to as pseudobulbs, as opposed to the true bulbs of such species as tulips and gladiolus. Once a new branch, or lead, has several pseudobulbs on it, you can separate them from the original bulb and pot as a new plant.

Always use a sharp, sterilized knife when dividing. Never cut more than one plant with a knife before resterilizing it over a hot flame. This is a good general horticultural practice that will reduce the spread of disease, particularly viruses. In orchid care, it is absolutely essential.

Older bulbs, those with flowering behind them, are called back bulbs. Their show is over—orchid bulbs flower only once. But by being made to feel that the new plants aren't doing well, back bulbs can be forced to generate more growth. Nick the rhizome part of the way through near the old bulb. This effectively reduces feedback from the new generation.

Nick rhizome part of the way through

Once new growth starts on back bulb, cut free and pot up separately

Back bulb propagation of cymbidium

Then once the back bulb's new growth starts rooting, cut the rhizome completely through and pot the new growth. The younger the back bulb, the higher the rate of success. Back bulbs can also be separated completely before new growth commences, particularly with large specimens such as cymbidiums. However, leaving them partially attached until growth is initiated reduces the shock for the plant and is a good insurance program for the beginner.

Orchid plants do, of course, reproduce from seeds—there are as many as several million dustlike seeds to each pod. But coaxing them to do so is quite exacting, and you need a nutrient solution as well as sterile conditions, since orchid seeds don't have stored in them enough food even to reach the seedling state. Best to wait till you've become really familiar with the plant before trying this form of propagation. Cattleyas, for instance, take five to seven years from seed to flower. That's a lot of patience.

. . . AND WHAT TO PUT THEM IN

One thing I learned from years of reading Nero Wolfe adventures before I became interested in orchids is that they grow in osmunda. I even looked the word up one day and found that it is a fiber from the roots of the royal swamp fern, *Osmunda regalis*. The question why orchids are grown in osmunda I didn't bother to pursue at the time.

There is a good reason, naturally. Epiphytic orchids are used to having their roots exposed to air. The osmunda, while retaining just the right amount of moisture, at the same time permits good air circulation. Fir and redwood barks, mixed usually two-thirds fir to one-third redwood, are often used as a potting medium today. It is easier to work with and less expensive than osmunda, but requires that you tend the plants with a nitrogen-heavy fertilizer. Unlike osmunda, the barks are deficient in nitrogen. A biweekly feeding with 30-10-10 fertilizer solution or, as is more the trend today, a very dilute solution of it used regularly for watering, will compensate for this. Another advantage of osmunda, however, is its ability to hold up for a long time. Once a potting medium breaks down, turning more or less to dust or mud slurry, you must repot. That means disturbing the plant, often slowing its growth.

Whichever potting medium you use, coarse sand, pea gravel, charcoal, Sponge-rok, or other looseners should be added to ensure good texture. Bark usually must have lime added to adjust the pH. For your first repottings it's a good idea to save yourself trouble by buying one of the commercial blends made up by firms that sell orchids.

As long as the potting medium is holding up, repotting is necessary only every second year or so. The time to do it is after flowering and before new root formation develops. Pick a pot about two inches greater in diameter than the base of your plant. If at all possible, use an orchid pot. It is notched along the bottom of the side to allow much better drainage and air circulation. If you use a regular pot, you'll have to enlarge the drainage hole considerably. This can be done with an ice pick or a tack hammer. It's an excellent way of building up your shard collection till you get the hang of it.

Lay down a good layer of crockery over the hole and fill the pot half full with moist mix. Unlike most potted plants, the orchids prefer their soil firmly compressed around the roots. There will be plenty of room for air circulation, since the potting soil is so chunky, but if you don't pack it down, the plant will be wobbly. Airsick orchids do not grow well. Therefore, unless the mix you use comes with specific instructions not to pack it, do so firmly with a blunt stick. Supply houses sell potting sticks, for those who want to feel really professional about it.

Trim off dead roots, the ones that feel empty and light, and clear out as much of the spent potting medium as possible from between the remaining roots. If you are switching potting mixes, it is essential that you clean away all the old mix, since the two may be incompatible in water-holding qualities. Set the plant, if it is a sympodial, so that the oldest bulb is against the edge of the pot and the roots are resting on the soil. If it is a monopodial orchid, it should be centered in the pot. Then carefully pour in more mix, working it tightly between the roots with your fingers. The trick is to fill all the cavities without breaking the brittle roots. Tamp down the soil again once the pot has been filled to within three-quarters of an inch to an inch of the rim. Be firm but gentle. Lastly, stick a wire stake into the soil and tie the plant to it. This will ensure that the plant does not wobble. Keep watering reduced and the plant out of direct sunlight until you see root growth commencing.

Orchids raised in osmunda need much less feeding than those in bark mixes. However, potting with this medium takes a bit more acquired skill, since you have to get a feel for breaking the osmunda into the right-sized chunks before potting. With either fir or osmunda, it's best to get a special orchid fertilizer and follow the specific directions for the brand used.

MESMERIZED BY MERISTEMS

Perusing the catalogs—and mail-order houses are the most common source of orchids—you'll come across the term "mericlones," and therein lies a most fascinating story. In the late 1950s the French plant physiologist Georges Morel discovered that under aseptic conditions he could cultivate the apical meristem, or growing point, of a cymbidium. It's somewhat the equivalent of cutting off your finger and watching another human being grow out from it.

Not only that, but once meristem growth reached the protocorm stage, that is, the stage where the cells have multiplied to form a little ball, but with no leaves or roots yet, Morel found the meristem could be divided again and again and again. The process was perfected on a commercial basis by the French firm of Vacherot & Lecoufle, and now plants that once cost hundreds of dollars, even a thousand, are available, for a fiftieth of the price, as mericlones. Meristemming isn't something you'll be doing in the kitchen, but at least you'll know that when you buy a clone, it's usually from a plant probably only a maharajah could have afforded back in the sixties. And it's absolutely identical to its parent in every quality.

SIXTEEN TO GET YOU STARTED

Ansellia gigantea 'Nilotica' (Leopard Orchid)
> MICROCLIMATE: Warm sun
> Orchid mix left to dry between waterings

Primarily from East Africa, *Ansellia gigantea* 'Nilotica' is often found growing on the unique *Hyphaene thebaica* palm, the only known genus of palm with a forked trunk. The palm fruit, with the taste and texture of gingerbread cookies, is bright orange. Add to that several *A. gigantea* 'nilotica' in bloom, with clusters of a hundred yellow and chocolate flowers flowing down on each spike, and you have a spectacular plant combination even P.T. Barnum would have had trouble dreaming up.

The orchid plant itself is fairly compact, usually one to two feet high. Given abundant natural light or lengthy days under good artificial illumination, the fleshy, bright yellow flowers about two inches across, barred and flecked with brown, are often produced in profusion several times a year. *A. gigantea* 'nilotica' takes no real rest period. Primary blooming times, however, are summer and winter.

Brassavola digbyana
> MICROCLIMATE: Temperate partial sun
> Orchid mix left to dry between waterings

The large white to apple green flowers four to six inches across are strikingly fringed with a "beard." Anywhere from one to seven flowers per raceme, or flower spike, bloom in spring and summer. Easy to grow if watered liberally and fed every two to three weeks. Excellent drainage is essential, for while the plants need a great deal of moisture around the roots, they must never be left sopping wet. After the main growing period, when new bulbs have stopped developing, the plants should be given a two-week dry rest period. Then resume watering, but not quite as generously. These plants do not like to be disturbed, so avoid dividing unnecessarily and wait at least till you're proficient at it.

> *Brassia gireoudiana* (Spider Orchid)
> MICROCLIMATE: Temperate partial sun
> Orchid mix kept constantly moist

Named after the eighteenth-century botanical illustrator William Brass, Esq., this flower has sepals and petals greatly attenuated, giving it a fantasylike appearance as well as its common name. Green-tinted yellow blooms with splashes of dark brown at the base erupt in racemes sometimes two feet long. Flowers freely in the spring and beyond. Long lasting though they may be, these energy-demanding blossoms should be removed once flowering is almost completed, before they can sap the bulbs of their energy and shrink them. Although easy to grow, brassias are very sensitive to stale soil. Repot whenever the compost in which they are growing breaks down. Do not use an oversized pot in the hopes of eliminating this chore. The plants like their feet bound a bit.

> *Cattleya bowringiana* (Cluster Cattleya)
> MICROCLIMATE: Temperate sun
> Orchid mix left to dry between waterings

Cattleyas are the familiar orchids from high-school proms. And they are almost synonymous with the word "orchid" itself. Still, at the risk of bringing down the wrath of old William Cattley's ghost on my plants, I think there are a lot more exciting genera to grow—a personal prejudice, I grant you.

Cattleyas are, however, easy enough to grow in the house as long as the relative humidity remains between 50 and 70 percent, which is about what you will need for all your orchids anyhow. And there has probably been more hybridization among the cattleyas than in any other orchid genus, which means there are numerous showy species to choose from, often at very reasonable prices.

C. bowringiana is a prolific late fall, early winter bloomer, with occasionally as many as twenty flowers on a stem, and a strong grower. The sepals and petals are rose purple, the lip a much darker maroon. In its native Central America, this orchid is almost always found on rocks close to running water. Its appetite for liquid refreshment is high. But once the new pseudobulbs are mature and the flowers shot, so to speak, watering should be cut back till the "eye," the bump that develops at the base of the pseudobulb, ruptures into new growth. The pseudobulbs should never be allowed to dry out completely, however.

Coelogyne cristata
  MICROCLIMATE: Cool partial sun
         Orchid mix kept constantly moist

Long-blossoming winter flowers which, except for their yellow centers, are almost as white as the snows of their native Nepalese Himalayas. An excellent easy-to-grow orchid for cooler locations, either on the windowsill or in a hanging basket. Sweetly fragrant, with flowers lasting over a month if not kept too warm.

Coelogynes are another genus with an aversion to being pushed around. The key to good flowering, besides a cool growing environment, is not to repot until absolutely necessary. Transplant shock can delay blooming by as much as three years. The rhizome does branch frequently, and the pseudobulbs may become too crowded. But in that case, rather than repotting, thin out older bulbs by cutting them away with a flame-sterilized knife and fill the empty spaces with fresh compost.

Cymbidium miniatures
  MICROCLIMATE: Temperate sun
         Orchid mix kept constantly moist

The miniature cymbidium hybrids are excellent starter orchids. They are manageable in size, with leaves rarely over two feet, and have graceful, colorful, long-lasting flowers. The plants are surprisingly adaptable, although they need high humidity and, for the best blooms, lots of bright sun, particularly in the summer. They need protection from direct sun during the intense noonday period, however, or they may sunburn. A glass curtain is the standard solution to this problem.

This is one genus in which numerous excellent quality mericlones are available to the beginner. Their cost, when one thinks orchids, is low.

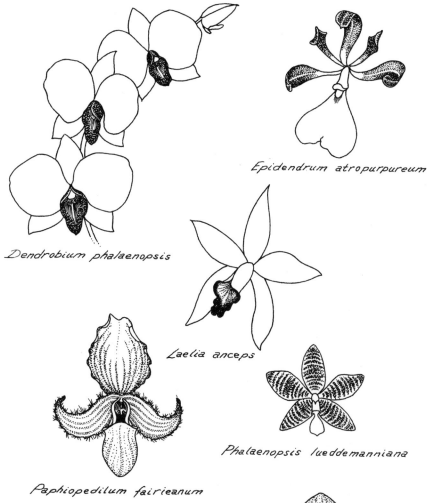

Dendrobium phalaenopsis

Epidendrum atropurpureum

Laelia anceps

Paphiopedilum fairieanum

Phalaenopsis lueddemanniana

Sophronitis coccinea

Vanda rothschildiana

Flower variations in orchids

Even ready-to-flower specimens usually run no more than a movie plus babysitter. And you'll have arching sprays of blooms for years and years. But make sure it's one of the miniature hybrids you're getting. Full-sized cymbidiums not only are unmanageable in their dimensions, they really need a cool greenhouse.

Dendrobium densiflorum

MICROCLIMATE: Temperate partial sun

Orchid mix left to dry between waterings

Another compact free-flowering, or profusely blooming, orchid from the Himalayas. Orange yellow flowers to two inches across, with as many as a hundred of them encircling the canes of one plant. The plant needs copious amounts of water, never standing, of course, while in active growth. After growth, the water should be withheld to harden the pseudo-bulbs and set flowers. Summers well outdoors.

Dendrobium phalaenopsis

MICROCLIMATE: Warm partial sun

Orchid mix left to dry between waterings

The 'Schroederianum' variety of this orchid is the famous carnivorous vampire orchid that had England in a stir during the 1890s. The first specimens arrived from the jungles of New Guinea growing out of a human skull—obvious inferences were drawn. The actual story involves a well-known collector of the time by the name of Micholitz. Traveling among the headhunters of New Guinea, he came upon the orchid in a sacred burial ground. After much nervous bartering, he was permitted to remove some specimens of the flower. It isn't clear whether the skull came as a necessary part of the trade.

The plant has stiff slender canes as long as three feet, with arching sprays of white to pale rose, purplish red, and magenta blooms. Flowers mainly in spring, often with an encore in fall. Does not require a resting period. Prefers a well-drained small pot—about skull sized, actually.

Epidendrum atropurpureum (Spice Orchid)

MICROCLIMATE: Temperate partial sun

Orchid mix left to dry between waterings

A free-blooming, easily cultivated evergreen epiphyte bearing many-flowered racemes. The blossoms are two to three inches across, predominantly chocolate colored with lighter borders and crimson centers. A fragrant delight during spring flowering. Blooms are long lasting, up to five weeks.

Epidendrum cochleatum goes *E. atropurpureum* one better. It is a spidery species with three-inch upside-down flowers resembling, if you prefer mollusk to insect images, an octopus. The flowers, which have a brown cockleshell lip and pale green petals, bloom primarily during winter. But with good light and growing conditions the plant is almost everblooming.

Laelia anceps
MICROCLIMATE: Temperate partial sun
Orchid mix left to dry between waterings

Plenty of light is the order of the day for *Laelia anceps*, a prolific and robust species of orchid from Mexico and Central America. Laelias as a whole resemble cattleyas, but the flowers are more brilliant in color, while not quite as full. You'll find a lot of crosses trying to get the best of both breeds. Very variable in color, with the winter flowers ranging from almost white to purple, depending on the specimen. Smallish pots make for the best growth. Propagated easily by division, but needs a rest after flowering.

Maxillaria variabilis
MICROCLIMATE: Temperate partial sun
Orchid mix kept constantly moist

Maxillarias are less common in collections than most of the orchids mentioned here. Yet the plants are relatively easy to grow. Do well in any of the following three potting mediums: osmunda, chunky tree fern, or bark mix. All should be firmly tamped down and tightly packed. Small yellow or white flowers, up to an inch in diameter, with dark red lip bloom throughout the year. Often almost everblooming.

Miltonia phalaenopsis (Pansy Face)
MICROCLIMATE: Temperate sun
Orchid mix kept constantly moist

From Colombia, these mountain flowers have been reported in some cases growing at elevations above fifteen thousand feet. Cool growers that need a good nighttime drop in temperature for best development. Since the roots are quite fine, sift out the coarsest potting components in their mix. Do not spray flowers, but keep overall humidity high. The plants do well under artificial light. Growth from clustered, flat pseudobulbs is grasslike, eight to twelve inches high. Flattened flowers two inches across have white sepals and petals with crimson-streaked lip. Bloom is in spring or summer for five weeks or more. Unlike most orchids, however, the lasting quality of the miltonias as cut flowers is poor.

Oncidium ornithorhynchum
MICROCLIMATE: Temperate partial sun
Orchid mix left to dry between waterings

Requiring less attention than most other orchid genera, oncidiums are excellent for beginners. The flowers are small but plentiful, in large bouquetlike arching sprays. *Oncidium ornithorhynchum* has fragrant, long-lasting fall and winter flowers rose to lilac colored with darker lip and yellow crest. Needs a rest period after growth for best flower production. Also likes a tight pot, firmly packed with osmunda.

Paphiopedilum fairieanum (Lady Slipper)
MICROCLIMATE: Temperate shade
Orchid mix kept constantly moist

Prefers it cool and does best with plenty of fresh air. Takes well to air conditioning as long as drafts are avoided. A compact species with pouch- or slipper-shaped flowers striped white and purple to brown. Blooming begins in summer and often goes on into the new year. Individual blossoms last four to six weeks. Since the plants form no pseudobulbs, constant moisture is required. Fertilize twice monthly with a weakened solution. Being a terrestrial orchid, it is potted most frequently in bark mixes almost as fine as soil. Does well under artificial light.

Phalaenopsis lueddemanniana
MICROCLIMATE: Warm shade
Orchid mix kept constantly moist

One of the so-called moth orchids from the Philippines, *Phalaenopsis lueddemanniana* is a monopodial with short clusters of waxy heavy-textured flowers whitish to yellow with cinnamon to amethyst markings.

They are long lasting, up to two months, and fragrant. Primary bloom is in spring or summer. But with the right care of the flower spike, a specimen can be kept flowering for as much as ten months. Rather than cutting back the spike at its base after flowering, the way you do with most orchid species, trim it just behind the faded flowers. This will usually force a side shoot from a lower node. The lateral stalk will duplicate the original display. In general, you should never cut away the spike until it withers, for another habit of the phalaenopsis is to occasionally generate plantlets, or keikis, on the old stems. They can be amputated and repotted once root growth is well established. Since this orchid is another one without a pseudobulb, it is crucial that the plant never be allowed to dry out. Humidity is on the whole much more crucial than light. Your specimen will be satisfied with less light than most popular orchids, but should have 70 percent humidity. Warmth is also needed except in the period just before flowering, when a nighttime drop to fifty-five degrees is beneficial to get things going.

Sophronitis coccinea
> MICROCLIMATE: Temperate partial sun
> Orchid mix kept constantly moist

Vivid scarlet blooms, one to a spike, are produced from September through winter. The plant is a dwarf epiphyte with a high water demand. Grows all year without rest. A little trickier than most, since it won't flower unless conditions are really humid and bright, but well worth trying as a next step after you've raised your first couple of orchid specimens.

A WORD ON VANDAS

Once you start getting those orchid catalogs, your eyes will probably keep wandering back to the genus *Vanda*, particularly such species as *Vanda rothschildiana*, one of the most popular of all blue hybrids. Well, they are beautiful. And they are relatively easy to grow. But when the instructions say they need at least six hours of very bright to direct sunlight a day, that's precisely what is meant. Even as much as five hours may not be enough to give you flowers. Best grown in a greenhouse. Now about getting a small greenhouse. . . .

THE CASE FOR A CASE

If you've gotten this far and find you absolutely can't raise the humidity in your house to a constant fifty degrees plus, consider a super-sized terrarium. A large glass case, either homemade or store bought, can become an ideal minienvironment for orchids. It is an excellent way to grow them under artificial light. Just remember they need good ventilation. You can't seal the case hermetically the way you would a regular terrarium. Give them a little access to outside air, best propelled by a small fan. Your orchids will give you in return a fine display of their exotic flowers.

THE ANSWER MAN

Orchid growing produces numerous specific small problems of a greatly varying nature. Write a question, leaving plenty of room for answer, on a self-addressed postage-paid postcard and stick it in an envelope addressed to the Question Box, American Orchid Society Bulletin, Botanical Museum of Harvard University, Cambridge, Massachusetts 02138. While you're at it, inquire about membership. The *American Orchid Society Bulletin* is one of the best specialty plant journals in the world.

Gesneriads: The Fuzzy-Leaved Favorites

The most popular of all houseplants may be the philodendron; the most popular *flowering* houseplant is almost certainly the African violet. Both came into vogue comparatively recently and through rather strange circumstances, the philodendron because of the Depression, the African violet after the invention of the fluorescent light.

Philodendron oxycardium, or heartleaf philodendron, was first taken to Europe from the West Indies by Captain William Bligh of *Mutiny on the Bounty* fame. But for some unknown reason it did not participate in the interior greening of Victorian England, remaining more or less a botanical garden specimen until the Great Depression. Then Florida nurserymen discovered that not only was it relatively pest-free and easy to grow, but it could be propagated for next to nothing. Millions of plants were shipped to five-and-ten-cent stores across the country. And with them the mass marketing of houseplants was launched.

African violets—not at all related to true violets—were introduced into the United States at the turn of the century. They remained splendid curiosities for the rich, since their culture and care seemed beyond the most patient amateur horticulturist. Because of their tropical origins, it was impossible to grow them in the unheated houses of the times.

However, central heating was making great inroads in American homes by the 1920s and 1930s. By the end of the Korean War, the African violet cult had truly begun to blossom. New hybrids were made almost everblooming. With as few as three plants you were assured flowers all year round. And more important, it was discovered they did even better under the recently developed fluorescent lights than they did in nature. Again millions of plants were sold. Local clubs sprang up overnight. And hybridization expanded to monstrous proportions. There are now thousands of varieties, many of them so much alike even their originators couldn't tell them apart.

NONVIOLETS FROM AFRICA

The Usambara, or African, violet was discovered by the Usambara Imperial District Captain of the German Empire, Baron Walter von Saint Paul-Illaire. In 1892 he dispatched either plants or seeds, most likely the latter, to his father in Silesia. The elder von Saint Paul was an enthusiastic amateur botanist. He grew the plants and took several specimens to the director of the local royal botanical gardens. The director, naming them *Saintpaulia* after their discoverer and adding *ionantha*, the Latin for "with violetlike flowers," exhibited them at the Ghent International Horticultural Exhibit a few years later. They drew rave reviews and admiring collectors, as they have ever since.

It was in the 1930s that the firm of Armacost and Royston in California began serious mass-scale hybridization of saintpaulias. By 1936 they had developed ten varieties, including Blue Boy, Norseman, and No. 32, all of which were to form the backbone of today's hybrid strains. By now, hybrids of saintpaulias have almost reached the point of absurdity. Furthermore, the names of some of the varieties are so kitschy as to convince most sane people that African violets are only for ladies' circle tea parties and grandmothers. After all, what do you do with 'Pooty-cat,' 'Pucker Up,' 'Wee Too,' 'Tinted Clouds,' 'Knit Wit,' and plants described as having "girl" foliage and "boy" foliage? I left them alone for a long while. Even now, although I do have some saintpaulias, I personally prefer growing other members of the diverse gesneriad family.

TRIPLE-X RATED

One reason there is such a profusion of hybrids in the genus *Saintpaulia* is the ease with which the plants are cross-pollinated. If you want to try your hand at pollinating flowers and growing new plants from the resulting seeds, here's excellent first-time-around material. Assuming you're interested simply in seeing how it's done, all you need is a single plant. Cross-pollination refers to introducing pollen from the anthers of one flower to the pistil of another flower. But nothing says they have to be on different plants (unless, of course, you're dealing with a species that carries flowers of only one sex on each plant). Cross-pollinating flowers on the same plant may occasionally produce interesting mutations in the following generation, not to mention the sports that can occur when cross-pollinating different hybrids.

All this is assuming, of course, either that you want the experience of playing bee to your flowers, with the resulting pleasure of growing plants from the seeds you helped develop, or that you plan to try eventually to develop an entirely new plant by crossing two exceptional specimens. If you just want extra plants like the ones you already have, then vegetative reproduction by cuttings or offsets is to be preferred. It guarantees you plants with the same qualities as the parent. For the beginner it is also often easier, not to mention quicker.

The fact that seed-grown plants often differ to a minor degree or more from their parents is evolutionary. To differ is one of the purposes of seeds, the main one, naturally, being sheer reproduction. With the constant genetic blending that occurs in sexual reproduction, new variants develop in each generation. Those best adapted to the changing environment or to new locations of dispersal are the ones that survive, thus strengthening, if at the same time altering, the family tree with each passing generation. To help ensure cross-pollination, and its subsequent benefits, many flowers are designed to minimze the chances of self-pollination.

But back to that single saintpaulia on your windowsill, the one whose future seed will probably *not* change the evolutionary direction of its whole genus. Pick up the pot and look at the plant closely. Hopefully, for simplicity's sake, it's a single-flowered variety rather than double. The flowers are bisexual. Each one has both anthers, the male organs, and a pistil, the female organ, surrounded by the colorful corolla we usually think of as the flower itself. In the case of the saintpaulia, this corolla appears to be composed of five petals. However, if you look closely you'll notice it's really only two, a two-lobed upper one and a three-lobed lower one to which the yellow pollen-filled anthers are attached. The pistil, on the other hand, comes right from the center of the flower, wherein is contained the ovary. To minimize self-pollination, the pistil grows out to one side of the flower center, away from the anthers, and if you look closely, you'll notice that the tip of the pistil, known as the stigma, is bent down as well as out. Since the sticky tip is where the pollen must land in order for seeds to develop, its angle further minimizes self-fertilization.

The easiest tools for pollination are a pair of small tweezers, a razor blade, curved fingernail scissors, and sometimes a piece of black cardboard or paper. A small, soft camel's-hair brush can be used in addition, but is not really necessary.

Select two good-looking flowers. You want them to have been open at full size for at least two or three weeks to make sure the pollen is fully developed. On the other hand, you don't want the flower to be spent. Some plants are very tricky that way, having only an hour or so in the flowers' existence that is just right for pollination. Saintpaulias are much more obliging. Almost any time during the flowers' long life will work.

THE OPERATION

The flowers are chosen and the tools ready—what next? Pollen picking, naturally. Some people remove the stamen and the whole corolla along with it, the rationale being, I suppose, that once the flower has been pollinated the corolla is no longer needed to attract insects and thus might as well be disposed of so it won't drain energy better put to use developing the seeds. Leaving the corolla on or taking it off seems to work equally well. But you might as well get into the habit of removing the anthers, since this is done pretty regularly on all future seed-bearing flowers to avoid accidental self-pollination.

A whole stamen can be readily removed with a snip of the scissors. Place it on a piece of black cardboard. With the tweezers, hold onto the filament, or shaft, beneath the anther, or pollen sack. Cut away the tip of the anther with the razor blade. As you do so, some golden to white powder will spill out onto the cardboard. If it stays in a ball and doesn't scatter like dust, the pollen wasn't ready. The dust can be picked up with the camel's-hair brush and gently deposited on the sticky tip of the stigma. By dint of careful brushwork you can stretch the pollen out to cover many, many stigmas.

Since I usually don't have that many plants to pollinate, I use a

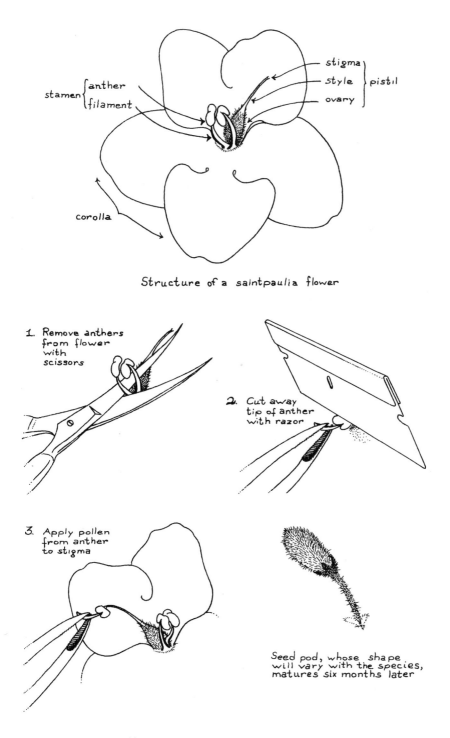

Structure of a saintpaulia flower

stigma ⎤
style ⎬ pistil
ovary ⎦

stamen ⎰ anther
       ⎱ filament

corolla

1. Remove anthers from flower with scissors

2. Cut away tip of anther with razor

3. Apply pollen from anther to stigma

Seed pod, whose shape will vary with the species, matures six months later

Hand-pollination of saintpaulias

coarser method. Once I've cut away part of the anther, I merely pick it up with the tweezers and push it gently on top of the stigma. While the stigma normally looks lighter, more translucent than the rest of the pistil, once it's covered with pollen the change is quite noticeable.

The pollen cells begin to grow down inside the pistil as soon as they've made contact. The rate of descent from stigma to ovary is quite rapid, as much as an inch in twenty-four hours in some plants. Once a pollen cell enters the ovary, fertilization occurs. But don't hold your breath. You won't notice the seedpod swelling for several weeks. Meanwhile you might as well put a small string tag on the plant to indicate the seeds' parentage. Label the seedpod even if you have only a few plants. It will take six to nine months for the seedpod to mature, and by then you could have scores of new plants to confuse the issue.

Springtime-pollinated saintpaulias take about six months to set a mature seedpod, fall-pollinated ones a little longer, usually up to nine months. The difference is probably due to generally slower growing conditions over the winter season. Of course, if you grow the plants under artificial light, most of the external seasonal variations will be eliminated. But there are also internal time variations introduced by the species involved.

Whatever amount of time your seedpod takes to mature, the plant during this time should be kept just a little drier than usual around the roots and given good air circulation. A still, cloying atmosphere can lead to softening and eventually rotting seedpods.

As it reaches maturity, the seedpod will begin to dry and shrivel. Once the withering has stopped completely and the pod has turned more or less evenly brown, it's done. Remove it from the flower, stalk and all. If you are impatient to be planting, the tiny dustlike seeds may be used at once. Normally, however, they are permitted a period of further drying, or after-ripening, of about four to six weeks.

Seedlings will usually flower the first year if well cared for. Store surplus seeds in small capped bottles—plastic vials from the pharmacist work well—in a cool place. A temperature of sixty degrees is ideal. Saintpaulia seeds will retain their viability for a year or more, those from some other plants less than a week.

YES, YOU CAN GET WATER ON THE LEAVES

The old adage about never getting water on those fuzzy leaves lest they be permanently maimed isn't true—unless the water is cold. Cold water on hairy leaves will produce spotting and ugly blemishes. But you shouldn't have been using cold water near the plants in the first place, or, for that matter, near any of your plants. Always use tepid water when tending houseplants.

Fuzzy leaves, like unfuzzy ones, may be washed with tepid water, leaving no evidence of your actions except cleaner leaves. Fill a bowl with a mild *soap* (not detergent) solution in lukewarm water. Turn the pot upside down and, holding the soil in place with your fingers, gently swirl the leaves in the cleaner. The leaves can be very brittle, by the way, so mind that word "gently." Let them drain well while the plant is still upside down; a little soapy water in the soil is beneficial, eliminating certain pests, but you don't want too much.

Apart from water spotting, there is a good reason for using the long-spouted watering can traditionally associated with saintpaulias for most of your gesneriads, and maybe even for plants in general. The leaves tend to fill out the pot grandiosely, and it's hard to get water in between them unless you literally pipe it in. Dumping a glassful of tepid water into the pot each time you water will wash the leaves; it also will probably rot the plant's crown. Excess water tends to lodge there to a much greater degree than rainwater in a plant's natural environment. And rotting crowns make for dead plants.

Another reason for the long spout is that you'll want to mix some fertilizer with the water twice a month when the plants begin to flower, and you don't want to get too much of this solution on the leaves. They are quite capable of absorbing some nutrients, but not too many at once; fertilizer salts simply poured on will collect, clogging the pores and discoloring the leaves.

BLASTING BUDS

Plants demand more light in their flowering stage than in their leafy state. But although light is usually the initiator of flower formation, it is not sufficient in itself to carry the process to completion. Without enough atmospheric humidity, the buds, once formed, will tend to blast rather than mature: that is, they will fall off before they have a chance to open.

Not all plants blast their buds when the air is too dry. But the gesneriads, and the saintpaulias in particular, are likely to. So make sure the humidity around your plants is high enough. For gesneriads 50 percent is about par. One preflowering warning symptom of low humidity is curling under of the plant's leaves.

Leaves that are severely distorted and twisted are more apt to be heralding a colony of resident cyclamen mites than mere dryness. The mites are extremely hard to control. Repeated dousing with malathion or rotenone will sometimes remedy the situation, but not as well as quickly disposing of the infected plant.

A HIRSUTE HANDFUL

Achimenes flava (Magic Flower)
   MICROCLIMATE: Warm partial sun in terrarium
                Humusy soil kept constantly moist

Primarily for warm greenhouses or terrariums, the achimenes really need a high-humidity atmosphere. They also seem to be particularly sensitive to pollution. However, they are well worth attempting for anyone growing a gesneriad collection, since *Achimenes flava* is one of the few yellow flowers in the family. The tubular petunialike blossoms are rather small. Usually they grow in pairs among the graceful trailing stems. Plant rhizomes during March, barely cover them with soil, and keep them constantly moist but not wet. As soon as growth starts, feed once a week with fertilizer. Less more often is the best fertilizer policy for gesneriads. Don't ever let the soil dry out, or your plants will go back into hibernation. But in fall, after flowering, stop all watering till the soil is powdery dry. Then dig up the rhizomes, breaking off any remaining withered foliage gently. You should find three to five new rhizomes for each one you planted. Store these at sixty degrees in a plastic bag filled with vermiculite and just a drop or two of water. Plant again the following March.

Hypocyrta nummularia (Goldfish Plant, Miniature Pouch Flower)
   MICROCLIMATE: Warm partial sun
                Humusy soil kept constantly moist

Naturally a bark-clinging epiphyte, *Hypocyrta nummularia* will do well in a hanging basket. Bears small hairy leaves, even smaller red orange flowers, to three-quarters of an inch. Bears goldfish-like flowers in summer, after which it should be pruned back, since the next season's flowers will appear on new growth. Sometimes loses leaves in fall dormancy, but then will bloom again come winter. Easily propagated from new, or soft-tip, cuttings.

    H. wettsteinii is unusual in that it has shiny smooth leaves with reddish undersides. So much for the fuzziness of the family. Both species are easy to grow. Both will probably be reclassified to the genus *Nemantan- thus* by the time you read this.

Kohleria strigosa (Cinnabar Tree Gloxinia)
MICROCLIMATE: Warm partial sun
Humusy soil kept constantly moist

The kohlerias as a whole are known in horticulture as tree gloxinias. Note the word "tree." The plants grow tall for gesneriads, sometimes over two feet, and in a rather scraggly fashion at that. Bloom primarily in summer and fall, but plants may become almost everblooming if old growth is continuously pruned back. The pruning will also keep a speci- men manageably sized for windowsill cultivation. The flowers are tubular, trumpet shaped, to an inch and a quarter long, and red with a five-lobed yellow throat with warm red leopard spots. If the plant goes into winter dormancy, store the rhizomes the same way you do the achimenes. And when pruning, plant the cuttings; they will readily form new plants. Also easily grown from seed when available.

The hybrid *Kohleria* 'Amabilis,' occasionally known horticulturally by its old name *Isoloma ceciliae*, is one of the loveliest and most floriferous of the kohlerias, with bronze-veined hairy green leaves and long-lasting yellow, rose, or red blossoms whose color is accentuated by their ribbed and spotted white throats.

Nautilocalyx lynchii (Black Alloplectus)
MICROCLIMATE: Warm partial sun
Humusy soil kept constantly moist

Interesting mostly as a specimen plant for those building up a collection, *Nautilocalyx* tends to be spindly and unattractive unless pinched back constantly. The short-lived creamy white flowers grow from the leaf axis and are not prominent. The hairy stems are purple at first, turning brown with maturity, the leaves bronze to blackish purple with conspicuous reddish veins.

Petrocosmea kerii (Hidden Violets)
MICROCLIMATE: Temperate partial sun
Humusy soil kept constantly moist

Unlike most gesneriads, *Petrocosmea kerii*, from the forest floors of the hill country straddling Thailand and Vietnam, needs a cool period for a month or so in winter to induce flowering. The plant will thrive in generally cooler conditions than its relatives. The flowers, however, are halfway buried on short stems among the rich quilted green leaves and are rather small, rarely exceeding half an inch in diameter. The three lower lobes are white, the upper two white with yellow spots, which is what makes the plant of special interest to the saintpaulia specialist. As yet there are no yellow saintpaulias—crossbreeding with *P. kerii* holds out the most hope for them.

Ramonda myconii (Alpine Gesneria)
MICROCLIMATE: Cool partial sun
Humusy soil left to dry between waterings

The only gesneriad winter-hardy in rock gardens. Originating in the Pyrenees, its cool-loving nature makes it unsuitable for anything but the unheated sun porch.

Rechsteineria various
MICROCLIMATE: Warm partial sun
Humusy soil kept constantly moist

As this book goes to press, the whole popular genus *Rechsteineria* is being eliminated by hard-working taxonomists ever refining our system of plant classification. *Rechsteineria cardinalis*, the cardinal flower, is now *Sinningia cardinalis*, *R. verticillata*, the double-decker flower, is now *S. ver-*

Rechsteineria leuchotricha

ticillata, and the Brazilian edelweiss *R. leuchotricha* has become a sinningia of the same given name.

The plants themselves have not changed. Neither has the method of cultivation, which is the same as for most gesneriads: rich loamy soil kept constantly moist with tepid water, a humid atmosphere, fertilization about twice a month, and good light but little direct sun.

> *Rehmannia angulata* (Foxglove Gloxinia)
> MICROCLIMATE: Cool sun
> Loamy soil kept constantly moist

Magnificent bell-shaped rosy red flowers form to three inches long. Throat spotted purple with yellow lines. Seeds sown in March will bloom the following March, but only if grown on a cool sun porch.

> *Saintpaulia* various (African Violet)
> MICROCLIMATE: Warm partial sun
> Humusy soil kept constantly moist

These are the gesneriads' claim to fame. Hybrids are too numerous to mention, except perhaps to say that I've found the Rhapsodies developed in Germany especially disease-free and robust, with erect flowers that do not drop. In fact, you must prune them off after they are spent. Cultivars, that is, varieties developed in cultivation and not available in nature, with dark foliage and flowers need more light than their pastel sisters.

Besides the original African violet, *Saintpaulia ionantha,* there are

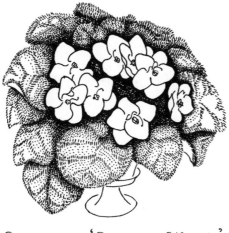

Saintpaulia 'Rhapsodie Elfriede'

fifteen to twenty other true species in the genus, depending on whose classification you use. All of them come from East Africa, primarily Tanzania. And although they are not as showy as the hybrids, they make an interesting collection. They also represent the gene bank from which further hybrids will be developed.

Sinningia speciosa (Gloxinia)
MICROCLIMATE: Warm partial sun
Humusy soil kept constantly moist

The popular gloxinias seen at the local florist's were named after P. B. Gloxyn of Germany in 1785. Unfortunately, one of his relatives must have beaten him in the botanical honorifics game, for about fifty years later it was discovered that an entirely different plant had been named gloxinia since the early 1700s. So the plant everybody today calls a gloxinia is actually a sinningia, while the real gloxinia, too large to be practical for indoor cultivation, remains untouted.

In their natural habitat of tropical Brazil, the flowers come in spring and summer, followed by leaf drop and dormancy. In the controlled climate of the house, tubers can be started any time of the year. The dormancy period of the new hybrids usually lasts only from a few days to a few weeks. When the last flower has blossomed, cut off the old leaves. If no new ones develop within a week, begin reducing watering. Give the plant no fertilizer and less water each time around. Once the soil is almost dry, put the pot in a dim cool spot, but not colder than fifty degrees. Check for new leaves weekly. Once they appear, repot the tubers in fresh soil. But get good fresh tubers, neither dry and hard nor soft and rotten. "Crisp" is probably the best word for prime specimens. Tubers should be covered with about half an inch of soil. While the sinningias are tuberous, they may be grown from seed as well, taking only six to eight months from seed to flower. May and June sowings should give you an excellent display of the large, velvety, bell-shaped flowers by Christmas.

Smithiantha cinnabarina (Red Velvet-Leaf Gesneriad, Temple Bells)
MICROCLIMATE: Warm partial sun
Humusy soil kept constantly moist

The flowers really do seem to grow from miniature spires emerging out of some of the plushest leaf rosettes in the plant world. The nodding

Smithiantha cinnabarina

bright scarlet flowers, borne on a red stalk, grow to an inch and a half. Cream-colored red-spotted throat. Plants bloom from November to April, after which they need a resting period usually one to two months long. Seeds are best planted in April or May for flowers the following winter and spring. Hybrids produce flowers ranging in color from cinnamon to yellow to scarlet. High humidity is an absolute must for smithianthas. Don't even attempt them if that in your home is under 50 percent—unless you have a large terrarium. The plants reach a foot or more in height.

Streptocarpus wendlandii (Royal Nodding Bells)
    MICROCLIMATE: Temperate partial sun in terrarium
            Loamy soil left to dry between waterings

I'd call this one the flowering leaf, for that's just what it is. The plant consists of a single large leaf. It reaches three feet by two feet if you give it enough room, the leaf curling almost carnivorously around the top of the pot. The corrugated blade is olive green and heavily hirsute. The leaf is so short it appears to be growing without a plant. The bright blue flowers rise on a tall stalk that seems to come almost from the center of the leaf itself. Numerous flowers on the branched stalk throughout the summer. Good in cool terrariums. Needs high humidity and lower tem-

Streptocarpus wendlandii

peratures than most of its relatives. Propagated from leaf sections—bye-bye plant—or seeds. No advanced gesneriad collection should be without one.

Grandmother's Classics Revisited

What can one say about geraniums and begonias besides that they were almost everybody's grandmother's favorites? Well, for one thing, since begonias are shade lovers, while geraniums thrive in the sun, between the two of them you can fill almost every window with a floral bouquet, not to mention an astounding variety of foliage. And these plants have come a long way since grandmother's day. New hybrids and varieties have been introduced by the hundreds. The diversity is so great that on seeing *Begonia kellermanii, B. coccinea*, an angel-wing begonia, and *B. luxurians*, or palm-leaf begonia, together for the first time, one's reactions would probably be that they weren't even related. Certainly none of them looks like the old standby *B. semperflorens* that the word "begonia" conjures up. And geraniums have undergone a similar explosion of hybridization.

The so-called geraniums, for all their appearance of having been around forever, are actually a fairly recent introduction in home horticulture. The true geranium comes from Greece, where it was first mentioned by Dioscorides in A.D. 64. This genus is characterized by a regular flower with five evenly spaced petals. The geranium familiar to most of

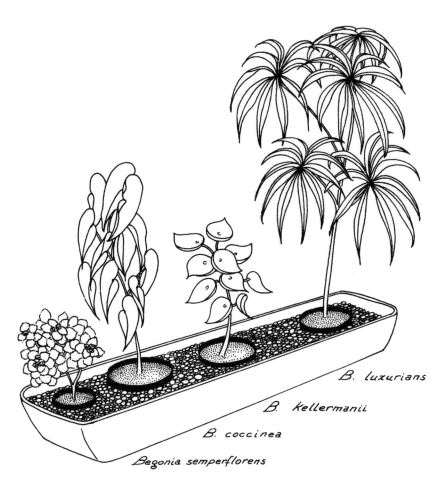

B. *luxurians*

B. *kellermanii*

B. *coccinea*

Begonia semperflorens

Leaf variation in begonias

us, on the other hand, comes from the Cape of Good Hope region of South Africa and was first brought to England in the sixteenth century. It is, properly speaking, a pelargonium and is characterized by having two upper flower petals considerably larger than the three lower ones, with a corresponding difference in stamen size, making the flower irregular and bisymmetrical. Also differentiating the two flowers is the long nectar tube of the pelargonium, which is fused to the flower stalk itself. After pollination, it forms the characteristic long seed case resembling a stork's bill—hence the genus name.

Now granted the differences between geraniums and pelargoniums aren't earth shattering for most people. But it's unlikely that someone who calls his car by its make would refer to it as a Ford if it were in fact a Plymouth, particularly if there were any teenagers in the family. So if you haven't grown the plants before, why not get into the habit of calling them pelargoniums right off the bat? If they're already sitting on your windowsill, it really wouldn't be snobbism to change the labels.

PEERING CLOSER AT PELARGONIUMS

By 1753 Linnaeus had listed twenty-five pelargoniums in his *Species Plantarum*. He included several of the scented-leaf varieties introduced to England in the 1630s. They had become important novelties on arrival, their foreign origin adding mystique to their aromatic growth. Since they were easy to propagate, commercial growers took them to their hearts and pocketbooks. All through the 1700s they flourished in gardens and cottage window boxes throughout Europe. Then it was discovered that oil extracted from the leaves of *Pelargonium capitatum* and *P. graveolens* could serve as a relatively inexpensive substitute for attar of roses, with four to six times as much yield by weight and easier harvesting. Massive fields of pelargoniums were planted in southern France and Turkey, and soon the pelargonium oils distilled at Grasse usurped a large share of the commercial rose oil market.

On the home front, meanwhile, the pelargonium craze reached its peak during the Victorian age. The two-toned leaves of the zonals, accompanied almost year round by riotous rose and vermilion flowers, matched well the rather gaudy taste of the period. The first tricolor leaves were hybridized in England during the 1850s, and by the 1860s hundreds of new varieties with extravagantly hued foliage had been developed.

At more or less the same time in the gardens of Henri Lecoq, Clermont-Ferrand, France, a double flower, with a greater number of petals than normal and thus fuller looking, appeared by spontaneous mutation on a young seedling. A spectacularly successful hybridizer, Victor Lemoine, got hold of some pollen from this flower and developed the—you guessed it—Victor Lemoine, the variety to become the forebear of so many of the doubles raised today.

And from the zonals and doubles modern hybridization has evolved such a number of crossbreeds that between them and the species, or natural, plants you could fill a whole house with nothing but pelargoniums. To this proliferation there has been one unfortunate side effect, however. The same plant sometimes bears different varietal names when purchased from different growers. If you happen to become an avid enough collector to run into this problem, your notebook will no doubt guide you in future purchases. Meanwhile, you'll probably be able to trade away duplicate specimens.

ZONED FOR CONTRAST

The so-called zonals are named for the circular, or banded, markings dividing the scalloped leaf into various color zones. The ones with the dark circular markings are the ones usually referred to as "common geraniums," growing as they do everywhere from garden borders to fire escapes.

The fancy-leaved zonals have more intricately patterned and colored leaves. They are classed together as *Pelargonium* x *hortorum* and derive mostly from a cross that resulted when the Duchess of Beaufort, who sponsored *P. inquinans*, got together with the Bishop of Compton, who was championing *P. zonale*, during the early 1700s. As a group they are divided again into the two major types of zonals, the standard and the French.

The French zonals developed spontaneously in France, naturally, around 1880. They are tetraploid, having a chromosome count of thirty-six rather than the normal eighteen. Vigorous growers, with larger stem stalks and more durable flowers than most common geraniums, the plants are also hardier and less susceptible to injury by pest and disease.

About those two numbers eighteen and thirty-six and the word "tetraploid": this isn't a book on genetics, but the subject is of interest because the occurrence of polyploidy (possession of more than the normal two sets of chromosomes) is not uncommon in plants. Chromosomes carry the inherited characteristics of a species within them and are the prime means through which new varieties and species evolve. When the chromosomes double, or triple or quadruple for that matter, plants superior to either parent often result. Gravenstein and Baldwin apples are examples; both are tetraploid, like the French zonal pelargoniums. Triploid grape and tomato vines produce fruit not only larger, but with a higher vitamin C content as well. Unfortunately, the rate of sterility in the seeds of polyploid plants is very high, which is why such plants are almost always reproduced vegetatively.

If you do try to raise plants from seed, it's always worthwhile to keep a lookout for one different from what its parentage would lead you to expect. Remember, the French zonals came about purely by accident. Had they escaped detection, they never would have become the popular plants they are today. Plant selection, one of man's endeavors ever since he gave up the nomadic life for one of agriculture, has produced superior strains in almost all crop plants, many of them turning out to be polyploid —and all without their cultivators' having the slightest awareness of genetics and chromosome theory, which didn't become subjects of knowledge until the rediscovery of Mendel's notes as recently as 1900.

Genetics, incidentally, although sometimes appearing formidable, is not a field devoid of humor. Recently I spent the better part of an afternoon walking around with a Cheshire-cat-like smile after reading about the early experiments of the Russian cytologist G. D. Karpechenko. In an attempt to synthesize an entirely new plant through hybridization, he selected for his project the radish *Raphanus sativus* and the cabbage *Brassica oleracea*, because of their similar morphologic characteristics and the fact that they both had nine pairs of chromosomes. The outcome of his testing was almost completely negative, most of the experimental plants being sterile. However, by the third generation he did end up with specimens carrying eighteen pairs of chromosomes. Furthermore, they produced highly fertile seeds. The entirely new plant was named raphanobrassica, and only one minor problem stood between it and a fabulous double crop: it had the leaves of a radish and roots of a cabbage.

But getting back to the pelargoniums, the fancy-leaved zonals took another great leap forward when crossed with *P. frutetorum*, discovered in 1931 in the Cape province of South Africa. Its color zones are particularly sharply defined, and the leaf prominently lobed. This species has

Pelargonium x *hortorum* 'Alpha'

been used extensively in the development of new zonals, labeled *P.* x *hortorum* like their predecessors.

Since there are by now hundreds of varieties of *P.* x *hortorum*, some with single, most with double flowers, I wouldn't even try to list them selectively here. Pick one that strikes your fancy, from *P.* x *hortorum* 'Alpha' with its golden dentate leaves ringed in brown and its free-blooming single red flowers to *P.* x *hortorum* 'Zip,' dark zoned and bearing single cerise blossoms. And for heaven's sake don't lose the label.

A PINCH IN TIME

Zonals all require more or less the same care. The only difference is that the fanciest-leaved varieties, with the brightest, most vivid color, tend to be a little more touchy than their plainer cousins and don't always propagate well. The plants need lots of sunlight to bring out their colors. But summer noons are a bit too hot for comfort. The ideal is plenty of morning sun, bright shade in the afternoon—which you'll find holds true for pelargoniums as a whole.

Since it is the new growth on fancy-leaved varieties that has the best color, you will want to pinch back the plants constantly to keep a wide spectrum growing. For that matter, all the pelargoniums need frequent pinching, to shape them; otherwise they will sprawl, looking leggy and ungainly.

WHERE HAVE I SMELLED THAT LEAF BEFORE?

Pinching back pelargoniums, you can't help but notice that their succulent stems and leaves are quite odoriferous. Some have such a specific fragrance that they are grown primarily for it. They are usually referred to as the scenteds. And their leaves are so filled with volatile aromatic oils that on a warm sunny day they may saturate the air with a tantalizing aroma without ever having been touched. More often, however, you will have to bruise the leaves slightly to get results. The ensuing fragrance, by which each plant is commonly known, can range from the ever popular rose scent of *P. graveolens*, the mint of *P. tomentosum*, the citrus of *P. crispum*, or the apple of *P. odoratissimum* to even ginger, pine, strawberry, or coconut, if your nose is sensitive enough and your imagination good.

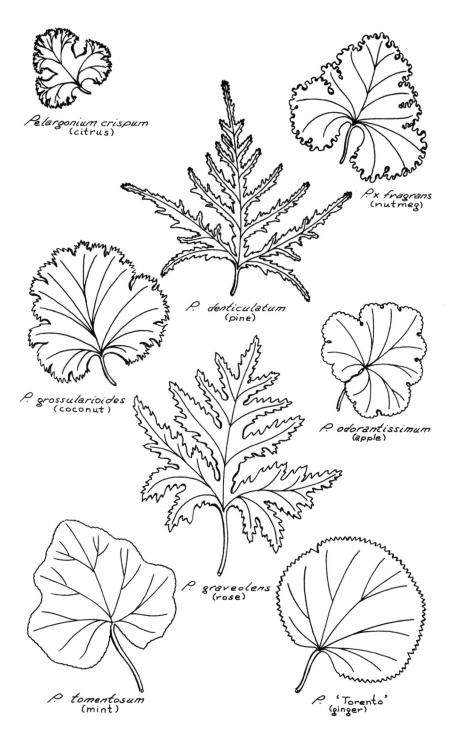

Pelargonium crispum
(citrus)

P. x fragrans
(nutmeg)

P. denticulatum
(pine)

P. grossularioides
(coconut)

P. odorantissimum
(apple)

P. graveolens
(rose)

P. tomentosum
(mint)

P. 'Torento'
(ginger)

Varieties of scented pelargoniums

THE IVY LEAVED

P. peltatum is called ivy leaved because of the resemblance of its leaves to those of *Hedera helix*, the true ivy. However, it goes the ivies one better by bearing a profusion of lavender, pink, cerise to almost white blossoms. It will bloom throughout the winter months as long as it is kept below seventy degrees by day and fifty-five degrees at night. That's of course one reason why grandma was much more successful at growing it than most people today: she didn't have central heating. Still, on a sun porch, or close to the window, where temperatures are often five to ten

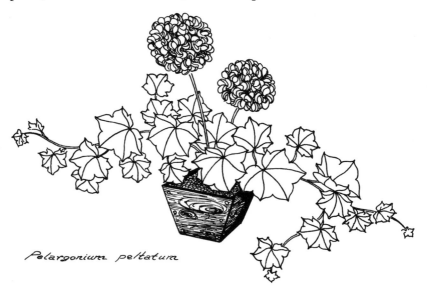

Pelargonium peltatum

degrees below those of the rest of the house, for once here's a plant that doesn't mind the dryness of central heating. Just remember to keep it cool and in full sun. If there's a really gray period between December and February, flowering will usually cease. Cut down on watering and pinch back the plant. Spring will launch a hundred blossoms.

ROYALTY ISN'T FOR EVERYONE

There is one group of pelargoniums that everybody calls pelargoniums. They are the Lady Washingtons, or Show pelargoniums. With their large pansylike flowers, they are probably the most showy of the whole genus. However, these *P. x domesticum* plants have one drawback: they are really unsuitable for home culture. There simply isn't enough light available indoors for them. You may not be able to resist trying one someday, but stick with other varieties until you've had several years of experience, or acquired a greenhouse, or moved to California, the one state where they thrive to the point of taking over whole gardens.

DWARFS FOR SMALL KITCHENS

Pelargoniums are usually associated with the kitchen windowsill. If your kitchen, like ours, is beginning to fill up with utensils, or if your home is already swamped with plants, dwarf pelargoniums, again varieties of *P.* x *hortorum*, may be your answer to the space problem. They stay small. Black Vesuvius, for instance, an old-time favorite from the late 1800s, produces an abundance of bright orange scarlet single flowers on top of dark green foliage, usually without ever growing more than six inches tall. It and many other dwarfs do very well under artificial lights.

SPECIAL SPECIES

If you begin collecting pelargoniums, no doubt you will eventually want to grow some of the natural species. After all, they are the origin of today's fancy varieties, and they are intriguing in their own right. For instance, there's *P. tetragonum*, the square-stalked cranesbill, which, as its popular name implies, has square stalks rather than the round ones to which we are accustomed. Then there's *P. echinatum*, the cactus geranium, its succulent arms covered with thorny stubble. It loses its deciduous leaves during resting periods, looking then, perhaps I should warn you, like a cross between a straggly cactus and something only a collector could love. Speaking of love, however, its white flowers bear heart-shaped maroon markings, giving the plant its other popular name, sweetheart geranium.

POTTING PELARGONIUMS

Most pelargoniums do not need a rest period. Their habit of flowering year round makes them a particular delight during the gray days of winter. If you're just beginning to grow pelargoniums, select standard zonals and dwarfs, specifically those listed as free flowering in the catalogs, for your winter blooms. You're looking for short-day plants that put on a good show with the briefer light of winter. If you are near a nursery featuring lots of pelargoniums, you can discuss flowering patterns when you go to buy the plants.

Plants by post, particularly orchids, are often sent bare root. Pelargoniums, on the other hand, especially since the advent of the plastic pot, usually arrive in their growing containers, most often two-and-a-quarter- to two-and-a-half-inch starter pots of inadequate size. Nevertheless, don't pot up to bigger containers right away. Give the plants a chance to rest from their travels. In two or three weeks they'll have forgotten the traumas of the United States postal system. Then move them to four-inch pots, three-inch ones for dwarf varieties. Even plants that have been with you several years should not call for anything bigger than a six-inch pot. Just repot them into the same pot—after it's been scrubbed—when fresh soil is needed.

Because of their drainage requirements, pelargoniums need several pieces of crock over the drainage hole in their pots to ensure that water will not collect. For the same reason, unglazed clay pots are preferable to plastic ones. All-purpose commercial potting soil works well for pelargoniums with the addition of one part coarse sand to every three parts soil for extra drainage. But don't use a soil mix formulated for African violets; it's too fluffy, and pelargoniums like somewhat firm soil. Likewise, pack the soil down when repotting, rather than just pouring it around the roots—pack, but don't pound, of course.

As for general care and upkeep, turn the pots frequently and pinch the plants back so they retain their balanced shape. Give them sunny mornings, shade at noon, and bright-shady afternoons. Let the soil dry out between waterings, and when you do water, souse. Feed frequently with a balanced fertilizer such as 20-20-20, using it at about half the strength recommended. Don't use a fertilizer high in nitrogen or blossoms will not develop. Pelargonium flowers, incidentally, react especially favorably to the plant hormone gibberellin. If you're interested in experimenting, spray the plants with a ten parts per million concentrate of gibberellin for larger, longer-lasting flowers. Cuttings of new growth can be taken during May and June to bloom in October.

Two things have changed in the kitchen since grandmother's day. The first is the stove. A gas stove is death to many plants, but particularly so to pelargoniums. Your pelargoniums will react to minute gas fumes of which you aren't even aware. So check your stove or keep them out of the kitchen. And as with all plants, it's a fine idea to open the window when you can and let in some fresh air. It's good for people too.

The second change since grandmother's day is that our houses are much warmer in winter. Pelargoniums don't like daytime temperatures over seventy-five degrees and prefer nights at around fifty degrees.

If your house is too warm for normal pelargoniums, don't despair. An interesting twist in the hybridization of pelargoniums is occurring at Iowa State University. There plants are being developed that are able to thrive in conditions warmer and more humid than the species in general can take. Look for *P. x hortorum* 'Cardinal,' 'Galaxie,' 'Skylark,' or 'Moonfrost,' to name a few of the varieties introduced recently by ISU.

THE BEGONIA BUNCH

Unlike pelargoniums, begonias are more or less shade loving, like considerable atmospheric moisture, and hate hard potting. So why are they together in one chapter?

Well, for one thing, people always seem to confuse the two. For another, most people who grow one grow both. They're definitely associated—if not on a botanical level.

Begonias are tropical flowering herbs with immense variety. Grouped within twelve hundred species and thousands of hybrids, specimens range from two-inch miniatures to giants over six feet tall with two-foot leaves. Their foliage is typically lopsided. Said by some to be mimics, their leaves often resemble those of other plants, such as maple, elm, and ivy. And *Begonia luxurians* has more than once been mistaken for a marijuana plant. I think probably these are simply cases of parallel evolution. After all, what reason would a begonia from Peru have for imitating a maple from Michigan?

Unlike most flowering houseplants, begonias bear separate male and female flowers. Interestingly enough, when days are short and night temperatures consequently lower, the plants produce a surfeit of male flowers. The blossoms appear superficially the same, but if you look at them closely, you'll readily discern the sticky receptive stigma of the female flower and the pollen-bearing anthers of the male counterpart. This segregation of the sexes makes natural cross-fertilization that much easier, and explains the number of varieties available—and why the plants are mostly propagated vegetatively.

Speaking of propagation, begonias can be reproduced by cuttings of tip, stem, or leaf. Leaf cuttings are the most fun, especially for children. The method works particularly well with Rex begonias, but almost all begonias, except some of the fibrous species, can be propagated from leaves. By slicing a leaf into arrowhead sections radiating from the stem

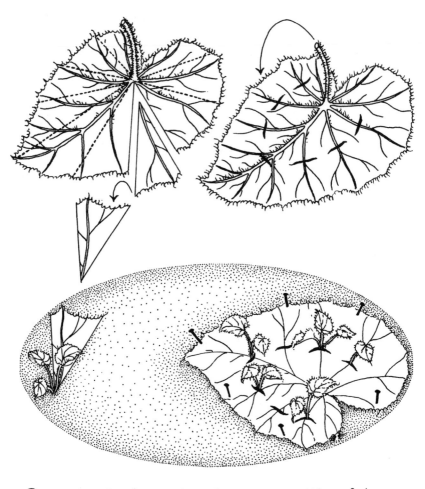

Propagating Rex begonia by wedge and vein cutting of leaves

and planting these point down in a pot, you'll get new plants that need no transplanting.

Vein cuttings yield more and are more intriguing. However, you have to transplant the delicate plantlets, which inevitably means losing some, though you'll still probably have plenty left. Pick off a leaf, lay it bottom side up so you can see the venation well, and make short slits through half a dozen of the largest veins, spacing the slits more or less evenly. Then turn the leaf right side up on a bed of moist sand. Poke the stem into the sand so it can continue to draw moisture and pin the edges of the leaf down to keep it in contact with the sand. Cover the pot with plastic and in two to three weeks new plants will develop at the slits. Leaf propagation is carried to its extreme in *B. hispida* 'Cucullifera,'

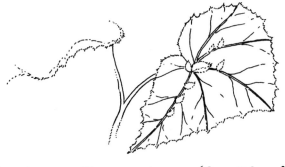

A mothering *Begonia hispida* 'Cucullifera' leaf

popularly known as the piggyback or crazy-leaf begonia, which doesn't wait for its leaves to be slit, but goes ahead growing new plants on the veins while the leaves are still on the parent plant.

THERE ARE BEGONIAS, AND THEN THERE ARE BEGONIAS

Horticulturally, begonias are divided into three groups on the basis of their root structure. The roots may be fibrous, forming a fine mat in the pot in the familiar way most houseplants do. Or they may be rhizomatous, with thick prostrate stems normally running belowground, but sometimes along the surface, from which both the stalks and the finer fibrous roots grow. The third variation in root structure is the tuberous. Thickened short tubers capable of storing a large quantity of food for the plant during its dormant period typically sprout numerous buds where future stem and leaf growth will emerge. A more common tuber, if you've never seen a begonia, is the potato. And like a potato, the begonia tuber can be divided, leaving an eye or two in each piece, to produce new plants.

WAXES ARE EASY

If your grandmother really did grow begonias, chances are they were one of the everblooming wax specimens, *B. semperflorens*. You'd know them by the leaves, nearly round, green to mahogany, and waxy, covering the numerous compact branches in profusion. Most of the earlier varieties carried single blossoms. They are still readily available. However, people nowadays seem to prefer the semidoubles, sometimes called crested, or the doubles, known variously and confusingly as rosebud or camellia.

For best flowering, the wax begonias like a few hours of sun during winter days, but come summer they must be shaded from the hot noonday blaze. Pot them in light, porous soil with a large percentage of sand. Begonias are succulent in structure if not in habitat. So although they need to be well watered, the soil should be allowed to just about dry out between waterings. Atmospheric humidity, on the other hand, is a constant must and should not fall below 50 percent.

ANGELS ON CANES

The wax begonias are fibrous rooted. So are the large-leaved ones commonly known as angel wings because they do look like the angel wings in old frescoes and on cherubic Christmas decorations. They grow thick, noded stems, from which the alternate name cane-stemmed begonias is derived. The plants will flower while still quite young, bearing heavy, drooping clusters of orange, coral, salmon, pink, or red blossoms. Tend them like wax begonias, preferably in clay pots to keep the soil from getting soggy and to allow enough root aeration. Pinching is needed to keep size down. You can make quite an attractive setting for the pendulous flowers by letting one or two of the canes grow as high as they want and keeping the rest of the plant low.

HIRSUTE SPLENDOR

The hairy-leaved begonias such as x 'Alto-Scharff' have a thicket of bristles on their leaves, sometimes on their flowers as well. The shorter-haired models are often referred to as felt-leaved begonias. Also fibrous in root structure, they are cared for like the waxes and angel wings.

RHIZOMES REST

There are numerous begonias of the rhizome type, but the most popular is the large-leaved Rex group. These are grown primarily for their colorful, often metallic, almost glowing foliage. They are the most shade loving of all begonias. Give them good light, but never expose them to direct sunlight, for bright sun will fade their foliage. Light, humusy, airy soil is a must, and since the roots do not go very deep, the plants grow well in three-quarter pots, which saves some space and money. Again a caution on overwatering: when you water, water well, but let the soil become quite dry before you venture toward it with the watering can again.

Come fall, the plants will begin to lose their leaves. Don't worry, you haven't mishandled them. Unlike the fibrous species, begonias of the rhizome variety sleep, or at least catnap, in winter. For some this means losing a few leaves, for others almost all the old foliage goes by the board. In either case, cut back your watering a bit and wait till spring. Once new shoots begin to develop, consider repotting to make sure the soil is rich and loose.

Rex begonias like daytime temperatures of seventy-five degrees, nights of sixty-five degrees. About five degrees of cooling off at night suits the other types fine.

TUBERS ARE TABOO

Tuberous begonias really aren't houseplants. Although they are sometimes sold as such, along with such gift specimens as the Christmas begonias, they require cool, humid conditions usually achievable only in a greenhouse or a well-controlled sun porch. In the summertime they do well in the garden. They might, just might, condescend to grow indoors for you. But why, unless they really challenge you, set yourself up for needless disillusionment when there are all those thousands of other begonias to choose from? Not to mention roses.

A Rose by Any Other Name May Not Be Extinct

The World Wildlife Fund estimates that twenty thousand species of plants, 10 percent of all known species, are in danger of becoming extinct this very minute. A phenomenal tragedy—not because of any immediate horticultural loss, since, except perhaps for some of the orchids, most of the species headed for biological oblivion are not particularly attractive or even useful house or garden plants. The tragedy is that we may never know what we lost, what might have come from these species. Plants and animals represent a basic cell and gene bank from which we have only begun to draw. Recently, for instance, a species of common, but dwindling, coral in the Caribbean was found to contain large quantities of a substance that potentially could reduce heart attack fatalities.

All of which would be a strange introduction to a chapter on roses were it not for the history of the miniature rose. A cultivar of *Rosa semperflorens* sometimes known as *R. lawranceana*, the Pompon de Paris, it was a favorite of British rose growers during the middle 1800s. Originally specimens had been brought to England by sea captains engaged in the China trade during the 1700s. The miniature rose was thought to have become extinct toward the end of the nineteenth century. People stopped growing it for a while, and since the original specimens were true mutant dwarfs and there was no wild variety, after a few decades there simply weren't any left. Still, things horticultural tend to run in cycles, and the time was ripe for a resurgence of interest in miniature roses when, in 1915, through one of those accidents of nature, the rose was discovered growing in a window box in the Swiss Alps by a Colonel Roulett. In that particular valley, so the story goes, it had been cultivated for several centuries. The rose was no doubt *R. chinensis* 'Minima,' mutant descendant of *R. semperflorens*, by now renamed *R. chinensis*.

Once the rose had been found again, no time was lost ensuring its survival. A Swiss nurseryman, Henri Correvon, took some cuttings of the lone known specimen and began propagating it. Rescued from oblivion, the rose then became known as *R. roulettii*, under which label it goes today—most of the time.

To this day you will find more than a little confusion about the nomenclature of miniature roses. Usually, however, they are sold by their varietal names, and here at least there is consistency, since most of the varieties are patented. Patented? Yes, well, more on that later, in case you're as vague as I once was on the subject of plant patenting. But meanwhile let's get the first miniature rose patented historically.

Jan de Vink of Holland began an intensive crossbreeding effort with some plants he received from Henri Correvon. In 1933 he at last achieved a specimen with all the qualities of bloom and diminutive size he wanted. It was introduced and patented in 1936 as Tom Thumb, the first and still most popular of the miniature roses.

And that's only a small fragment of rose history. The flower's symbolism, from the War of the Roses to the gold rose-studded decorations of the Order of the Garter and the Order of the Indian Empire, permeates more of Western man's past than any other flower. England, particularly, is traditionally rose crazed, and it's hard to imagine an English cottage without its rose garden. Even common Latin terms like sub rosa really do refer to the flower. Roses were a common sight at Roman orgies. At the same time, they somehow came to symbolize secrecy. A conversation held below (sub) a hanging rose was deemed highly confidential. But as for growing rose miniatures indoors, the secrets are few and easy to conquer.

BAPTISM

Chances are you'll purchase your rose miniatures by mail, for relatively few nurseries or plant stores stock these specialty items. When the plants arrive and before you unpack them, fill a deep bowl with cool water and mix in a little very fine soil to make a soup. You can use plain water, but the mud slurry coats the roots better and reduces transplant shock. If it tends to lump, spicing it up with a drop or two of liquid detergent often helps, the detergent acting as a wetting agent. But don't use too much.

Unpack the dormant plants and plunge them as far as their root tops in the slurry. If they look dry or wilted, soak for up to twenty-four hours. The preplanting dip is vital, since rose roots are very sensitive to water deprivation. I once unpacked a plant before I got the dunking bowl ready. Called away by my daughter Genevieve for a minute that stretched out to an hour, I returned to find that the sun had made its way across the kitchen table. The roots hadn't been exposed for more than half an hour, yet the plant failed to survive. Its still-packed sibling had its roots properly dunked and thrived.

Plant in an unglazed clay pot. Some plants accept plastic pots, but roses are not among them. The evaporation through the clay sides is needed both to aerate the rose roots and to cool them for good growth. For the same reason, and to ensure better-than-average drainage, use several pieces of crock, rather than just one or two, to cover the drainage hole in the bottom of the pot. Choose a small container. Although the roots should not be crowded, there also shouldn't be much room left around them once they are laid out in the soil .

Use a soil mix of two parts potting soil, two parts peat moss, and one part sharp sand. It is often recommended that the soil mix include parakeet gravel containing charcoal, but I am not among the proponents of this addition. Although charcoal will help keep the soil from turning sour in case of overwatering, roses like acid soil, whereas charcoal tends to neutralize it.

MULCHING INDOORS?

Mulching is a common outdoor practice that can be transplanted indoors with great benefit, especially to your roses. A half-inch layer of redwood chips, cocoa hulls, or like material will reduce soil evaporation, increase humidity, and keep the shallow feeder roots from drying out. There are two points to bear in mind, however. First, if you are going to mulch, plan on it before you pot; keep the soil level low enough so you can add your mulch and still leave enough pot rim for easy watering. Second, to check when the plant needs watering, feel the foil underneath the mulch. The top layer of mulch will dry before the soil does, and if you check only the mulch, you will overwater your roses.

TWO MUSTS

To bloom, miniature roses need even and regular sources of light and moisture. On a windowsill, this means at least five full hours of sunlight a day in summer. If you don't have it, don't try roses, at least not by the window. You can try them under good artificial light, however. If you give them enough of it, they will thrive. My personal preference is for Vita-Lite fluorescent tubes, made by Duro-Lite, suspended about six or seven inches above the plant tops. The artificial day should be extended to about fourteen to sixteen hours.

Even fluorescent lights produce enough heat to require that the plants be grown in a pebble tray. Fill a deep tray with pebbles (I get marble chips or rough aquarium gravel at the local pet store) and set the pots on top of them. Add water to submerge the pebbles. At its maximum the water level should barely touch the pots. Evaporation from the tray will enshroud the roses in a minicloud of their own, keeping the moisture level where they like it.

Although they prefer a humid atmosphere, it's not a good idea to mist the plants directly as you do most of your other houseplants. Moist leaves seem to encourage fungous diseases in roses. And while on the subject of wetness, don't water the plants so much that the soil becomes sopping. But don't let it become bone dry, either, even for only a day, or you are apt to have a dead rose on your hands. The safest tack is to water heavily enough for the water to run straight through the pot and into the pebble tray. This is why good drainage and a loose soil mixture are so important.

THEY CAN'T TAKE THE HEAT SO KEEP THEM OUT OF THE KITCHEN

It seems, no matter where our family lives, the kitchen turns out to be one of the sunniest and most pleasant rooms, so we spend a lot of time there. In part this may be an association built up around our liking for good food. Whatever the case, although the sun is right, everything else is wrong with the kitchen as far as roses are concerned. They dislike gas intensely. Just as the canaries in the coal mines of old expired before the miners even realized there was gas in the air, so a rose will die from a whiff so slight you wouldn't notice it.

One of the things that makes a kitchen cozy is its warmth on a cold winter's eve. Unfortunately, warmth is another problem for roses. If the temperature stays above seventy-five degrees for too long, they will go into semidormancy. Miniature roses grown indoors normally take a rest come midwinter, but they may well languish in summer too if not kept cool enough. A climate anywhere between fifty-five and seventy degrees is fine. So long as the temperature drops to below sixty degrees at night, everything should go bloomingly.

SIX WEEKS TO SHOWTIME

One of the beauties of miniature roses, besides their profusion of flowers, is that you don't have to wait forever for some color. Given good growing conditions, most varieties will bloom six or seven weeks after settling into their new pots. The blossoms open one or two at a time until the plant is covered with them. Pinch off each flower as soon as it fades. This promotes more flowering. Besides, wilted flowers attract fungi to a plant that is otherwise quite pest-free indoors.

With regular fertilization your rose plants should send out another flush of flowers soon after the first is done. Except for the short initial rest period after potting, they can be encouraged to flower almost constantly.

VARIATIONS ON A THEME

All the miniature rose varieties are probably descendants in one way or another of *R. roulettii*. The exact genealogy I leave up to the rosarians; since they do not yet agree among themselves, I see no reason they should agree with me. In any case, miniature roses are always sold under their variety or trade names.

Baby Betsy McCall

Light pink, one-inch-diameter flowers begin appearing when this plant is four to five inches tall. A fine bloomer introduced by Jackson and Perkins in 1960 with patent number 1984. Moderate fragrance.

Baby Darling

Although they have no fragrance, the orange to coral double flowers are a real delight. They may reach a diameter of two inches on a plant around twelve to sixteen inches tall, which makes this one of the bigger miniatures. Also comes in a climbing variety up to three feet high. Patent number 2682 in 1964.

Bit o' Sunshine

Bears fragrant, bright butter-yellow flowers an inch and a half across with around fifty petals. The bush itself grows to roughly sixteen inches in height. Introduced in 1956 under patent number 1631.

Cinderella

Pink with white edging, this full double rose has forty-five to sixty petals per flower on a prickleless bush reaching ten inches at maturity. Moderate spicy fragrance. A cross between the original Tom Thumb and Cecile Brunner, both produced by Jan de Vink. Rated 9.3 (out of 10) for perfection by the *American Rose Annual*, putting it very close to the top of the heap. Patent number 1051 in 1952.

Scarlet Gem

Brilliant scarlet flowers to an inch and a half in diameter with around fifty pointed petals having slight folds down the center. Few prickles. Introduced in 1961 with patent right reserved.

Tom Thumb miniature rose

Tom Thumb

The first of the new breed of miniature roses remains two to six inches tall at maturity. No collection should be without it. Simple ten- to twenty-petaled crimson flowers with numerous yellow stamens. Grows without prickles. The original cross of *R. roulettii* x 'Gloria Mundi' by Jan de Vink. Patent number 169 in 1934, now expired.

MULTIPLICATION AND PATENTS

What is all this talk about patents and flowers? If you're like me, you probably used to think of patents in terms of automated left-handed pipe cleaners and ultrasonic shoe polishers, but there are, as I discovered some time back, plant patents as well. These originally applied only to vegetative reproductions. That is, you were allowed to raise a patented plant from seed, but if you grew one from a cutting, you had to pay the royalty. Vegetative reproduction assures new plants true to the parent, while propagation from seed rarely does in roses, which explains why the rose has been patented more than any other flower. The patent laws have recently been changed, however, and now varieties grown from seed can be patented as well as those from cuttings. If the propagation urge gets you, remember a patent is good for seventeen years from date of issue, and, to play fair, you shouldn't grow your own for that period unless you contact the original breeder and pay the nominal royalty. On the other hand, maybe you can start a breeding program of your own to develop a truly thornless rose. After all, Burbank came up with a thornless cactus.

The Durable Ones: Cacti and Other Succulents

Succulents in general and cacti in particular are often considered "neglect-able" houseplants. And it's true they will survive under conditions nothing short of their plastic counterfeits would tolerate. They will subsist in a wide temperature range. They may naturally grow in air that's quite dry, but will go right on greening your apartment even if its relative humidity is a constant 100 percent. Often they will survive in light far too poor for many other plants. However, the key word here is "survive."

To thrive, rather than just survive, succulents need some care too. But tending them is easy and the rewards are bountiful, for succulents have some of the most beautiful blossoms of all flowering plants.

When I was a kid my father had a long ceramic tray of what must have been the most neglected cacti in the world. It was a random mixture, including some round ones that were probably gymnocalyciums or parodias and some opuntias. They sat on top of the radiator cover in a sunny window for ten to twelve years. Every few years they'd send out some new stems, which fascinated me, since by the time that irregular event came around I'd entirely forgotten that these green little pincushions were indeed alive and growing. Care on my father's part consisted of watering every few months and, since the planter made a convenient ashtray, a daily shower of cigarette ashes. "The ash is full of potassium," he explained, "excellent for their growth."

By the time my family moved, some dozen years later, the terra firma in the cactus planter had been reduced to an American Tobacco Company slag heap. Yet the cacti had struggled on valiantly all that time. They had even multiplied, although they bore no fruit. The opuntias dropped a branch here and a branch there, and new plants took root.

Shortly after the big move, my father cold turkeyed his smoking. Once the plants, as well as the family, were settled into their new quarters, a marvelous change occurred. Properly potted and cared for, the cacti bloomed within a year or two. And then they were truly a sight to behold. For there is hardly another family of plants as intriguing and full of contrast as the bare cacti and their grandiose floral display.

WHAT IS A SUCCULENT?

Almost all cacti are succulents, but far from all succulents are cacti. In fact, succulents aren't *all* anything. The word is derived from the Latin *suculentus*, meaning juicy or fleshy, and is applied to any number of plants that have adapted themselves to the rigors of living with a water problem. Succulents can be found in such diverse families as lilies, milkweeds, and pelargoniums. A design for survival is their common characteristic. They are apt to be more stem than leaf, and since all their parts are thicker and more three-dimensional than those of other plants, they are able to store water as a precaution against periods of drought.

If you think of succulents in terms of their structure you'll avoid one prevalent fallacy: namely, that all succulents come from arid desert regions. Many do, it's true, but others come from plant-rich jungle areas where either seasonal droughts are common or the succulent's habitat is so high up in the trees that its clinging roots can snitch moisture from the supporting bark only during the heaviest rainstorms. Still other species grow at altitudes where cold and wind limit the water supply.

Besides the size and shape of their leaves, succulents are adapted in other ways to their harsh environment. All plants transpire water through the millions of pores that lace their leaves, many small ones losing as much as their own weight in water each day. Succulents long ago accommodated themselves to water shortages by drastically reducing the number of pores, or stomata, from the millions found in the average leaf.

In many cases the remaining stomata were buried beneath a thin layer of wax coating the leaves.

The stomata couldn't be eliminated completely, of course, because transpiration is as essential to the life of a plant as respiration to that of a human. But with fewer and smaller pores the plant's transpiration was reduced considerably. In turn, the overall activity of the plant was reduced as well—try breathing slowly after running for twenty minutes. This means succulents are among the slowest-growing houseplants.

There was one more logical step for certain succulents to take. Those living in the desert rapidly acquired a reputation as delicacies, and on that fact turned their further evolution. They were the juiciest things around in the eyes of the local animal inhabitants—until they developed stiff hairs and thorns to ward off predators. At this point we have mostly cacti.

WHAT IS A CACTUS?

Cacti grow all over North and South America, traditionally reaching from the Arctic Circle to Patagonia. Now it seems patently obvious to me that if they grow in Patagonia, which is the southernmost region of Argentina, they should grow somewhere in the Hoste island/Wollaston Islands area of Chile as well. This is the Cape Horn region just below Patagonia, and I refuse to believe that a species so enduring and stubborn could have conquered two continents and left this little spot untouched. Someday I'm going down there to check it out myself. Meanwhile, if you happen to be south of Tierra del Fuego and find some spiny specimens, please let me know.

Where cacti definitely drew the line, however, was at crossing oceans. One could humorously attribute this to a natural dislike of water and probably not be too far off the track. For seeds of plants so accustomed to the dry torpor of the desert could reasonably be expected to fare poorly if awash at sea more than a day or so. As for vegetative reproduction by whole cacti drifting across the seas, that would fare no better. As you can readily verify, an overwatered cactus rots quickly.

Of course, this does nothing to explain how the other succulents have managed worldwide distribution. Still, the fact remains that the cactus is as American as the western movie filmed on its native territory. And I, for one, would like very much to know why. Perhaps it has something to do with the way we classify plants. After all, it is a somewhat arbitrary system, a development of man's powers of observation and organization.

Nature didn't grow a cactus. It grew something that we called a cactus.

Specifically the characteristics that define the Cactaceae family are five. First, cacti are all dicotyledons. That is, when a cactus seed sprouts, it always has two initial embryo leaves. Second, the plants develop with small pincushionlike structures on their stems called areoles. Each areole has twin growing points that produce spines, hooked climbing spines, flowers, branches, or a combination of any two. Third, cacti are perennial, living for many years rather than just one or two. Fourth, when they bloom, the flowers are usually composed of an indefinite number of petals in a symmetrical round pattern. And fifth, the fleshy fruit, which always forms below or behind the flower, is a one-celled berry, the seeds distributed randomly without design throughout it. And there you have the definition of a cactus. If your desert-loving plant doesn't meet all five qualifications, it doesn't make Cactaceae status.

Some plants that at first glance would not appear to be cacti nevertheless meet these qualifications and indeed are members of the Cactaceae, albeit very special ones. They aren't even succulents. The pereskias, leafy cacti from Central and South America, are living bits of history. Representing the cacti in their early stages of evolutionary defense, these (for instance, *Pereskia aculeata*) look more like woody shrubs than cacti.

TOUGH TOPS, TENDER ROOTS

In contrast to their hardy, resilient, visible upper growth, the succulents' subterranean structure is delicate and tender. The surest way to kill a cactus is to damage its roots. You may become aware of this sooner than you think if you purchase your specimens from a mail-order house. Shipping cacti bare root is a common practice, and one not detrimental as long as you treat the roots right. But it means being extra careful when handling them, trimming off neatly any bruised or broken ones and *not* watering the plant right away after potting. Any other houseplant should be given a good soil drenching as soon as it is repotted, to help the roots settle in snugly. But try it with a succulent and the roots will rot, killing the plant. When the soil remains dry for a couple of days after potting, any bruised roots have a chance to toughen up and heal.

Of course, there has to be an exception even to the exception. The jungle genera such as epiphyllums, schlumbergeras, and zygocactuses, which include among others the Christmas cactus, should be watered lightly right after potting, preferably by misting the top of the soil rather than pouring water into the pot.

TIGHT SHOES MAKE THEM BLOOM

Flowering leads to fruit, which leads in turn to seed. It's all part of the cycle of reproduction, one of the most important elements of survival, since no plant lives forever. When a succulent, particularly a cactus, is thriving and cozy in your home, it's likely to put off blooming for a year or more. After all, if things are going well, why expend the extra energy to put on a floral display and raise a horde of potential competitors? Conversely, a specimen that is really maltreated won't have the energy to spare and will also delay its blooming.

To ensure the best conditions for both blooming and overall well-being, a pretty standard rule exists for the size of a cactus pot. For round or barrel-shaped cacti, the pot should be an inch wider all around than the plant itself. For tall plants, the best results are usually procured by using a pot whose diameter is about half the height of the plant, slightly less for really tall specimens.

Which leads to the inevitable question of what kind of pot to pot in. Quite often one's first introduction to succulents comes in the form of a dish garden—hopefully not one decorated with a ceramic burro or a bridge across a dried-out riverbed. Such prepackaged novelties rarely survive at home, since most have been hastily assembled from a collection of cacti and other plants whose soil requirements and general care are quite different from each other's. The hodgepodge assortment combined with poor to nonexistent drainage and not enough soil usually leads to horticultural disaster within a month or two.

Not that you can't let your dreams wander out on a minilandscape of your own choosing. But select compatible plants. Don't try growing ferns with succulents, for instance, or even jungle cacti with desert species. And if you must use a dish that has no bottom drainage, get a deep one and fill the entire bottom half with nothing but a mixture of broken crockery and charcoal; then add the soil layer. Bonsai suppliers usually have a good stock of suitable dishes that are visually attractive, yet plain enough in design not to detract from the natural beauty of the plants. A few small stones or some weathered wood will add contrasting texture and form to your dish garden. But, again, don't let them dominate the plants. Simplicity is the key to the beauty of deserts.

For individual plants, unglazed clay pots are your best choice. Particularly good are orchid pots, which provide not only extra drainage, but excellent areation as well. More about them and the whys and wherefores of plant containers further on.

NOT JUST SAND

Into the pot must go, of course, soil as well as the plant. Now desert soils are much richer than one would suppose. Their content of mineral nutrients is often far higher than that of the rich black river delta mud one usually thinks of as good soil. What they lack for normal plants to thrive is large quantities of organic matter. Heavily organic soils retain moisture copiously enough to rot cactus roots. What cacti need is nutrient-rich soil low in organic matter, not just sand.

There are many sparse, loose soil mixtures suitable for cacti and other succulents. I've found the commercial premixed varieties to be quite good as long as they have sizable particles. If the blend looks like dust, you'll end up with concrete as soon as you pot something in it. Shop elsewhere or make up your own mix.

A good general cactus mix for the desert and alpine varieties is one part sharp sand, one part soil, and one part leaf mold, with a tablespoonful of bone meal per quart as a good slow-release fertilizer. For jungle varieties add one more part leaf mold. These are only guidelines. Don't be afraid of experimenting. It's the only way really to get a feel for growing things.

Remember, however, unlike the soil used for other houseplants the potting mixture for a desert cactus *should be dry when you set the plant in it*. Likewise, rather than leaving a high rim of pot above the soil level, bring the soil up almost to the brim itself. This will help keep you from overwatering. It will also keep most succulents from bruising themselves against the pot. Bruising usually won't harm them, but the resulting scars detract from the specimens' overall appearance.

Some cactus and succulent growers like to scatter a thin layer of round pebbles on the soil's surface to further protect the plants from bruising and rot. Many of them feel it enhances the plant's looks, too. As with almost all ideas about indoor gardening, the practice has its adherents and its detractors. Personally I prefer not to use pebbles; they eliminate the possibility of readily checking the soil's moisture.

Because water, at those intermittent times it makes its way to the desert, rarely gets a chance to seep deeply into the ground, the roots of succulents, cacti in particular, tend to stay close to the surface. Unlike the deep taproot system of so many temperate zone plants, the roots of desert varieties tend to spread out in a horizontal fan. Accordingly, the soil layer in the pots should not be too deep. Rather than using one small shard or two to cover the drainage hole of the pot, it's a good idea to fill the entire bottom quarter of the pot with a mixture of charcoal and pieces of broken pottery or small, very angular stones. Not only does this encourage the growth of shallow roots, but it's an extra safeguard for good drainage as well.

LESS LIGHT THAN YOU MIGHT THINK

Most people, associating cacti with bright wastelands, instinctively give them, and succulents in general, as much light as possible. And it's true that since the amount of chlorophyll-filled green surface area exposed to light is considerably less than that of most plants, succulents need good light in order to manufacture their food. However, even the desert species usually seek out a spot shaded for part of the day by a rock or hillside. Epiphytic jungle cacti, which normally grow in the dapple light of the treetops, and some of the more temperate species do best with considerably less than the daily six hours of sunlight recommended for desert plants. This six hours, incidentally, usually includes some shade during the midday sun. Cacti, if not more sensible than mad dogs and Englishmen, at least entertain different preferences.

What if you don't have good southern exposure with full sun in your home or apartment? Does that mean no cacti? Certainly not. First of all, you can grow any of the jungle cacti as well as the orchid cacti cleisto-cactuses and epiphyllums. Second, you can use artificial light. I have a nice old mammillaria sitting by my reading chair, where for years it has thrived thirty inches from a hundred-watt incandescent bulb, with very little daylight as supplement. I've grown accustomed to its place and so has it in its own lazy way. It hasn't bloomed, however. Frankly, that's due to neglect. And one of the reasons for my benign neglect is that cacti aren't supposed to bloom under artificial light. So of course I wanted to give it a try. Well, it seems that old rumor was true. At least till recently.

The elements in the light spectrum needed for cacti to bloom are the near-ultraviolet rays. Traditional fluorescent bulbs, even those specifically designed for indoor gardening, do not supply these. However, the new Vita-Lite does. According to George Kalmbacher of the Brooklyn Botanic Gardens, writing for the *Cactus and Succulent Journal*, good blooms were obtained from a variety of cacti and succulents, including euphorbias, using four forty-watt Vita-Lite tubes twelve inches above the plants, with a daily on duration of sixteen hours. Besides flowering, the general tone and color of the plants were improved as well.

In nature the sun does not shine for the same length of time each day. Photoperiodism, the plant's reaction to the lengthening of spring days and the shortening of fall ones, the annual cycle of diurnal time changes, controls most plants' dormancy period, with the exception of some species that are habitués of the equator. With the shortening of the days, dormancy begins to set in. During the briefest days of the year, the plant rests. Then, as the days lengthen again, the plant once more begins to grow. Sometime after this renewed activity, flowering commences. Exactly when—spring, summer, or even fall—depends on the particular species. Interestingly, if not surprisingly, enough, plants brought north directly from the Southern Hemisphere, where summer comes in December, have a growing period reversed from that of their Northern Hemisphere cousins. Some of them may need over a year to get into the swing of things up here.

A CAMEL GOES ON THE WAGON

A succulent you know nothing about can be well cared for if you judge its water requirements by the thickness of its leaves. The thicker they are, the closer they come to being spheroid, the less water the plant will need.

When in doubt, water less. Succulents, the camels of the plant world, will recover from underwatering. Overwater them, and root rot sets in. To help reduce chances of overwatering, if you use saucers under the pots, make them deep ones and spread a layer of pebbles for the pot to sit on. You should water a succulent enough so that water drains out the bottom of the pot, but the pot should never be left standing in a puddle.

Watering your succulents right not only provides them with moisture, but aerates the soil as well. A few heavy waterings are better than many light ones. Really douse the soil. Excess water will drain out. Then let the soil dehydrate almost completely before watering again. The new flood will percolate down through soil that has gone dry, forcing out accumulated carbon dioxide and pulling fresh air with it. How long to wait depends on the particular environment your home provides. If, when you scratch the soil away gently to a depth of about an inch it seems parched, water. If not, wait. Once you've had the plant awhile you'll have a good feel for the frequency with which it needs moisture and you can stop scratching like a chicken.

Spring and summer are the main growing seasons for most succulents, and these are the times they need water regularly to replenish the supply in their stems and trunks. Succulents are more than 95 percent water, by the way. Once the coolness of fall sets in, they begin hibernating. Cut back on the liquid diet severely. Give them just enough to keep them from shriveling. They need the rest period in order to blossom again come spring. Young plants can go several weeks without watering. Older ones, particularly the cacti, can go even longer, often from November to February, with nary a drop to drink if your home is not very dry.

Along with the winter water shortage, the heat should be cut back. In modern centrally heated buildings this means placing the plants close to the windows where the temperature drops at night. But don't let them actually touch the glass on a night when it might go below freezing outside.

Water succulents' soil directly, using tepid water. Avoid getting any on the plants themselves. It can cause discoloration, particularly if your water is very hard.

Once in a while you may have to spray the plants to clean them. However, a shower should not be given frequently, and only early in the morning so that excess moisture will have a chance to evaporate before the sun hits the plants; otherwise you may end up with burn marks. Evening spray cleaning is not advisable; if there are any small, open scars, the moisture may well induce rot before the plants dry off the next day. A small watercolor paintbrush is convenient for cleaning all but the hairiest cacti, the little *Cephalocereus senilis*.

NOT ALWAYS TORRID

If you've ever been out in the desert, you know it can get mighty cold at night. Cacti know, too. In fact, they wouldn't have it any other way. The most dramatic example of this preference I've seen among the cacti is the opuntia of South Dakota that thrives in places where winter nights drop to forty degrees below zero.

Many succulents grow at high altitudes. Here again the days may be blazing and the nights freezing. Most succulents, even those whose habitat is less lofty, prefer their nights at least cool, particularly in the wintertime, when fifty degrees or so is just cozy. If your house doesn't get quite so cool, that's all right. The daily cycle is what counts. There should be a ten-degree drop or more from daytime to nighttime temperatures.

Besides the actual temperature fluctuations, the change in the weather aids atmospheric circulation, and if there's one thing cacti and succulents like, it's fresh air. Good ventilation is essential for prime growth. But avoid drafts. And again, cacti and succulents will survive without the air-ing. We're talking here about optimum conditions and results.

There is, as usual, one exception, the jungle cacti, typified by flat, leaflike stems and accustomed to the warmer things in life. A drop below fifty-five or even sixty degrees at night can temporarily arrest their devel-opment. They still like good air circulation, however, owing probably to a lifelong habit of swinging back and forth at the jungle's treetop levels.

TEN EASY SPINY ONES FOR THE BEGINNER

The following terrestrial cacti will give you an interesting repre-sentative collection of shapes. Some are easier to find than others, so you may have to look around a bit, but not much.

> *Aporocactus flagelliformis* (Rattail Cactus)
> MICROCLIMATE: Warm sun
> Sandy soil left to dry between waterings

Originating in Mexico, this cactus has hanging branches thin by com-parison with their length, usually an inch or less in diameter, but up to four or five feet long if grown in a hanging basket. Branches will creep slowly into neighboring pots if so allowed. Stems break off readily, form-ing new plants. Small reddish spines. A profusion of bright red flowers in spring.

> *Astrophytum capricorne* (Bishop's Cap, Goat's Horn, Star Cactus)
> MICROCLIMATE: Warm sun
> Sandy soil left to dry between waterings

A smooth, globular plant with small white freckles and many very long, curving, sickle-shaped spines. The white scales are natural, so don't worry about the "water spots." Plants three inches or more in diameter bear beautiful red and yellow flowers near their tops. Summer blossoming is followed by woolly fruit yielding easy-to-germinate seeds.

Astrophytum capricorne

Cephalocereus senilis (Bearded Cactus, Beetle Cactus, Old Man
Cactus)
MICROCLIMATE: Warm sun
Sandy soil left to dry between waterings

A slender, closely ribbed gray green cactus with translucent spines. The
whole plant is covered from head to foot with felted white hair not unlike
the angel hair on Christmas trees of old. A poor bloomer, but still worth
having for the coiffure. Doesn't like the kitchen windowsill, where the
myriad hairs tend to act as grease traps for kitchen vapors and cooking
oils. Accumulating grease will quietly kill the plant. By the same token,
the cactus should be kept dust-free wherever it resides.

Chamaecereus silvestri (Peanut Cactus)
MICROCLIMATE: Temperate sun
Sandy soil left to dry between waterings

Small cylindrical green branches grow from the base. They are covered
all year round by rows of soft bristlelike spines, and in spring by a profusion of open-faced scarlet flowers sometimes lasting almost a month.
The joints are easily detached and rooted for new plants.

Mammillaria bocasana (Pincushion, Powder Puff)
    MICROCLIMATE: Temperate sun
                       Sandy soil left to dry between waterings

The mammillarias are some of the easiest-to-grow pot cacti. Their seeds just burst with vitality, and the plants remain manageable in size. *Mammillaria bocasana* is covered with silky white hair and brown fishhook spines. Tiny cream-colored flowers grow in a halolike circle around the top of the plant in spring and summer. These in turn give way to strange, long fruit looking like diminutive hot-pink snap beans. Mammillarias are best propagated using their abundant seeds.

Mammillaria parkinsonii (Owl's Eyes)
    MICROCLIMATE: Temperate sun
                       Sandy soil left to dry between waterings

Originally grows round, then cylindrical with age. The owl's eyes are the neat woolly white areoles from which grow white spines. The plant exudes a milky white sap if cut. That doesn't mean you have to nick yours to verify it. I just toss this bit of information in for the purist, because the milky fluid is supposed to be one of the distinguishing characteristics of euphorbias—which are not cacti at all—to help separate them from the Cactaceae. Just goes to show you never can tell.

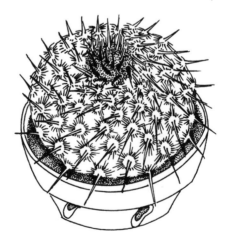

Mammillaria parkinsonii

Notocactus scopa 'Cristata' (Spiraled Silver Ball)
>MICROCLIMATE: Temperate sun
>Sandy soil left to dry between waterings

Usually grafted onto another species for rootstock to promote growth, this Brazilian cactus looks like a giant hairy caterpillar curled up asleep. As its name states, it is the cristate form of *Notocactus scopa*. That is, it has grown crested appendages rather than remaining globular. The rest of the genus are globular. All are easy to grow. New plants from seeds.

Opuntia microdasys (Bunny Ears, Gold Plush, Prickly Pear)
>MICROCLIMATE: Temperate sun
>Sandy soil left to dry between waterings

Fleshy, flat, oval joints up to six inches long are covered with neat rows of brown glochidia, or barbed bristles. They look soft. But watch out. Although not hard like spines, they have a nasty habit of burrowing under your skin. Difficult to coax into bloom, but visually nice, and easy to grow so long as you guard against rot. Propagate by joint cuttings.

Notocactus scopa 'Cristata' grafted onto *Trichocereus spachianus*

Rebutia kupperiana (Crown Cactus, Red Crown)
    MICROCLIMATE: Temperate sun
                  Sandy soil left to dry between waterings

The open, brilliant red flower of this miniature cactus from the Andes is larger than the young plant itself. Always spectacular, if somewhat strange. Great for those who have only one small window with full sun. The plant is quite happy in a two-inch pot for the first couple of years, so you can grow a lot of specimens on one narrow ledge. The scarlet flowers bloom in profusion from April to July. Grow new plants from seeds or offsets.

Trichocereus spachianus (Torch Cactus)
    MICROCLIMATE: Warm sun
                  Sandy soil left to dry between waterings

A very cactusy-looking cactus with tall slender close-ribbed columns growing up to four feet high. More mundanely, *Trichocereus spachianus* is often used for rootstock in grafting other cacti. White flowers, but not easily come by except in a greenhouse. As cacti go, however, this one is a fairly rapid indoor grower.

Opuntia microdasys

EIGHT EASY OTHER SUCCULENTS

Aeonium haworthii (Pinwheel)
> MICROCLIMATE: Temperate sun
> Sandy soil left to dry between waterings

Thick, red-edged blue green leaves form rosettes up to three inches in diameter at the end of short, woody-looking branches. The plant enjoys an outing to the terrace or yard in summer, although the move is not necessary. Overall shape is that of a miniature tree around two feet high at its maximum.

Crassula argentea (Chinese Rubber Plant, Jade Plant, Money Tree, Silver Crassula)
> MICROCLIMATE: Temperate sun
> Sandy soil left to dry between waterings

The real jade plant, although many other crassulas are called by the same popular name. In horticultural circles *Crassula argentea* is often referred to as the *C. arborescens*. Names aside, from the standpoint of care it is one of the best all-around houseplants. Propagates easily from cuttings,

Crassula argentea

and under optimum conditions, as well as several generations of owners, will branch and fork till it is a shrub eight to ten feet in height. Most housebound specimens remain a more manageable size. Clusters of pale pink blossoms form in winter and spring.

Crassula perforata (Necklace Vine)
    MICROCLIMATE: Temperate sun
                     Sandy soil left to dry between waterings

Looks like a wire sculpture studded with triangular marzipan leaves. Likes cool winters. For a plant, unusually well suited to air conditioning. Will even tolerate some drafts. Grows best in a small container.

Euphorbia splendens 'Bojeri' (Dwarf Crown of Thorns)
    MICROCLIMATE: Warm sun
                     Sandy soil left to dry between waterings

More leafy, compact, and showy than its larger counterpart, the full-sized *Euphorbia splendens*, this gray plant with deep green leaves comes from Madagascar. As well as being small enough to handle easily, *E. splendens* 'Bojeri' is less likely to shed its leaves. Propagate by cuttings, but watch out for the milky white sap; some people have a strong skin reaction to contact with it. Rinse off sap in tepid water. Let each cutting dry thoroughly and the wound heal, or form a callus, before sticking it in the rooting mix. Bottom heat is a great aid in getting cuttings to root.

Haworthia papillosa (Crystal Cactus, Pearly Dots)
    MICROCLIMATE: Temperate partial sun
                     Loamy soil left to dry between waterings

A very pretty, small, sculptured rosette whose deep green leaves are covered with even rows of white sugary-looking dots. Propagates from leaf cuttings or suckers. Water more generously than you would most desert succulents, particularly during the summer growing period. The plant takes a short rest period, during which it will be less thirsty.

Hoodia rosea (African Hat Plant)
    MICROCLIMATE: Warm sun
                     Sandy soil left to dry between waterings

Leafless, cactuslike succulent forming a cluster of stems. The star-to-saucer-shaped rust brown flowers are spectacular, reaching three inches in diameter on an eight-inch plant. For propagation, seeds must be fresh, since they do not retain their viability long.

Kalanchoë tomentosa (Lamb's Ears, Panda Plant)
    MICROCLIMATE: Warm sun
                         Sandy soil left to dry between waterings

A different species from the more common *Kalanchoë blossfeldiana* with its many scarlet flowers usually seen in shops around Christmas. *K. tomentosa* has delightful, soft, soupspoon-shaped leaves covered by a fine, white felt and edged with brown toothlike markings. The leaves are an easy means of propagation. Simply lay them individually on a bed of sand. New plantlets will form at the leaf base.

Sedum x *orpetii* (Giant Burro's Tail, Lamb's Tail, Live Forever, Stonecrop)
    MICROCLIMATE: Warm sun
                         Sandy soil left to dry between waterings

Probably the most popular sedum is *Sedum morganianum*, the burro's tail, whose long, full branches are so often seen tumbling down from a hanging basket. Unfortunately, the plump leaves also come tumbling down if you so much as touch the plant, leaving behind them stems that

Kalanchoë tomentosa

might more descriptively be called rat's tails. To solve this problem, S. *morganianum* was crossed with S. *treleasei*. The resulting S. x *orpetii* is much to be preferred, since the fatter, more open-spaced leaves cling tightly to the branches. Even so, you shouldn't knock the plant about if you wish it to retain its fullness. Propagates easily from any fallen leaf. Just stick the leaf in sand.

THE FLOWERING STONES

In South Africa there's a group of plants that look just like small stones or pebbles. Coming in all varieties, from sandstone, quartz, and iron ore to limestone, they so carefully mimic their mineral models that, except during flowering, you'd walk right by without noticing them.

The most fascinating genus is *Lithops*, the "windowed" plants. Small paired leaves form inverted cones. In their natural habitat the only things

Sedum x orpetii

showing are the round, pebbly tops of these cones. The rest of the plants are buried. The tops are like skylights, letting the sun shine on through to deep inside the plants, where the chlorophyll cells remain protected.

Pot stone plants contrary to their natural habit, keeping only the roots buried. Choose a container you can live with awhile, for you don't want to repot these plants if you can help it. Use a soil mixture of two parts fine sand and one part soil. If possible, to show the plants' natural camouflage, top the soil with pebbles matching in color and shape the particular species of *Lithops* you are growing.

Although the stone plants like warmth during the day, keep night temperatures around fifty degrees during the wintertime. Water very sparingly except in late summer and fall. These are among the least water-tolerant of all plants. During winter dormancy they can go without water for several months. At the same time, however, watch for shriveling and dehydration. Plenty of sun and *very little fertilizer* will give you the healthiest plants. The autumn flowers you'll find not only beautiful and surprisingly large, but usually very fragrant as well.

Although over twenty genera of stone-mimicking plants are known, the indoor gardener is limited by necessity to those plants readily avail-able. These usually include only three genera besides *Lithops: Conophytum, Fenestraria,* and *Pleiospilos.* All are intriguing additions to a collection of succulents. But remember the master key to growing them successfully: don't repot unless it's absolutely necessary.

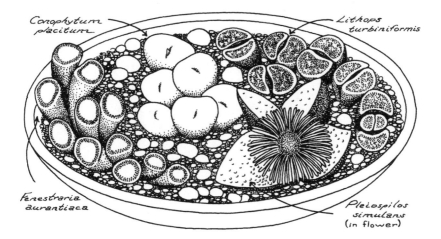

Stone-mimicking plants

'TIS THE SEASON FOR CACTI

There's been such a confusion among Christmas, Easter, and Thanksgiving cacti lately that one mail-order firm has begun advertising a "Chreaster cactus." The holiday cacti are all epiphytic jungle varieties, with a liking for bright light but not prolonged direct sun. Also, unlike their desert cousins, they prefer soil kept constantly moist, though never wet. The soil itself should be a rich, humusy mixture like that you would use for other epiphytic jungle plants. Fertilize lightly every two weeks during the growing season, from late spring through August. Good air circulation is essential.

Being photoperiodic, these cacti need long nights and short days to encourage them to blossom. Long nights in this case means thirteen hours or more. For best results use grandma's old double-eight plan: eight weeks with only eight hours of light a day before you want the flowers. You may have to tuck the plant in a cool closet every night during that couple of months. For really good blooms, no light means no light. Even sixty seconds of light in the middle of the night is enough to disturb the plant's somnolence. Night temperatures should be kept between fifty and

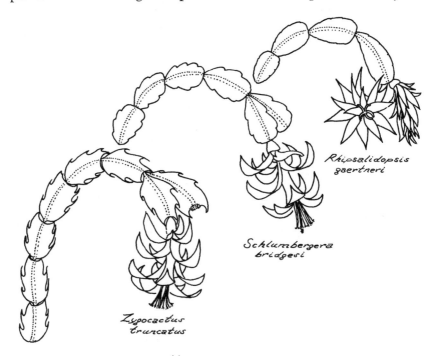

Rhipsalidopsis gaertneri

Schlumbergera bridgesi

Zygocactus truncatus

Holiday cacti

sixty degrees, but if you can keep tight control over the light cycle they can go as high as sixty-five degrees. Supply just enough water to keep the leaves from shriveling.

Oh yes, about which cactus is which. . . . Well, according to latest nomenclature, *Zygocactus truncatus*, whose flat, jointed leaves have saw-toothed edges, is the Thanksgiving cactus. *Schlumbergera bridgesi* has rounded teeth and is the Christmas cactus. *Rhipsalidopsis gaertneri* is the toothless Easter cactus. When buying these cacti, check the plant's teeth if you want blooms for the right holiday.

ORCHID CACTI

Similar in appearance to the holiday cacti are *Epiphyllum*, or orchid, cacti. Their blooms are even more impressive and carry on the show through spring and well into summer. Although the genus has only twelve species, these cross easily with other genera. Hybrids are common, with iridescent blossoms in every color except true blue and deep yellow, and from two to ten inches in diameter.

The plants need a rich, friable soil such as equal parts of loam, peat moss, and sand or perlite. One spoonful of steamed bone meal per four inches of pot is a good idea, since epiphyllums need plenty of phosphorus. Fertilize with a low-nitrogen compound every second week during the growing season, which begins in March. At the same time, moisture must be maintained to a high degree. Keep in good bright light, but with little direct sun except during summer. Remember the plant comes from a jungle environment.

Orchid cacti rest November to February. They should be kept cool then; about fifty degrees is good. During the summer, if night temperatures do not drop below fifty-five degrees, these cacti love to be outside for a few months of fresh air. On the opposite side of the wall, *Epiphyllum* species do well indoors under artificial light, even flowering under Vita-Lite or Gro-Lux bulbs, as long as air circulation is good.

The plants may have to be staked, since the leaflike stems tend to get out of hand, appearing ready to crawl every which way. Crawl they do, as a matter of fact. In Brazil, growing wild, an epiphyllum starts more or less at ground level, throws a stem out and up, and anchors wherever it makes contact with something higher. Then another stem and another reach up. Over the years a plant will disperse, with the new stems taking root. Eventually pieces of the plant in the form of new off-shoots make their way to a comfortable niche high in the crotch of a tree.

If this gives you the idea orchid cacti might do well in a hanging basket, right you are. Should they become too long and rattailed looking, pinch off the stems at the leaf joints. This will encourage them to fork and branch, at the same time giving you easy-to-root cuttings.

WHEN A CACTUS IS NOT A CACTUS

The cacti's appearance is enough to turn almost any hungry animal away to less spiny pastures. Their defensive spines are, in fact, so effective that other plants try to camouflage themselves as cacti in order to escape munching predators. They also parallel the cacti's thick, water-retentive shapes. Called convergence, this development of similar characteristics in unrelated plants (and animals as well) owing to the similarity of their environment sometimes produces remarkable false twins. The phenomenon is particularly evident among succulents.

There are members of the spurge family, called euphorbias, that would fool anyone at first glance. They parallel the cacti they are mimicking right down to a set of false spines. The only way you can tell them apart easily is by making a small incision in the stem. If the plant is really a cactus, the liquid inside will be clear. If it's a euphorbia, the fluid will be milky—like that of a poinsettia, which resembles a cactus not at all but which also happens to be a euphorbia.

If it sounds like a bit much to bother about, perhaps it is, when you're first beginning to collect succulents. Once you're hooked, though, curiosity will get the better of you, I'm almost sure.

Carl Olaf Bromel's Bounty

What family of houseplants is pestproof, objects only a little to dry air, can survive for weeks forgotten in a dark corner, blooms under artificial light, and has dazzling flower spikes that last as long as half a year? Bromeliads is the answer, as almost any European plant lover will tell you. Oddly enough, although bromeliads originated in the Americas, somehow they remained strangers in their own land, at least as far as living indoors goes. Even their name was the gift of a Swedish botanist, Carl Olaf Bromel. But all that seems to be changing now. Bromeliads are coming into their own on their native soil, so to speak, and a specimen or two added to your plant collection is certainly worth considering.

Generally known as the pineapple family, from their most popular edible member, the bromeliads are a distinctive group of epiphytic and ground-dwelling plants with hardy, brightly colored leaves. Admittedly, Spanish moss looks a bit more like a discarded Brillo pad than verdant splendor, but, after all, there are exceptions in all families.

STRAPHANGERS

The main roots of bromeliads, particularly the epiphytic varieties growing high in the treetops, are small and not very numerous, but tenacious and strong. Their primary function is to anchor the plant, be it in a treetop or a rocky crevice. Only secondarily do they serve to gather nutrients, and they do it so poorly that the plant can survive, even grow slowly for a considerable time without them. Some species such as *Tillandsia usneoides*, the native-American Spanish moss, have given up on their roots altogether and no longer have any.

When you pot offshoots, the small roots can make it difficult to anchor the plants properly in the loose friable soil they prefer. Yet anchor them you must, since the new plants will grow very hesitantly till they have a firm grip on things. To this end it's a good idea to staple each down with some wire shaped into an inverted U or with the proverbial

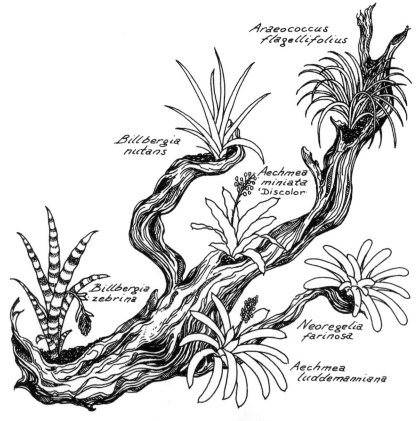

A bromeliad "tree"

hairpin if there's one handy. A tight shoe suits a bromeliad best, so always choose a smaller-than-normal pot for it. Bromeliad trees—driftwood, or an artful stump or two, with the plants secured to niches and small pockets—can look very attractive. However, since the roots are then not protected by a surrounding pot from drying out, they should be misted once or twice a day.

As to soil for the bromeliads, the prime considerations are aeration and avoiding root rot. Almost any soil mix will do as long as it's heavily laced with sharp sand, perlite, vermiculite, or broken crockery. Basically the plants prefer a humusy soil, since in the wild most of them have their roots buried only in the vegetative scraps that get trapped in their own clinging web.

THEIR CUP RUNNETH OVER

The typical bromeliad has leaves arranged in a rosette. Since the plant is a true shrub, the rosette is mounted on a stem, although usually such a short one that it's hard to tell. Crucial to the bromeliad's survival, in the wild as well as in the home, is the cup, or funnel, formed at the center of the plant by these leaves. It serves the same function as a water tank on top of an apartment building, ensuring that the vital liquid is available when needed. This is one of the reasons bromeliads can do quite well in a dry house. They supply their own moisture cloud.

Basic plant care entails making sure the reservoir always contains water. The soil, by contrast, should be watered sparingly. Usually I just fill the rosette to overflowing, letting the excess take care of the soil's needs.

DIETING BY THE SCALES

The leafy rosette of a bromeliad in its outdoor habitat fills with a lot of things besides water: misdirected ants, slugs that slipped off the plant's side, leaves, flower pollen, and so on. Their decay supplies the plant with necessary minerals. So in the home, supplying the reservoir with liquid fertilizer about once a month is just natural. But remember, six pollen grains, one leaf, and a pinch of ant do not a very strong brew make. Avoid chemical fertilizers; instead use fish emulsion. Even this should be diluted to anywhere from a fifth to a tenth its normal strength. Try the weakest dilution first. If there's no adverse reaction from the plant, you can try a stronger solution.

Water and nutrients are absorbed by the plant through a group of specialized scales. Don't confuse these rightful scales with pests such as mealybugs or the insect kind of scales. They are located primarily in the cup, but on some bromeliads they cover the leaves almost entirely like a woolly scurf.

I've found that spraying the leaves with diluted fertilizer at the same time I fertilize the rosette makes for healthy, more attractive plants, as long as I spray them with plain water a few days later. But very hard water will form a scum, blocking the scales and slowly killing the plant. Remember that rainwater is distilled water. You need not rob your steam iron supply; just bear in mind that, while the plants need minerals, there is a limit to what they can absorb. Also they dislike the flavor of chlorine, so if you are in one of those communities whose water system is so heavily chlorinated that you can smell it, let the water stand overnight so the chlorine can volatilize before you offer it to your plants. They like the taste of insecticides even less, and will usually die after the first application. Eliminate any insects, which shouldn't really be a problem in the first place, by brushing them off.

Most plants need good root aeration, and the bromeliads are no exception. But with hungry leaves to feed, they also like good ventilation aboveground. They are accustomed to it from the treetops and expect to get some of their nourishment that way.

FLOWER POWER

The key to making bromeliads flower is forcing the leaves to stop growing. Interestingly enough, beta-hydroxyethyl-hydrazine, one of the components of the liquid fuel that gives space rockets their zip, does just that. But while beta-hydroxyethyl-hydrazine is an invaluable aid to commercial growers, it isn't exactly available for home use.

There is, however, a convenient way to induce flowering at home. Enclose a mature bromeliad specimen in a plastic bag together with a couple of very ripe apples for five or six days. As the apples ripen, they give off small quantities of ethylene, which counteracts the plant's natural growth hormones. Obviously, if things aren't going well enough for the plant to grow, something has to be done to keep the species alive. So the plant blooms. It usually takes a month or two, once you remove the bag, for the flower to develop.

Three things should be kept in mind when forcing the bloom. First, to further inhibit growth, empty the rosette of water before packing up the plant. Second, keep the plant out of direct sunlight during the time it is enclosed in plastic, or it will bake. Remember it's not getting any air circulation. And third, apples generate more ethylene on warm sunny days, so early summer is one of the best times for the project.

IT'S THE BLOOMING END

One of the things your local florist or plant man may not have told you is that once a bromeliad flowers, *c'est fini.* Don't let that stop you from buying one already in bloom, the first time at least. It's worth not having to wait for the main feature. And it's not really the end of the line, for like all living things, bromeliads do reproduce—in two ways, at that, as do most of the more primitive and more stubborn plants. Many bromeliads can be grown from the seeds that develop after they have bloomed. The majority will also produce offshoots, sometimes called pups.

The key in rooting offshoots is to wait till they are well established before cutting them off. This sometimes means waiting till the main plant has withered back. Some people find the sight ugly, but personally I find a plant putting forth new life with its dying breath, so to speak, and in somewhat purple prose, quite a little miracle.

Offshoots will usually be mature enough to bloom by their second or third year. Plants raised from seed may take as long as five years to flower. The flowers on many species actually do not last more than a day before falling off, incidentally; but they are often insignificant compared with the colorful spike and the bracts surrounding them, and it is these that last for months.

PLAYING BEE

Most outdoor bromeliads have their brilliant seeds dispersed by birds, which find them tasty morsels. To this end the berries are temptingly colored. The really fascinating aspect of their coloration, moreover, is that, particularly in the aechmeas, they only acquire their strong, highly visible coloring if they are fertile. Sterile berries remain pale. No use wasting bird power.

Since you may have a shortage of insects around the house, not to mention birds, if you wish to grow new plants indoors from your own seed you may have to do the pollinating job yourself in order to ensure a good harvest. But the pollen must be transferred only when it is dry, and only to a stigma that is moist and sticky. Commercially, the pollen is removed with tweezers as soon as a flower opens, allowed to dry for a couple of hours on a sterile surface, and then reinserted onto a sticky stigma.

ELEVEN INDESTRUCTIBLE ONES

Aechmea fasciata (Silver Vase)
MICROCLIMATE: Warm partial sun
Humusy soil kept constantly moist

Aechmeas are very popular, colorfully foliaged epiphytic bromeliads that look just the way one expects a bromeliad to look. *Aechmea fasciata*, probably the easiest one to grow, has an urn-shaped rosette of toothed green foliage striated with silvery white. The flower stalk is erect and grows considerably higher than the plant itself before the blue flowers emerge above the pink bracts, or flower leaves. A spectacular show usually commences after a short dry period in the summer. The rose-colored flower bracts last three to five months before the display is over. The plant will offset readily and can also be propagated by seed to reach flowering maturity in the third or fourth year.

Aechmea fasciata

Aechmea luddemanniana
> MICROCLIMATE: Warm partial sun
> Humusy soil kept constantly moist

Narrower, less clownishly colored leaves, green with a darker green mottle. A striking bloomer. After flowering there is a second feature of well formed elongated white berries that gradually turn bright purple. They last for months.

Aechmea miniata 'Discolor' (Purplish Coralberry)
> MICROCLIMATE: Warm partial sun
> Humusy soil kept constantly moist

A more open rosette of olive green leaves with pale red undersides. Light blue flowers, followed by rounded red berries that seem almost iridescent when the sun hits them. Both blossoms and berries are long lasting.

Araeococcus flagellifolius
> MICROCLIMATE: Temperate sun
> Humusy soil left to dry between waterings

Slender, very stiff whiplike leaves up to four feet long. Needs a minimum of four hours of direct sunlight daily for the leaves to develop their best bronze brown color. The flower structure resembles that of the lily of the valley in that bottom flowers open first and an elongated stem keeps producing more buds until at last the terminal bud forms the final flower. The erect racemes bear light red bracts, pink flowers, and eventually blue green berries.

Billbergia nutans (Indoor Oats, Queen's Tears)
> MICROCLIMATE: Temperate partial sun
> Humusy soil left to dry between waterings

A petite species with relatively few slender silvery bronze leaves turning to bright red in full sunlight. It has an arching flower stalk with a pendant inflorescence of multiple flowers on a common stem. The blossoms are green, edged in violet. Blooms last only a couple of weeks, but the plant itself is very tolerant of neglect. Keep its soil moist, but do not water the cup when the plant is in flower, since that would shorten the bloom's duration.

Billbergia zebrina (Zebra Urn)
MICROCLIMATE: Warm partial sun
Humusy soil left to dry between waterings

Long, fluted purplish brown leaves crossbanded in silvery white and sharply serrated. The nodding flowers are violet, surrounded by rosy red bracts. Propagated by means of suckers, but wait until they develop a good root system. Though this can take the better part of a year, it means better and quicker growth when they are finally on their own.

Cryptanthus zonatus 'Zebrinus' (Earth Star, Pheasant Leaf)
MICROCLIMATE: Warm partial sun
Humusy soil left to dry between waterings

A terrestrial bromeliad rarely more than a foot in diameter. It grows into a flattened rosette with wavy bronze purple leaves dominated by silver white cross-stripes. Flowers are white, but small, and hidden in the rosette rather than displayed on a tall spike. The name cryptanthus, in fact, means hidden flower.

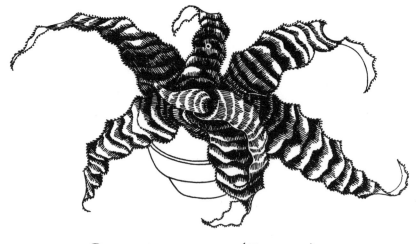

Cryptanthus zonatus 'Zebrinus'

Neoregelia carolinea
> MICROCLIMATE: Warm partial sun
> Humusy soil kept constantly moist

As spring blooming approaches, the flaring nestlike rosette of this bromeliad changes color, the metallic brown green leaves turning a brilliant deep red toward the rosette's center. The white-edged violet flowers form one or two at a time from a large disc deep within the center of the water-filled cup. Definitely a plant to look down on. Needs good light for maximum leaf coloration, which it will then retain for many months.

Neoregelia farinosa (Crimson Cup)
> MICROCLIMATE: Warm partial sun
> Humusy soil kept constantly moist

Similar to *Neoregelia carolinea*, but the leaves are blunter, more purplish than brown, and their preflowering display is a more brilliant crimson. Purple flowers. Propagated by seed or more readily by sucker.

Nidularium innocentii (Black Amazonian Bird's Nest)
> MICROCLIMATE: Warm shade
> Humusy soil left to dry between waterings

A shade-loving epiphytic bromeliad that does better than most in poor light. There are several varieties, including the miniature *Nidularium in-*

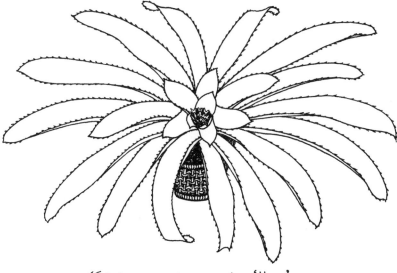

Nidularium innocentii 'Nana'

nocentii 'nana' and the white-banded *N. innocentii* 'lineatum.' All have a distinctive nest of low leaves at the center of the rosette. *N. innocentii* var. 'innocentii' appears far from innocent in color, its leaves being on occasion almost black. Wonderful contrast is provided by the short rust-colored bracts and the white flowers.

Vriesia x *mariae* (Painted Feather)
MICROCLIMATE: Warm partial sun
Humusy soil left to dry between waterings

Hybrids are still not very common among bromeliads. This is perhaps one reason why the bromeliads have taken time to gain popularity here. There is a tendency on the part of many growers to prefer hybrids as being "improved" for indoor use. So for hybrid lovers, here's a bromeliad that has been crossed for improvement. Light green to pink-tinted foliage and a striking long-lasting spike rose colored at the base, with small yellow flowers forming a flat boat-shaped inflorescence. The red and yellow bracts, which in themselves look like flowers, last for months; the small yellow real flowers are again short lived. Vriesias as a whole need more humidity than many other bromeliads; 50 percent or so is about right.

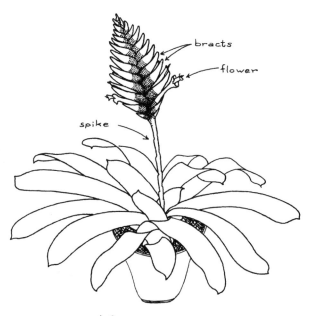

Vriesia x *mariae*

HAVE YOUR PLANT AND SALAD TOO

Pineapple tops discarded after the fruit has been eaten will grow readily. In fact, that's the way the pineapple spread throughout the Pacific islands and Asia following its discovery in America. Sailors and explorers with sloppy habits threw the remains of their meals over their shoulders, and had they returned in a year or so to the site of their banquets, they would have found new pineapple plants where the old tops took root and grew.

To root pineapples at home, cut off about half an inch of the pineapple itself along with the top. Scrape out as much of the flesh as possible and then let the shell dry out for two or three days. A scar will be formed that will prevent mold when the top is planted. After drying, pin the pineapple top down to a pot of soil with a couple of straight pins. Try to anchor it firmly enough so it doesn't wobble. Wobbly tops take longer to root. Water the soil regularly—the pineapple is not an epiphytic bromeliad—but let the soil become quite dry between waterings, to promote rooting. Unfortunately, the reproductive cycle usually ends indoors with a new plant. Pineapples need blazing full sun to reach maturity and set good fruit. Even without it they make nice houseplants, are about as inexpensive a type of greenery as you would find, and though the plant wouldn't make it with Dole, there's always a chance you'll get a small pineapple.

Water
Water
Everywhere

It had been raining on and off for over a week when, bored with indoor confinement, Genevieve converted the tubbed avocado tree in her room into a sandbox. The renovation occurred during what is euphemistically known in our house as quiet time, an attempt by the harried parents to continue in different guise the age-old tradition of an afternoon nap. When we opened the door to her room, a thin layer of evenly sifted potting soil covered everything from bed to desk, including, of course, Genevieve. There ensued a lengthy discussion, over the roar of the vacuum cleaner, on how plants need the soil in their pots to live and therefore we couldn't go spreading it around for other purposes. It seemed to sink in.

However, about an hour later she pointed to some cuttings of *Iresine herbstii*, "Irene herb" to her, and *Gynura aurantiaca* 'Sarmentosa' sitting rooted in a vase on the windowsill. "They don't need dirt to grow."

Now if there's one thing I don't particularly appreciate, it's being outfoxed by a three-year-old, which seems to be occurring with some frequency these days. But it so happens she was right. There are a number of houseplants that can be grown in just water if you are so inclined.

Raising them this way won't give you a riot of colorful flowers, but it's a good method for those who feel they always give their plants too much or too little water. After all, if they're sitting in it up to their waist, there's no question of degree. Either the plants have water—in which case they grow—or they have no water—in which case they crumple into a state not unlike that of a used grocery bag.

THE LIQUID DIET

Aristotle left his mark on almost every thought man had for centuries and centuries after his time. Unfortunately, like so many of the ancient philosopher-scientists, he was wrong as often as he was right, if not more often. For the longest time men followed Aristotle in believing that plants somehow derived their food from the soil. Even today many people who have had no reason to ponder where the plants do get their three squares accept the notion automatically. Yet as early as 1514 Cardinal Nicolas of Cusa suggested that plants derive their nourishment from water rather than soil.

In 1684 the Flemish Jean-Baptiste Van Helmont set out to prove it in an experiment you can duplicate—if you have a large enough living room. First he took two hundred pounds of dirt and baked it dry. In it he planted a five-pound willow shoot, covering the container so nothing could enter except the water he supplied. After five years, the tree weighed one hundred sixty-nine pounds, three ounces; the soil weighed one hundred ninety-nine pounds, fourteen ounces. Obviously the willow's extra one hundred sixty-four pounds, one ounce had to come from somewhere, and everyone was agreed on at least one point: the plant couldn't live on air. Van Helmont decided it had to come from the water the tree devoured. Well, he was more correct than Aristotle, but he still had only a one-course meal.

Only at the turn of this century was it discovered that plants synthesize their own food, using water and carbon dioxide from the earth's atmosphere. The power behind the manufacture is sunshine, which is why the process, appropriately enough, is known as photosynthesis. So within its tolerance, the more sun a plant gets, the better it grows—as long as there's enough water on hand.

DIET SUPPLEMENTS

Why does anyone bother with fertilizer then? Well, it's about those two ounces of dirt that were left unaccounted for by Van Helmont. They represent mineral salts absorbed by the plant, used in its structural components, the synthesis of amino acids and proteins, and so on. Minerals are essential to a plant's life and growth, but only in minute quantities. A dozen or so manganese molecules, for instance, will probably last the average houseplant for a year. And since the slightest trace in the soil will do, such minerals are known as trace elements.

Not surprisingly, considering his diet, a man needs more or less the same minerals as do the plants he eats. And much as he may take a mineral supplement with his breakfast, a plant may need a fertilizer compound. When the plant is grown in water, in fact, it is dependent on one to supply the trace as well as the three major elements, nitrogen, phosphorus, and potassium.

When adding fertilizer to your plant's water, remember that Van Helmont's willow used only two ounces in five years. Don't overfertilize. Next to overwatering, overfertilization is probably the biggest cause of houseplant death.

Even in the great outdoors, an excess of one mineral or another in the soil can produce a marked effect on the plants in that locale. For instance, soil particularly rich in boron will produce plants two to three times their normal size, with exceptionally dark green leaves. Russian geologists report using this phenomenon as a prospecting tool in their search for new mine locations.

For regular earthbound plants, any fertilizer will do if used according to the directions or, probably better yet, slightly weaker and less frequently than called for by the directions. For your water-lodged plants, however, you must use a soluble fertilizer, one that mixes with water instantly, as opposed to slow-dissolving powders or tablets. I've used Spoonit and Peters with good results. The Peters adds a crystal-blue tint to the water; the Spoonit, green. Use a formula with trace elements, and mix it up at half-strength.

THE TRANSFORMATION

When you're ready to switch the potted plant on your windowsill from a creature of terrestrial habits to one of at least semiaquatic nature, all you do is knock it out of its pot and stick it up to its old soil level in a basin of tepid water—that's what I was told when I first tried growing plants in water. There was only one problem with the advice: after I had let my plant soak, carefully worked all the soil off the roots, and washed them, I was left with two gallons of mud slurry. What I had not been told was how to get rid of it. (The building superintendent had already balked about the sphagnum moss that slipped through my fingers and stopped up the sink.) Late that night I slunk past the elevator man with a covered bucket and watered the ginkgo in front of the building.

Now I pick most of the soil off the root ball with a pencil point and dispose of it in the garbage. Usually, if I have taken care to let the soil in the pot dry out a bit before the transformation, there is so little soil left after the picking that I can wash it off under tepid running water without giving the grease trap in my sink gustatory upset. This doesn't really harm the plants, but it is aesthetically somewhat displeasing. The roots must be really clean, or little particles of dirt will cloud the potting water. Of course, if you're working with a plant cutting, you've already eliminated the dirt problem.

Now for a pot. Almost any glass or glazed ceramic container will do for growing plants in water. Roots are somewhat inhibited by light— which is not surprising, considering their normal buried state—so tinted glass or semiopaque planters usually give you the lushest growth. Stainless-steel or silver vases are fine too, but the fertilizer may pit the insides, and, of course, you don't get to watch the roots grow.

Fill your container with tepid water. It isn't really necessary to let the water stand overnight. Although this does permit chlorine to escape, the amount of chlorine in most city water is not enough to affect a plant. It more or less has to smell like the pool at the local YMCA to be harmful to the greens.

If you're using a wide-mouthed container that allows the plant to lean erratically to one side, fill the bottom quarter or third with clear marbles or washed aquarium gravel and anchor the stem and roots in it. A thin layer of charcoal underneath, or simply mixed in with the marbles or gravel, will help keep the water clear and at the same time prevent its becoming too acid. Charcoal floats, as I discovered the first time I used it, so be sure to presoak it for several days, until it reaches the sinking stage. If you pour boiling water over it before setting it to soak, the charcoal will get waterlogged and sink more quickly.

Once the gravel and plant are in place, trickle the nutrient solution into the container. Only the stem and roots of the plant should be in water, not the leaves. Submerged leaves will rot, so pinch off any below the surface. When because of evaporation the water level falls, refill the container. Don't add more nutrient solution, or the concentration will become too high. Wait till you change the water.

AIRING THE PLANTS

Potted plants need watering. Water plants, on the other hand, need airing. The process can be pretty haphazard, however. They won't mind. About once a month or every six weeks, you can change the nutrient solution. The fresh water will be oxygenated. The change will also keep the water from going stale and slimy or collecting algae, as sometimes happens with all those good nutrients floating around just waiting to be gobbled up.

Changing the water in a planter that has a gravel layer can often be a nuisance: the gravel shifts around, making a mess. Unless algae have joined your garden, you can skip the water change, just adding a little fresh nutrient solution every two or three months to keep the plants well fed. But if you don't change solutions, get hold of a kitchen baster, an automobile battery syringe, or for that matter even a bicycle pump, and squirt some air into the water every week or so. You can't overaerate the water, so don't worry about doing it too often, but do it gently enough so the bubbles don't stir up all the gravel.

Curiously enough, the oxygen in the water isn't really for the plant per se. It's just that the roots can't absorb the *water* unless there are plenty of oxygen molecules around.

SWIMMERS

A lot of plants will grow in water, particularly those that can be propagated by cuttings. Some particularly easy ones to try are *Iresine herbstii*, or blood leaf; *Cyperus alternifolius*, the umbrella plant; syngoniums, or arrowheads; aglaonemas, the Chinese evergreens; coleus; dracaenas; dieffenbachias; the various ivies; as well as philodendrons. For flowers try sinningias—make sure not to submerge the crown—and begonias, although in my opinion small flowering plants are more trouble to grow hydroponically than they are worth. Just out of curiosity I'm going to experiment with a cactus one of these days.

THE ENDLESS STRAW

If you stand a vase of water next to your swimming plant, you'll notice the water in the plant container disappears much faster than that in the one filled with plain water. This is because the plant's roots draw up much more water than the plant actually uses. They do it with con-

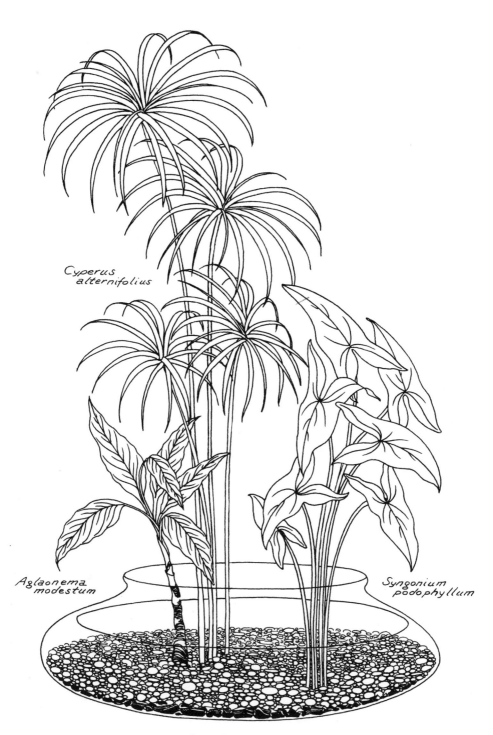

Cyperus
alternifolius

Aglaonema
modestum

Syngonium
podophyllum

A water garden

siderable force and by various means, one of them being root pressure.

If you happen to have a large spare tomato plant growing in the yard sometime, decapitate it a few inches from the ground. Attach a piece of clear plastic tubing over it and keep the tube vertical. The plant will keep pumping water for a couple of days, raising the liquid level in the tube to several feet.

There are a lot of roots behind the phenomenon, by the way. One single rye plant, for instance, has been estimated to have fourteen billion root hairs with a total surface of almost four hundred square yards. Try to visualize it. I can't really, but there it is.

Water in a plant can move with considerable speed. That's what saves the day when you notice your neglected cyclamen bent over double from lack of water and rush to give it a good root dousing. It literally sops up the water, often springing back upright in less than an hour. The water rushes up from the roots through xylem tubes in the stems that serve a function somewhat parallel to that of veins and arteries. The velocity of the water traveling through them is really amazing when one thinks of a plant as just sitting there. It's been timed at up to two feet per minute. Watch the tip of the second hand on the average-sized electric clock. That's how fast the water can be translocated in your plant.

So what happens to all this water? It leaves the plant through small porelike openings in the leaves called stomata, by the process called transpiration. Transpiration serves much the same function as perspiration in an animal. It cools the plant. Each leaf is, among myriad other things, a mini air-conditioning unit that keeps the plant from getting roasted in the hot noonday sun.

Most of the stomata are located on the undersides of the leaves, a few on top. Urban grime and dirt clog the stomata, cutting down transpiration and making for less healthy growth. That's why you should dust and wash your plants' leaves with a mild soap (not detergent) solution or plain water occasionally, particularly the underside, which, being of no real decorative benefit, is often ignored.

One last thought on plants and water: an acre of corn will transpire three hundred twenty-five thousand gallons of water in one growing season. In other words, thirteen hundred tons of it—enough to flood the selfsame acre eleven inches deep if it were poured back on all at once. That's a powerful lot of transpiration. Not to mention a lot of cooling power. Raise enough plants in your house and you can probably lower the summer temperature a couple of degrees with green air conditioning alone.

Easier Than Plastic

If you were a plant, one of the first things you'd discover is that it takes a lot less effort just to be green and comfortable than to burst forth in bloom. To a plant, energy means light. And to flower, plants need lots of it. But there are many plants content to grow on and on, thriving in relative dimness and with not much care. These foliage plants, as they are known, are ideal for offices, presently undergoing their biggest greening since the Boston fern boom of the Victorian age. They are also good for rooms or crannies in the home on which old King Sol never shines.

LOW-LIGHT SPECIALS

The key to growing attractive foliage plants in low-light-intensity areas is a vacation in brighter light for a couple of months once a year. Healthy new growth during this time will fill out the plants. All of the following need minimal care for maximum green.

Aglaonema modestum (Chinese Evergreen)
    MICROCLIMATE: Temperate shade
                         Loamy soil left to dry between waterings

The plant may grow slowly, but it survives under light conditions usually considered suitable only for mushrooms. Has durable, leathery, waxy green leaves shaped like a narrower version of the dieffenbachia's, a plant with which on first glance it can easily be confused. The flower, normally infrequent in indoor culture, is composed of a cream-colored spadix and green spathe. Aglaonemas as a whole lend themselves admirably to water culture, or hydroponics, and are one of the best beginner's plants for this endeavor.

Aspidistra elatior (Cast-Iron Plant, Parlor Palm)
    MICROCLIMATE: Temperate shade
                         Loamy soil kept constantly moist

The common name's reference to cast iron aptly states this plant's most popular quality. It's tough. Except for that, and the purple bell-shaped flowers that occasionally emerge at soil level, it's a rather unremarkable houseplant. With leathery dark green leaves sprouting directly from the soil rather than from a trunk, the plant remains relatively small. For that dark, cool, even drafty corner where nothing else seems willing to grow. *Aspidistra elatior* 'variegata' adds a bit more color to its surroundings, being a version with alternate white and green striping on the leaves.

Beaucarnea recurvata (Bottle Palm, Elephant's Foot, Ponytail)
    MICROCLIMATE: Warm partial sun
                         Loamy soil kept constantly moist

Grows with one to several trunks swollen at the base for water storage, to enable the plant to survive droughts. The brown gray wrinkly skinned plant is surmounted by a dense rosette of narrow, thin, concave leaves. Related to yuccas, it can go for a year without water in the wild. Indoors, it wouldn't dream of doing so. Nevertheless, it is one of the most durable houseplants, if not always readily available. Easily, though not quickly, grown from seeds, should the plant itself not be procurable.

Cissus antarctica (Grape Ivy, Kangaroo Ivy, Kangaroo Treebine, Kangaroo Vine, Treebine)

MICROCLIMATE: Temperate partial sun
Loamy soil left to dry between waterings

Although it needs fairly good light, *Cissus antarctica* has one quality that should endear it to anyone who has problems putting air conditioning and plants together in the same room. Its name aside, even the reversal of temperatures in an office kept cool during summer days and left to warm up at night does not seem to affect it. Forms a slow-climbing vine that may be staked or allowed to hang. Bears sturdy bright green leaves up to six inches long. Also attractive in hanging baskets.

Beaucarnea recurvata

C. rhombifolia, a close relative commonly known as grape ivy or Venezuela treebine, has a smaller, three-part leaf. This vine trains well and can do with slightly less light.

Dieffenbachia amoena et al. (Dumb Cane, Mother-in-law's Tongue, Tuftroot)
MICROCLIMATE: Warm shade
Loamy soil left to dry between waterings

One of the hardiest plant genera for the dry, well-heated apartments prevalent today, the dieffenbachia has become to the second half of the twentieth century what the Boston fern was to the nineteenth with its cool, humid homes. The plant grows five feet tall under optimum conditions. The long leaves are splashed with cream, and variegation tends to increase in most species under good light. About the only thing that can go wrong with a dieffenbachia is root rot, which can be avoided by making sure the soil dries out between waterings. Propagates readily from side suckers or from sections of cane laid horizontally on moist sand.

The common name dumb cane comes from the fact that nibbling on a dieffenbachia plant will quite literally strike you dumb. The sap contains calcium oxalate, which, although not a toxic poison, causes swelling and intense pain. The plant is one of the few I won't grow because I have children in the house.

Dizygotheca elegantissima (False Aralia, Finger Aralia, Spider Aralia, Split-Leaf Maple, Threadleaf False Aralia)
MICROCLIMATE: Warm partial sun
Loamy soil kept constantly moist

The lately acquired name false aralia must be giving this airy tree an identity crisis, since it really does belong to the Araliaceae, the aralias. But identity crises should be nothing new for it; its home, the Melanesian-populated New Hebrides, is ruled—jointly or disjointedly—as a condominium by the British and the French. *Dizygotheca elegantissima* grows to twenty-five feet in the wilds, but will remain a much more manageable three to six feet indoors. The narrow-fingered coppery red leaves, on thin, almost quaking stems, provide interesting contrast against the rich green of most of the other foliage plants. The lower leaves will be lost eventually—or almost instantly if exposed to a cold draft. Propagates best from seed.

Dracaena marginata (Dragon Lily, Madagascar Dragon Tree)
  MICROCLIMATE: Warm partial sun
              Loamy soil kept constantly wet

A slender trunk branches off into canes with dense rosettes of long stiff leaves edged in red. The canes tend to twist and bend, creating rather wild specimens resembling palm trees that grew during a hurricane. Keep the plant warm in a small pot, and except for watering let it be.

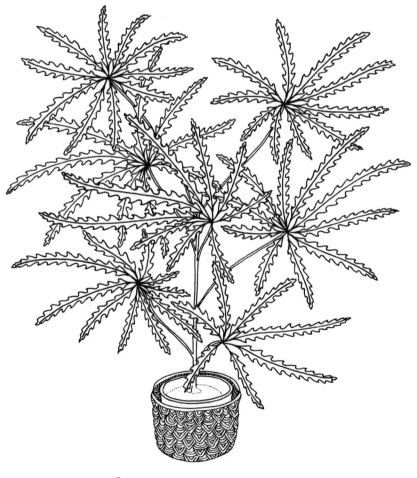

Dizygotheca elegantissima

Grows very slowly, so choose a plant to start with about the size you'll want it.

There are a dozen other dracaenas that make good low-light house-plants, including *Dracaena massangeana* and *D. deremensis* 'Warneckei,' which does well in air-conditioned areas. *D. goldieana* has wide leaves crossbanded with uneven white to light green stripes growing along the full length of the trunk. Unlike other dracaenas, however, it does not do well except in a greenhouse.

Dracaena marginata

Ficus elastica (India Rubber Fig, Rubber Plant, Wideleaf Rubber Plant)
    MICROCLIMATE: Warm sun
                     Loamy soil left to dry between waterings

Here's a typical example of what happens with light variability. *Ficus elastica* has a reputation for growing under very low light conditions, which it does. But the more light it gets, the sturdier its growth and the more luxuriant its foliage: with several hours of full sun a day the plant is at its splendid best. The broad, heavy leaves grow to a foot or more in length. A glossy deep green upper surface is accompanied by a lighter lower one with pink to reddish midrib. Since the specimens sold by nurseries and plant stores are all domestic varieties, the actual characteristics may vary considerably from plant to plant. There is even a variegated version, although it is not too common, in part because it needs more light than its all-green counterpart and also because it is particularly cold-sensitive. As long as you let the soil become almost dry between waterings, it hardly matters where you grow the *F. elastica*. In a dark corner or in a south window, it should do well.

Grevillea robusta (Silk Oak)
    MICROCLIMATE: Temperate sun
                     Loamy soil left to dry between waterings

A dainty, lacy tree from Australia, *Grevillea robusta* looks almost like a tree fern. Particularly reminiscent of one are the new shoots, covered with a silvery white down that gives the leaves a gray, rather than green, color. Likes sun and fresh air, but is generally very easy to please.

Monstera deliciosa (Ceriman, Mexican Breadfruit, Swiss Cheese Plant)
    MICROCLIMATE: Warm partial sun
                     Loamy soil kept constantly moist

A lot of flat things with holes in them pick up an association with Swiss cheese. This large-leafed plant is no exception. The leaves when young are in one piece and normal looking, hence it is often confused with a philodendron. But with maturity the leaves begin developing oblong holes or even long slashes. Like so many other tropical American jungle plants, this one is a climber, forming long hanging aerial roots. The plant can be kept more or less in its pot with pruning or be allowed to scramble helter-skelter up a rough-surfaced pole. Does most of its climbing as a juvenile. *Monstera deliciosa* will grow in poor light and under adverse conditions, but giving it plenty of good light is the only way to encourage large split leaves. The plant adjusts its growing to the illumination rather than the calendar, however, so with two plants, one bright location, and one dark one, you can have your cheese and eat it too by switching the pots occasionally. Kept in a constantly bright spot, *M. deliciosa* will bear cone-shaped fruit supposedly with a flavor reminiscent of pineapple.

Pandanus veitchii (Screw Pine)
    MICROCLIMATE: Warm partial sun
                     Sandy soil left to dry between waterings

Grows into a large crown of leathery, finely serrated leaves. Stilt roots that grow above the soil develop with age, helping to anchor and prop up the plant, so give it a fairly large pot. In order to maintain the creamy white bands that typify the leaf of this variegated version, the soil must be heavily watered. Should you forget its watering, the plant will change its appearance drastically, sending out only green growth. However, it will continue to grow well even after it loses its stripes.

Peperomia various
    MICROCLIMATE: Warm partial sun
                     Loamy soil left to dry between waterings

Numerous species of the semisucculent peperomias are available for home culture. All of them are pretty hard to kill except by overwatering. Even then they will merely start dropping leaves until there are only one or two left, while the plant hangs on for dear life. Of course, that wouldn't make the most attractive specimen, so don't overwater. Leaves of the various species range from silvery to red, quilted to shiny to hairy, banded, blotched, or variegated.

Philodendron various
    MICROCLIMATE: Warm partial sun
                     Loamy soil kept constantly moist

Let's face it, we all have our likes and dislikes—and I've never liked philodendrons, maybe because my dentist really did keep one in his

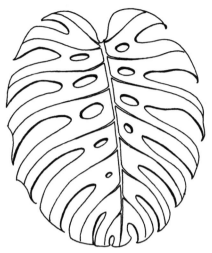

Monstera deliciosa (often confused with philodendron)

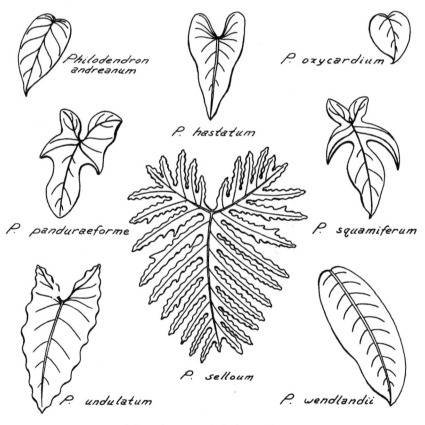

Philodendron andreanum

P. oxycardium

P. hastatum

P. panduraeforme

P. squamiferum

P. undulatum

P. selloum

P. wendlandii

Varieties of philodendron

office. Grow them if you must. There are about four hundred species, mostly hybridized, that will do well as houseplants. As long as they are warm, even though they survive air conditioning quite well, and get some light, there isn't much that can go wrong with philodendrons.

Pilea cadierei (Aluminum Plant, Clearweed, Watermelon Pilea)
MICROCLIMATE: Warm partial sun
Loamy soil kept constantly moist

A handy desk-sized plant from Vietnam. It is rapid growing and has thick, succulent, quilted leaves that look as if someone had stroked the blue green background of each one individually with a paint roller of aluminum paint. A very tolerant personal touch to any office. If your desk is crowded, there would still be room for *Pilea cadierei* 'minima,' an attractive miniature cultivar.

Pittosporum tobira (Australian Laurel, Japanese Pittosporum, Mock Orange)
MICROCLIMATE: Temperate sun
Loamy soil left to dry between waterings

A tough evergreen whose densely branching form will accent any room. Grows well in anything from full sun to the shade of a forty-watt bulb in a closet (appropriately ventilated). The creamy white flower clusters that bud on the branch tips in spring, however, will only develop with sun. They fill your room with orange-blossom fragrance. Pittosporums are slow growers—very slow with low light intensities.

Podocarpus macrophylla (Bamboo Juniper, Buddhist Pine, Japanese Yew)
MICROCLIMATE: Temperate sun
Loamy soil left to dry between waterings

A diecious—that is, having separate male and female plants—evergreen conifer whose needlelike leaves add contrast to the larger-leafed plants, like ficus and aglaonemas. The branches form a dense mass, particularly on the smaller-needled *Podocarpus macrophylla* 'Maki.' Both lend themselves to pruning and shaping if you are so inclined. Buy only well-established tubbed plants. Newly transplanted specimens may be difficult to acclimate.

Pittosporum tobira

Rhoeo spathacea (Boat Lily, Man in a Boat, Moses in the Cradle, Oyster Plant)

MICROCLIMATE: Temperate partial sun
Loamy soil kept constantly moist

Small shell-shaped bracts, the specialized leaves sheltering the flowers, look not unlike cradles or boats. They develop toward the center of the leaf rosette on and off during the year. There are several Moseses per cradle, however, since the bracts are filled with flowers. Very tolerant, and worth growing for the unusual blossom arrangement, which may appear any time of the year. Easily propagated by seeds as well as by suckers. Sometimes sold under its old horticultural name *Rhoeo discolor*.

Sansevieria trifasciata (Angola Hemp, Bowstring Hemp, Mother-in-law's Tongue, Snake Plant, Zebra Lily)

MICROCLIMATE: Warm partial sun
Loamy soil left to dry between waterings

This one really is easier to care for than plastic. Being a living plant, it doesn't get as dusty as a fake and the colors don't fade. It also grows slightly faster, but not much. Probably the most durable of all houseplants. As always, however, there is a difference between survival and thriving. Under favorable conditions, the long leathery leaves may grow to four feet, at which point they are almost lethal.

Schefflera venulosa (Octopus Tree, Seven Fingers, Umbrella Plant)
    MICROCLIMATE: Warm partial sun
                        Loamy soil left to dry between waterings

When you buy a young schefflera, it's more apt to be, in reality, *Brassaia actinophylla*. Not that it makes much difference, since the culture of the two is more or less the same. You'll know for sure what you've got only when the plant matures. The real schefflera will never have more than eight leaflets per leaf; the brassaia may have as many as sixteen. And, oh yes, the brassaia can grow up to a hundred feet high if you have the room. If the leaves suddenly drop off, the plant has been overwatered or is too cold. It is also prone to mealybugs.

Scindapsus aureus (Devil's Ivy, Golden Pothos, Hunter's Robe,
                    Pothos, Solomon Islands Ivy Arum)
    MICROCLIMATE: Warm partial sun
                        Humusy soil left to dry between waterings

Another hardy climbing vine. This one loves it warm. A boiler room would suit it fine if there were some light. Will grow in poor light conditions; will grow spectacularly in good ones. The vine is easily trained up a trellis; also makes a good hanging plant. The green and yellow variegated leaves should be cleaned when dusty if you want the best color pattern to be retained. For the same reason, the soil must be allowed to dry between waterings.

Spathyphyllum various (Peace Lily)
    MICROCLIMATE: Warm partial sun
                        Loamy soil kept constantly moist

One of the plants most adaptable to low-light conditions. Does well in air conditioning, dry rooms, and almost any other hostile environment you care to give it—as long as it gets plenty to drink. Grows vigorously, usually forming clumps, with a succession of white to green spathes surrounding the erect club-shaped spadix.

Spathyphyllum floribundum is a dwarf variety that maintains itself at a foot or so, while S. *cochlearispathum* is at the other end of the scale with its long, corrugated light green leaves reaching six feet—which is about as tall as your bamboos will grow in the opposite, sunny corner.

Leave Us
Not Be
Bamboozled

As a child growing up with a favorite story about a striped tiger who bamboozled hunters by hiding in a clump of bamboo, where his camouflage made him invisible among the plants' slender canes and dark shadows, I inevitably associated the verb with the plant. But although the similarity of spelling would seem at first glance to indicate a philologic association, there isn't any. "Bamboozle" is actually an old hobo term meaning to confuse or trick, and comes from reversing the vowels of "bumbazzle," which in turn is derived from "bombast," which means silly language with little substance.

As it turns out, however, my childish explanation was almost as good as anyone else's, since no one knows for certain where the word "bamboo" comes from, though it is used as a variant wherever the plants are grown. The best etymologists have been able to come up with is "bambus" in the 1598 English translation of explorer Linschoten's journal *Navigatio ac Itinerarium*. Which hopefully leaves you neither bamboozled nor bambooless, since this oft neglected plant is perfect for giving an exotic look to any sunny corner of your house.

Bamboos are evergreens belonging to the grass family, the single most useful group of plants to man. And the bamboos themselves aren't exactly the laggards in the family when it comes to helping man in the tropics. They supply food, in the form of the familiar bamboo shoots sliced or diced in various Chinese dishes, timber and thatch for housing, cooking utensils, farm implements, weapons, musical instruments, paper, toys, and numerous other artifacts of civilization—not to mention the simple old-fashioned catfish pole.

ESSENTIALLY HOLLOW

Most bamboo culms, or canes, are naturally hollow between the nodes. It is this quality plus their hardness and fast-growing nature that makes them so useful. A machete or an ax is all that is needed to turn bamboo into simple water pipes or whole dwellings, yet the material itself is hard enough to be used as a tool with which to shape other materials. Most ancient Chinese jade carvings were done with fine abrasives and bamboo knives whose long-lasting points and flexibility let the artisan turn his imagination into delicate and intricate designs. The same jade can hardly be scratched with machine-tool-quality steel. The hollowness of bamboo gave it one of the most important roles in founding the silk industry of the Western world. Silk was a monopoly of China until A.D. 522, when two Nestorian monks smuggled some silkworm eggs out of the Central Kingdom to the Byzantine court of Emperor Justin hidden within their walking staffs—naturally enough made of bamboo.

WATCH IT GROW BEFORE YOUR VERY EYES

Bamboo's fast growth assures a steady supply of material. In fact, bamboo is one plant you can actually almost see grow. The most rapidly maturing species are the tropical or semitropical ones—sometimes difficult to grow as well as to get. *Bambusa tulda* of India is on record as having added an inch and a half to its height in a single hour. And *Phyllostachys mitis* has been known to raise its head twenty inches in one twenty-four-hour period in its native habitat of North Africa, making bamboos the speediest-growing plants known. But even the common varieties make rapid-action additions to your windowsill garden.

RUNNING AWAY WITH IT

The rhizomes, which like the culms are hollow, develop after the first season's growth in bamboo seedlings, or from the old rhizome in vegetatively reproduced plants. The typically ivory-colored root rhizomes swell with the growing season, storing food produced by the diminutive leaves. Like their aboveground equivalents, these underground canes are jointed. The next year's growth develops from the internodal sections, with both new roots and culms breaking out at more or less the same time.

Of particular interest is the tip of the rhizome, which is sharp and hard as a chisel. Pumping moisture through the tip to loosen the soil in the best hydraulic engineering fashion, the rhizome drives through the hardest soil, spreading new growth around like a weed. However, it's not quite strong enough to split rock, so when it encounters one the rhizome is deflected up. In the case of running bamboos, the first major group, it grows toward the surface and then along the ground for a while before burying itself again. This can make walking through some bamboo groves a real hazard, the aerial wickets seeming almost to be developed for catching boot tips and tripping people.

In a houseplant the looping rhizome presents you with another problem. Reaching the edge of the pot, it may just go round and round the periphery. More likely, however, it will simply run right out of the pot and along your windowsill looking for more soil in which to burrow.

Normally, in the wilds, rhizome tips break through the surface soil when the growing season commences, to establish new islands of culms. Since they readily reproduce vegetatively, if your bamboo does crawl out of its pot, let a rhizome go until it's about eight or twelve inches long. Then cut it off and bury it in a fresh pot horizontally, like an L on its side, beneath three to five inches of soil, with the growing tip just breaking through the surface. Water well. The tip will form your first new culm. The best time to propagate is after December but before spring growth begins. Incidentally, hormone rooting powders do not seem to speed up rhizome growth.

There is a second large group of bamboos known as clump bamboos. These are primarily tropical and, as the name implies, have a clumping habit. They do not climb out of their pots as readily and are in many ways more manageable as houseplants, if not as hardy as their fleet-footed friends. Propagation is by division. Wait for warm spring weather if possible. It's not necessary, but it increases your chances of success.

Cut back the old culms to half their height, making sure, however, to leave at least two internodes intact. Then split the clump in half or thirds. The clumps can be very tough, so be prepared for work. You probably won't have to resort to the tactics employed by some of the tropical research stations, where several sticks of dynamite have occasionally been used to loosen a clump sufficiently for splitting, but you will need sharp shears.

SLIP THEM SOME SILICA

The bamboos are heavy feeders, and do best with regular application of fertilizer during their spring and summer growing period. Outdoor tests in Japan have shown that fertilized stands will outgrow their unfertilized neighbors three to one. Even more amazing are the results of adding a little silica to their diet. Although not a plant food in the ordinary sense of the words, silica gives bamboos a real growth boost, which is not surprising, since it is one of the main structural components of these unusual plants. The bamboos are very efficient in extracting silica from the soil. They will rapidly exhaust any that is available in the potting mix, and additional quantities should be provided. Get some calcium silicate from a chemical supply house, add a teaspoonful to a quart of water, and thoroughly douse your bamboos once a month from April through August.

ALWAYS THIRSTY

Bamboos prefer an open, loamy soil with good drainage, and heavy watering during the main growing season. In some cases it may even be necessary to water them twice a day during the six to eight weeks of most intensive development. Two pests to watch for when watering are slugs and snails. Bamboos are surprisingly problem-free, but if slugs have any access to your plants, they will be drawn to the juicy new shoots as fast as a Chinese chef.

Bamboo's one ill-mannered trait is shedding leaves when it is grown indoors. While the naked canes are more exotic than ugly, leaf drop can be minimized in all species by making sure the soil is never allowed to become dry. *Pseudosasa japonica* has the least predisposition toward baldness.

THE CLUMPS AND THE RUNNERS

Arundinaria nitida (Glossy Leaf China Cane)
MICROCLIMATE: Temperate partial sun
Loamy soil kept constantly moist

One of the most graceful hardy bamboos, *Arundinaria nitida* is said to flower only once every hundred years in its native China. It has never been known to flower elsewhere. The species was introduced into England from the Imperial Botanic Gardens at St. Petersburg in 1889, and from there into the United States. The trim dusky purple canes are slender, growing out of a compact clump. They bear a paper-thin tasseled foliage only on the top half, which at fifteen feet above the ground in their native habitat waves around in the slightest breeze like gossamer threads. The long fine leaves are very light-sensitive, and when exposed to direct sunlight, they fold up until it passes. First-season canes remain whips, but by the second or third year numerous branches and twigs develop at the nodes.

A. *murielae* is very similar to A. *nitida*, and the two species are often confused. However, A. *murielae* has canes that are pale green rather than purplish brown.

Arundinaria pygmaea (Dwarf Bamboo, Pygmy Bamboo)
MICROCLIMATE: Temperate sun
Loamy soil kept constantly moist

An aggressive spreader sometimes classified as *Sasa pygmaea*, this dwarf bamboo is being tried as an easy-to-care-for lawn substitute. The canes are rarely over ten inches high and an eighth of an inch in diameter, while the leaves are up to five inches long and covered with fine hairs. It grows densely enough in a field to be mowed. Among the smallest of all bamboos, it will grow taller indoors under more liberal light than in its native Japan. Easily propagated by division.

Bambusa multiplex (Horai-Chiku, Oriental Hedge Bamboo)
MICROCLIMATE: Temperate sun
Loamy soil kept constantly moist

Originally from China, this bamboo is one of the most commonly cultivated garden bamboos in the United States. In California, it has been known to withstand temperature drops into the high teens. It is a clump-type bamboo with compact growth, good for tubs or pots. A graceful grower normally four to five feet high, but up to forty feet high with canes an inch and a half in diameter under ideal conditions. New shoots, bitter and not really edible, develop in June and July. *Bambusa multiplex* is a highly variable species, with between six and ten forms presently recognized as distinct. All of them have thin-walled green canes with a ring of hairs at the leaf bases. The leaves themselves, growing the full length of the canes, range from one to six inches long and have a silvery sheen on the bottom side. One large, two medium, and numerous small branches are par after the first growing season.

The most popular varieties include 'Riviereorum,' the dwarf best suited for indoor cultivation; 'Fernleaf,' known for its feathery foliage; and 'Silverstripe,' distinguished by the white threadlike stripes on the canes and brown lines on the leaves. Somewhat rarer is 'Silverstripe fern-leaf' with its white-striated leaves, combining the features of 'Fernleaf' and 'Silverstripe.' All need a cool location as well as a constant and heavy water supply. Propagate so readily that freshly cut culms used as field props for other plants often take root, forming fresh clumps.

Bambusa ventricosa (Buddha's-Belly Bamboo)
    MICROCLIMATE: Temperate sun
                      Loamy soil kept constantly moist

Tends to dwarf when grown in pots, remaining a manageable three to six feet as opposed to a maximum of fifty under natural conditions, but does well indoors. The common name comes from the round swelling at

Bambusa ventricosa

the nodes of the canes, most prominent when the plant is stunted from growing in poor soil. The canes are a distinctive dark olive green and bear leaves up to seven inches long.

Bambusa vulgaris (Feathery Bamboo)
MICROCLIMATE: Temperate sun
Loamy soil kept constantly moist

One of the most widely grown ornamental bamboos in the tropics, with graceful branching canes, each having a base diameter of almost half a foot, in an open clump reaching up eighty feet or more. But again, it will remain manageable as a houseplant, dwarfing naturally in a tub. If the canes look as if they're going to go through your ceiling, cut them back, and a lush new growth will develop from the spreading rhizomes. Often grown like a tree, with all but one branched main cane cut back.

Phyllostachys aurea (Fish-Pole Bamboo, Golden Bamboo, *Hotei-Chiku, Taibo-Chiku*)
MICROCLIMATE: Temperate sun
Loamy soil kept constantly moist

Unique among the bamboos in that cylindrical swellings just below the joints form almost a handgrip—which indeed they do when the poles are used for fishing. It's a good idea to put all bamboos outside for the summer wherever possible. But *Phyllostahcys aurea* is hardy enough to be left outside in a sunny spot until the temperatures fall below ten degrees. New shoots, edible, form in May, developing into very stiff canes up to twelve feet high. They are yellow to bright green, depending on the amount of sun, and the internodes are deeply grooved. Known in Japan, where it has been grown for centuries, as *Hotei-Chiku*, the bamboo of fairyland, or *Taibo-Chiku*, the phoenix bamboo. Introduced into the United States in 1822 by G. H. Todd of Montgomery, Alabama, it soon became a staple tool of river fishermen throughout the South. Indoors it will grow large enough for you to take the day off fishing—in the aquarium.

Phyllostachys nigra (Black Bamboo, *Kuro-Chiku*, Umbrella Bamboo)
MICROCLIMATE: Temperate sun
Loamy soil kept constantly moist

Interesting because of its black canes. When young, they are green, slowly becoming speckled with black, eventually acquiring the even black look of polished ebony. Once used extensively for umbrella shafts, the *Phyllostachys nigra* is now grown primarily for its decorative value, being, so they tell me, particularly popular in gardens along the resorts of the Crimea. Does well in tubs, with its paper-thin dark green foliage, usually borne on pairs of branches from each node, complementing the exotic black canes.

Phyllostachys aurea

Phyllostachys sulphurea (Moso Bamboo, Sulfur Bamboo, Yellow Running Bamboo)
    MICROCLIMATE: Temperate sun
                 Loamy soil kept constantly moist

Characterized by golden-yellow culms and thin green internodal grooves. Has yellow branches usually borne in pairs at each node. Culms are arching and graceful, with leaves averaging three to four inches long and half an inch wide. New brownish yellow shoots appear from May through summer. They are edible.

Most bamboo shoots are edible, incidentally. But many of them also contain large quantities of cyanogen, a volatile form of cyanide that must be driven off by cooking. That is why they are not eaten raw.

Pseudosasa japonica (Arrow Bamboo, Hardy Metake Bamboo)
    MICROCLIMATE: Cool-temperate sun
                 Loamy soil kept constantly moist

Sometimes known as *Arundinaria japonica*, particularly in England, this is the easiest of all bamboos to grow indoors. The leaves, up to twelve inches long, are broader in proportion to the canes than those of most bamboos, while the thin-walled canes themselves arch gracefully with age just the way you always imagined bamboo would do. The canes are shiny olive green the first year, turning more matte with age. The plant sends out deep green shoots edged with purple from April on. While the running rhizomes don't go far, they offer an easy means of propagation.

Sasa veitchii (Kumazasa Bamboo)
    MICROCLIMATE: Temperate partial sun
                 Loamy soil kept constantly moist

The sasas as a whole are not the best of indoor bamboos, for one reason: their leaf tips and margins wither during the winter. It doesn't harm the plant, fresh leaves replacing the old in spring, but many people object to the weathered look. Still, the dwarf habit of the sasas makes them good container plants, and their relatively heavy leaves weight the canes down into very graceful arches. *Sasa veitchii* carries single branches with leaves up to ten inches long by a little over two inches wide. They are smooth and glossy. Grows densely when potted and can do well with a little less sun than most bamboos.

FLOWERS—WELL, LET'S SEE, WHAT DECADE IS IT?

The individual flowers of bamboo are small and inconspicuous. However, they grow in groups of three or four to a spikelet, and numerous spikelets develop together in a raceme or larger cluster. These can be quite beautiful and, as in the case of *Phyllostachys castillonis* (which can't be grown indoors), look like enormous, maybe fifteen-foot, sprays of oats. The seeds, not produced often or in great quantity, resemble date pits.

The chances of getting bamboo to flower indoors are slim, but probably no more so than for those cultured outdoors; the flowering habits of these plants are irregular, to say the least. Bamboos may flower once and then not bloom again for another ten or twenty or even fifty years. *Arundinaria nitida*, you will recall, is believed by the Chinese of its native region to flower only once every hundred years. To boot, the time between flowerings is never constant. *A. falconeri*, the falconer bamboo, for instance, has bloomed at intervals of fourteen, thirty-nine, and seven years.

An even more curious fact is that when a species of bamboo flowers in one country, the same species usually blooms all over the world. For instance, in 1876 *A. spathiflora*, or the spathe bamboo, flowered in England; although it had not done so for a long time, that year it also flowered in France, Spain, North Africa, and Sikkim. Actually there is a simple explanation for this phenomenon. Since seeds are so rarely set, the majority of cultivated bamboo plants are propagated vegetatively. As clones, the plants retain the botanical identity and flower characteristics of their parent. When one flowers, they all do.

A TOUCH OF GINGER

The ginger family, or Zingiberaceae, is quite distinct from the grass family to which bamboo belongs. But ginger, like bamboo shoots, is essential to much of Chinese cuisine, and *Zingiber officinale*, from which the commercial edible tubers come, looks rather like a bamboo, so why not stick them in this chapter? Growing ginger gives you a chance to have bamboolike plants—with which to bamboozle your guests—where there is less than full sun. Like the bamboos, by the way, all the gingers are best propagated by division.

Costus igneus (Fiery Costus, Spiral Flag)
    MICROCLIMATE: Warm partial sun
                    Loamy soil kept constantly moist

Has wide, bright, shiny green leaves with red undersides growing on stout red to maroon stems. They say a redhead should never wear orange, but this plant has bright orange flowers up to three inches across that don't jar with the foliage. Remains small and compact, usually under two feet, even in its native Brazil.

Costus speciosus (Caneweed, Spiral Flag, Spiral Ginger, Stepladder
        Plant)
    MICROCLIMATE: Warm partial sun
                    Loamy soil kept constantly moist

Costus species are characterized by the spiral arrangement of the leaves growing up the stem. The pattern is accentuated in *C. speciosus*, whose glossy slender pointed leaves visually form a spiral staircase to the tip of the plant. The dense flower spikes are white with yellow centers and red bracts.

Costus speciosus

Curcuma roscoeana (Hidden Lily, Turmeric)
    MICROCLIMATE: Warm partial sun in terrarium
                    Loamy soil kept constantly moist

Produced from tuberous roots, this plant usually has six to eight lance-like ribbed leaves on long stalks. Although the yellow flowers are hardly visible, being almost completely buried in the stacked-cuplike bracts, the bracts themselves are very showy, gradually changing from green to a vivid scarlet orange with maturity. Needs 50 percent humidity or better to thrive.

Hedychium gardnerianum (India Ginger Lily, Kahili Ginger)
    MICROCLIMATE: Warm partial sun in terrarium
                    Loamy soil kept constantly moist

Another species that needs at least 50 percent humidity, also lots of room. The canes can reach six feet, with leaves a foot and a half long, but usually stay more manageable when tubbed indoors. Worth a try because of the delightful yellow flowers with long red filaments on spikes over a foot in length.

    Hedychium coronarium, the garland flower of Hawaiian leis, has the same size problem, but again it is worth a try because of the numerous aromatic flowers, this time white with little yellow hearts on their lips.

Kaempferia roscoeana (Peacock Plant, Resurrection Lily)
    MICROCLIMATE: Warm partial sun
                    Loamy soil kept constantly moist

Grown primarily for its foliage, this plant bears a profusion of small lavender flowers throughout the summer. The flowers are overshadowed by the leaves, and last only a day each. Unlike most of the other gingers, *Kaempferia roscoeana* in no way resembles bamboo, since there are no canes. Rather the leaves emerge in pairs directly from the roots. The leaves are a bronzed chocolate, zoned pale green, with iridescent veins. The plant is best grown on a pebble tray for extra moisture.

Zingiber officinale (Canton Ginger)
    MICROCLIMATE: Warm partial sun
                    Sandy soil kept constantly moist

    This is the real McCoy. I started mine by purchasing two ginger roots in Chinatown and planting one in the beef with vegetables and the other in a six-inch pot. The potted one produces eight to ten tuberlike roots each fall before dormancy. We harvest enough for our winter needs and plant the extra one. Not a particularly attractive plant, since the bamboolike leaves tend to yellow, but it's almost indestructible as long as it is kept warm, and it does make its pungent addition to the larder.

GROWING IN 2/5 TIME

If you decide to grow *Costus speciosus*, perhaps you should know that it suffers from an extreme case of phyllotaxy. Leaves do not grow on a plant in a random fashion. Some grow in opposite pairs, but most, surprisingly enough, grow in a spiral defined by precise mathematical proportions that vary from genus to genus. Only one leaf grows at each node in this spiral arrangement technically known as phyllotaxy. Sometimes alternate leaves are on opposite sides of the stem; to go from one leaf to one directly below it would involve one circuit of the stem and two leaves. This is expressed by the ratio 1/2. On another plant two circuits of the stem and five leaves may be necessary to reach another leaf directly above or below the starting node. This would be a ratio of 2/5.

The known leaf arrangements fall into the following series: 1/2, 1/3, 2/5, 3/8, 5/13, 8/21, and 13/34. That series happens to be the Fibonacci series. Now—even if you had as much trouble with math as I did—bear with the leaves a moment longer. The Fibonacci series is generated by adding the denominators and the numerators of two fractions to obtain the next one. For instance, 1/2 + 1/3 gives you 2/5, and so on. If you keep this up, you approach a fraction equal to 0.38197, which just happens to be that classical Greek architectural ideal known as the golden mean. And if each successive leaf formed this exact angle around the stem in relation to its predecessor, *no leaf would ever be exactly above any other*. Which is, of course, one of the main points of "plant design," namely, to maximize the leaves' exposure to sunlight, to try to make sure that one leaf doesn't shade the other and render photosynthesis less efficient. Ah, nature, where were you when I tried thatching my first tree house?

UP, UP AND . . .

The bamboolike plants not only add an Oriental touch to a room, they give it a vertical accent as well. Inevitably your eyes wander from the pot up the long canes to empty space at the top. So why not fill that space with some hanging plants that come tumbling down again?

Hang 'Em High

Babylon had the right idea when it decided to hang its gardens. For one of the most attractive ways to display plants is to suspend them at various levels—framed in the window, beneath pole lamps, or even, if a plant is massive enough, cascading from an overhead chandelier. It adds an instant lushness to a room that hardly anything else can equal. However, a barrel cactus in a dangling basket looks plain uncomfortable. A cyclamen looks fine on the windowsill, good on a wall bracket, and lanky, even somewhat shabby, when suspended so you have to peer up at it. And a worm's-eye view of African violets is simply boring. So when you hang plants, be sure to choose ones that look as though they belong up there.

There are numerous species that trail naturally in the wilds, either growing epiphytically on trees or just flowing comfortably from rocky crags and crevices among mountain canyons. Why they developed their pendulous habit is a question to which I haven't yet found a satisfactory answer. Not that the subject isn't brought up at least once a week by my three-year-old daughter Genevieve as the *Ceropegia woodii* in her window grows ever longer. The real answer will no doubt be forthcoming soon; but for the moment at least, I satisfy myself, if not Genevieve, by saying that as the branches grow they get tired of sticking straight out and just hang down.

CHINNING PLANTS

Speaking of the direction down, as opposed to up, as in hanging, a pot of soil is heavy, particularly after it has been watered. When securing a hanging plant, be sure the plaster or the window frame is strong enough to take the strain. And remember there's no such thing as too big a hook or bolt.

Recently we moved to an apartment with elegant but ancient window frames. They were so rotten the curtain rods stayed up mostly on hope. Maybe that was what gave me the idea. In any case, I discovered that a chinning bar, readily available at any sporting goods store, is the perfect solution for hanging plants from window frames of questionable weight-bearing ability. It can support a couple of hundred pounds, fits into the window frame with ease, and doesn't need screws or bolts to hold it up, which means it doesn't leave any scars. If the bathroom-chrome finish doesn't go with your decor, it can be spray-painted a suitable color. This eliminates distracting glare on sunny days.

CLIFFHANGERS

Another handy way of suspending plants is from cast-iron replicas of the old swinging wall brackets once used for kerosene lamps. These can be attached to a window frame in a staggered arrangement at various levels, with the additional advantage that they can be swung to and fro. If you want to get your plants away from the cold windowpanes during long winter nights, all you have to do is swing the brackets, plants and all, into the room. The extra foot or so of distance from the panes can make all the difference between a healthy plant and one with frostbite. Come sunny morning, you just swing the plants back in place. If you have a lot of brackets in a window, this swing feature is also handy if you want to look outside.

STRATOSPHERIC PROBLEMS

There is an amazing difference between growing conditions on the windowsill and those just a couple of feet higher where your hanging plants are. Various parts of a room are never the same temperature, and hot air always rises. A room is a minienvironment complete with ground-level air masses, where you normally grow your plants, and an indoor stratosphere of sorts where the air circulation is noticeably greater, the temperatures higher, and there's more dust to boot—all potential problems for your plants.

Hanging plants and those on wall brackets need to be watered more often than others. On a particularly scorching day I've found those in a south window sometimes need watering twice, after breakfast and dinner. Usually once a day is sufficient, where for those sitting on the ledge below once every two or three days is fine.

I dislike plastic pots enough to stick with clay for my hanging plants. But if you feel it makes no difference, here's one place where the plastic ones come in handy. Since they are not porous, the amount of water lost through pot transpiration is minimal, which means you can water less often. It also means less air circulation around roots and a slightly slower-growing plant.

If you do get plastic pots, those with built-in saucers are convenient for catching excess water, and the whole affair is a little more manageable than a saucer under a clay pot. In any case, don't leave out the saucer, except in a greenhouse or sun porch, where drips don't count, for hanging plants must, like all others, be doused thoroughly enough so the water runs all the way through the soil and out the drainage hole. However, I must admit I often skip the saucers under my higher plants, simply arranging them so the water will drip into a large pot on the sill below. Sometimes, of course, it misses its aim by a little.

THE DRIP

Watering hanging plants can be a nuisance, if one well compensated for by their lushness. For plants at eye level, a small kitchen stool raises you in one step to a height where you can see what's going on in the pot. The type of stool that rides on little wheels that retract when you step on it is particularly handy, since you can just push it along with your foot from plant to plant. A watering can with a long spout and no rose is also a great asset. And a battery-testing bulb from your local auto supply store or a kitchen baster in conjunction with a bucket are also good for squirting water into hard-to-reach pots.

Back in my school days I used to take cold showers to toughen up. I found them then rather a shock; now I find them quite unpleasant. Most of your plants, particularly the tropical ones, feel the way I do about cold water, so although putting ice cubes in their pots and letting them melt may seem a clever way to avoid drips, don't do it. Besides giving the plants chills, ice-watering can induce rot and generally slow down growth. Stick with tepid water; it's the best for all houseplants.

THE DANGLERS

Aeschynanthus lobbianus (Basket Vine, Lipstick Vine)
    MICROCLIMATE: Warm partial sun
                     Humusy soil kept constantly moist

An epiphyte from the island of Java with opposite dark green leaves on semiwoody stems two feet or longer. Summer blooms form at the tips of the stems. They are composed of scarlet flowers set in duller red, hairy, silklike calyxes. At maturity the deep creamy yellow of the flowers' throats is exposed. A good cutting taken in spring will fill a basket, come winter, if grown under sunny, warm, moist conditions.

    Aeschynanthus marmoratus, the marbled basket vine from Burma, is grown more for its yellow-netted dark green leaves, maroon on their undersides, than for the occasional green and chocolate flowers, which blend in with the foliage to the point where flowering sometimes goes unnoticed. The scarlet basket vine *A. pulcher* is similar to *A. lobbianus*, but often blooms in winter as well as in summertime. Numerous hybrids.

Begonia solananthera (Brazilian Heart)
    MICROCLIMATE: Temperate partial sun
                     Humusy soil kept constantly moist

The number of begonias available is truly staggering, and quite a few of them are of the trailing variety. *Begonia solananthera* with its smooth heart-shaped leaves and profusion of fragrant white winter flowers is one of the more spectacular.

    Others you might want to try are *B. limmingheiana*, with late-winter coral blossoms, and the crinkly leafed *B. radicans*. Try, too, some of the numerous hybrids constantly being developed.

Campanula isophylla 'Mayii' (Italian Bell Flower, Ligurian Bell Flower)

MICROCLIMATE: Cool sun
Loamy soil kept constantly moist

Well worth growing if you can supply the two conditions of coolness and plenty of light. Otherwise this plant with its pretty blue flowers is more suited to a cool sun porch than to actual indoor cultivation. It will produce a profusion of flowers tumbling from its basket. The show goes on for several months in summer and fall, although individual blossoms last only a day. Native to the limestone-based Italian Alps, which should be a hint of what to enrich the soil with for best growth. Propagate by cuttings in spring.

Ceropegia woodii (Heart Vine, Rosary Vine, String of Hearts)

MICROCLIMATE: Warm partial sun
Humusy soil left to dry between waterings

The ceropegias belong to the milkweed family, and while they shouldn't be considered indoor weeds, they really aren't much prettier. *Ceropegia*

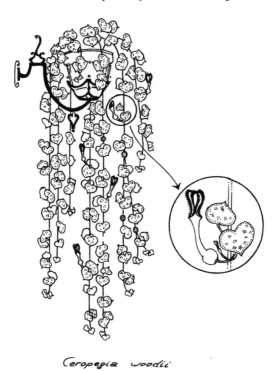

Ceropegia woodii

woodii is the most attractive of the lot, but even it is grown primarily as a curio for its rather interesting plump silver-speckled, blue green, heart-shaped leaves. It is one of the most durable of all houseplants, a second reason for its popularity. Small nutlike tubers form at the nodes of the long thin stems. These will produce new plants when buried in soil. Our cat Adolphus manages to prune *C. woodii* whenever it trails over two feet from its basket. I simply bury part of the broken-off strand with the parent plant to add fullness. The last piece I found behind the couch, where it looked like it had been for a couple of weeks, and still it rooted. Watch for vines pinching in or shriveling where they drape over the pot's edge. If they seem to be withering, cut off and replant the lower length of the strands.

Chlorophytum elatum 'Vittatum'

Chlorophytum comosum (Air Plant, Spider Plant)
   MICROCLIMATE: Temperate partial sun
                 Loamy soil kept constantly moist

Another toughie, originating in South Africa, that will survive considerable neglect. The plant sends up long wiry arching flower stalks from a
central rosette. These become pendant once blooming is completed. The
tiny white lily-shaped flowers are inconspicuous, but the stolons, or new
plants, develop in chains along the flower stalks, hence the common name
spider plant. The plantlets will take root readily if potted, either while
still attached to the mother plant or right after being cut free.

For more foliage variety, try *Chlorophytum elatum* 'Vittatum,' the
bracket plant. It has banded green and white leaves.

Columnea arguta
   MICROCLIMATE: Warm sun
                 Humusy soil kept constantly moist

Unlike most columneas, *Columnea arguta* has waxy leaves. They are
pointed, around an inch and a half long, and bronzed in appearance.
They grow densely on slender stems measuring up to five feet. The
flowers, red and tubular, are almost twice the length of the leaves. Bloom
in fall on old growth. *C. arguta* can do well with slightly less moisture
than the other columnea species, but even so it should have 50 percent
humidity. Leaf loss is a sure sign that the climate is too dry.

C. gloriosa, C. hirta, and *C. microphylla* are all of the hairy-leafed
variety and a little more delicate when it comes to indoor cultivation.
Easiest of all the columneas to grow are the hybrids such as the everblooming yellow-flowered *C.* x 'Cornellian' and *C.* x 'Cayugan,' the reddish winter-to-spring bloomer, developed at Cornell University in 1959.

Episcia reptans (Flame Violet)
   MICROCLIMATE: Warm partial sun
                 Humusy soil kept constantly moist

The episcias are members of the gesneriads grown as much for their
attractive foliage as for their flowers. *Episcia reptans,* with its broad,
quilted brown green leaves overlaid with silver venation, was the first of
the genus to become popular horticulturally. The flowers are bright blood
red with a fringed corolla pinkish in the interior.

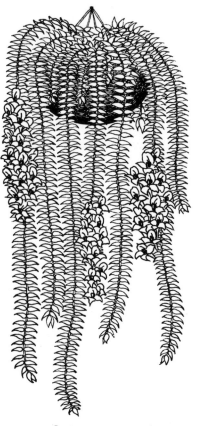

Columnea arguta

The episcias develop stolons with runners in a fashion similar to the strawberry plant. For sheer charm, these are best left on until your window runs out of room, since they form a dense cascade of foliage difficult for any other plant to rival. There are several species and numerous varieties available. All of them need at least 50 percent humidity. Give them 75 percent and they grow even more abundantly.

Gynura aurantiaca 'Sarmentosa' (Java Velvet Plant, Purple Passion Vine)

MICROCLIMATE: Warm, sun

Loamy soil kept constantly moist

Make sure you get the 'Sarmentosa' variety, the others are reluctant danglers. The angled stems creep out of the pot with soft, fleshy lobed leaves. The purple of the common name comes from the color of the undersides

Gynura aurantiaca 'Sarmentosa'

and the bristles covering the metallic dark green leaves. Where the "passion" comes from I have no idea, except that in a way the plant does look somewhat passionate. Needs to be pinched back frequently to remain bushy and full. Even two- or three-inch cuttings will take root readily, so getting new plants is less of a problem than giving them away once you start pruning. Come to think about it, maybe that's where the passion comes from.

Hoya carnosa (Wax Plant)
  MICROCLIMATE: Temperate partial sun
          Loamy soil left to dry between waterings

A popular and durable plant good not only for hanging baskets but for training on wire supports or window trellises as well. It has thick leathery waxy leaves to three inches long, and fragrant shiny pinkish white wheels of flowers from June through September. The flowers are borne only on the previous years' growth and need good sun and lots of water daily to develop fully. Do not move the plants or turn them while in bud, since this tends to make the blossoms drop. Also don't cut off the dead flowers. Let them fall, then remove them. New flowers will appear on the same spurs the following year. Let plants rest in winter, cutting back water and eliminating fertilizer.

Lantana delicatissima (Trailing Lantana)
      MICROCLIMATE: Temperate sun
                     Loamy soil left to dry between waterings

The clusters of small fragrant lilac flowers are up to two inches in diameter and will keep coming all year round if the plant is kept in a sunny location. Unfortunately, so will the red spiders and the white flies if the air is too dry. Isolate the plant when you buy it and look it over carefully for pests before you expose your other greenery to potential infestation. After that, mist the leaves once a day to minimize the risk of inhabitation. Personally I'd rather pass this one up in spite of its everblooming quality.

Manettia inflata

Manettia inflata (Firecracker Plant)
    MICROCLIMATE: Warm partial sun
                    Loamy soil kept constantly moist

A fast grower from southern Brazil, *Manettia inflata* bears tubular waxy red flowers, the lower part covered densely with bristles, the tip a vivid yellow. Blooms almost continuously in a sunny window. Even if you keep pinching, the plants look their best when less than three years old, so you may want to start new ones in spring from cuttings to use as replacements.

Russelia equisetiformis (Coral Plant, Fountain Bush)
    MICROCLIMATE: Temperate sun
                    Loamy soil left to dry between waterings

Composed of whiplike, almost square stems with leaves reduced to small scales on the branches. Cascades to four feet, bearing fiery red tubular flowers almost year round. Propagates readily from cuttings, but use only the tip and first six inches for best results.

Schizocentron elegans (Spanish Shawl)
    MICROCLIMATE: Temperate partial sun
                    Humusy soil kept constantly moist

Forms a dense trailing mass of small leaves bearing a profusion of large magenta-colored flowers in spring and summer. In the high humidity in which the plant thrives, the stem nodes will often form adventitious roots before a cutting is even taken. Needs sun, but also a cool window. Pinch often to keep full.

Tradescantia various (Inch Plants, Spiderwort)
    MICROCLIMATE: Temperate sun
                    Loamy soil left to dry between waterings

The common name inch plant derives from the plant's habit of growing so quickly it seems to inch along. Numerous species and varieties are available. All do well under most indoor conditions, thrive and develop their best leaf color in cool sun.
    Tradescantia albiflora 'Albovittate' has three- to four-inch bluish green leaves with white margins. *T. blossfeldiana* has four-inch olive green leaves with purplish undersides, and white to purple three-petaled

flowers almost constantly in bloom. *T. velutina* is covered with white hairs, as is *T. sillamontana*, on which the threads of the upper leaf surfaces are so fine they look like gossamer.

> *Zebrina pendula* (Silvery Wandering Jew)
> MICROCLIMATE: Temperate sun
> Loamy soil left to dry between waterings

The zebrinas are some of the easiest to grow of all houseplants. Kept for their foliage rather than their flowers, they have leaves ranging from silver-banded green, as in *Zebrina pendula*, to mixtures of purple, red, pink, green, and yellow. Pinch often and root several cuttings in one pot for fullest results. Like the tradescantias, which they resemble, zebrinas produce the most colorful foliage when grown under good light conditions.

HANG 'EM LOW

As long as we're up there with the hanging plants, let's see what else we can drape around the room, at a slightly lower level perhaps. Across from the grove of bamboo might go a climbing ivy, for instance. . . .

The Ivy League

There are numerous plants sold as ivies. Most of them aren't really ivies at all. The true ivies, belonging to the genus *Hedera*, are distinguished by evergreen woody vines growing aerial rootlets that cling readily to any textured surface they touch. Two characteristics of the hederas are particularly interesting. One is that they lose their vining habit when they run out of climbing supports. Branches begin to grow out from the old climbing trunk in the fashion of trees. The leaves even change their shape, from lobed to plain ovate. It is then that the plant flowers and bears its small berrylike fruit. A second characteristic of the true ivies is what Darwin called circumnutation. This is present in all the higher plants to some degree. But it's in the climbing plants that it really shows its style.

ROUND AND ROUND WE GO

We're used to thinking of plants, at least most of them, as simply sitting there day after day, growing ever so slowly and unspectacularly. Actually, although their roots may be stodgily anchored in the ground, plants lead a much more active life than one might suspect. The turning of leaves and growing stems, the constant bending toward light, or phototropism, is readily observed by the watchful in windowsill-grown plants. The bending is caused by a combination of cell elongation and turgor, or the pressure of liquids within the cells, triggered by the growth hormone auxin. Usually phototropism occurs over a period of days and passes unnoticed. But some leaves will turn completely around in a day if the plant is turned. This reaction enables the plant to keep the broad side of the leaves exposed to sunlight, thereby maximizing photosynthesis and food production.

Circumnutation is the continuous bending of a plant in a kind of screwy spiral, or helix. As noted by Darwin, a plant you see leaning slightly north on the first observation "will be found gradually to bend more and more easterly until it faces east; and so onwards to the south, then to the west and back to the north." * This movement occurs in all parts of a growing plant. Even the underground sprout of a seedling circumnutates; this almost drill-like turning helps it break through the surface of the soil.

Darwin further hypothesized that circumnutation stemmed from the dissimilar rate of growth of various cells and changes in turgor. Several other factors a bit too complicated to go into here are involved. But what counts is that circumnutation and phototropism in all probability act together to exaggerate the motion of climbing plants such as ivies compared with, say, tulips. It's this slow-motion flailing around that lets the plant reach out to grab something to climb up on. If it is a plant with tendrils, which are leaves modified for grasping, a circumnutating tendril wraps itself around the something, or a protrusion therefrom, supporting the whole plant.

THE IVIES

The genus *Hedera* contains many easy-to-care-for varieties to grow indoors. Almost all of them are hybrids of *H. helix*.

Hedera canariensis arborescens 'Variegata' (Ghost Tree, Variegated Algerian Ivy)
      MICROCLIMATE: Temperate partial sun
                            Loamy soil left to dry between waterings

Not a climber, but rather a pendant ivy whose ovate stiff lacquered-looking leaves are variegated light green with cream. Very durable—and

---

* Charles Darwin, *The Power of Movement in Plants* (New York: D. Appleton and Company, 1881), p. 1.

slow growing. Propagation is from half-hard cuttings, that is, cuttings not entirely new, but not yet woody. *H. canariensis* 'Variegata,' known as Hagenburger's ivy, is a climbing version, and one of the most popular indoor ivies. Native to the Canary islands and the western Mediterranean region, it tolerates either warmth or coolness, dryness or humidity, shade or sun. Visually, perhaps, not the most exciting plant, but there's no doubt that it will grow, even thrive, with minimum care. The vine itself is reddish, and the leaves, which grow up to six inches long, have a green or gray green center surrrounded by a zone of blue green and edged with a marginal variation of creamy white occasionally tinted pink.

> *Hedera helix* (English ivy)
> MICROCLIMATE: Temperate partial sun
> Loamy soil kept constantly moist

Used as a groundcover throughout the temperate world, *Hedera helix* is also a good plant to grow indoors *as long as* it doesn't get too warm, preferably not above seventy degrees except in summer. High temperatures are conducive to infestation by red spider mites, particularly if the house is dry. Dryness induces leaf dropping as well. On the other hand, the plant, because of its semitemperate origins, doesn't mind air conditioning or drafts.

Several varieties do particularly well as houseplants. 'Conglomerata,' a slow-growing, almost shrubby plant, is the one often seen surviving neglected on the desks of mutual fund managers. 'Curlilocks' is another bushy variety, this one with crested parsleylike leaves. 'Glacier,' a variegated vine, sprouts triangular leaves. 'Hahn's Self-Branching' divides continuously at the growing tip, making it an ideal tree for dish gardens. There are 'Manda's Crested,' with reddish stalks and rosy-edged leaves, and 'Patricia,' which sends out an incessant stream of draping reddish branches. There are more. . . .

THE INTERLOPERS

As if there weren't enough ivy varieties to choose from, florists and plant retailers have added numerous other plants to the family simply by selling them as ivies. For the most part the adoptive ivies have the same cultural requirements, are equally hardy, if not more so, and possess the climbing or trailing characteristics one associates with the word "ivy." They also circumnutate a lot.

Coleus rehneltianus (Trailing Coleus)
    MICROCLIMATE: Temperate sun
                     Loamy soil kept constantly moist

This is a trailing version of the familiar coleus, or painted nettles. The square stems start out erect, then bend over and begin to creep. It's best to buy one already creeping, or you may find you have a species that is normally upright. Pinch heavily to keep compact.

The 'Lord Falmouth' variety has round, toothed, rosy-centered carmine leaves up to an inch and a half long. 'Trailing Queen' has slightly larger leaves carmine at the center, emerald green at the margins, all overlaid with a brownish purple marble pattern.

Cymbalaria muralis (Kenilworth Ivy)
    MICROCLIMATE: Cool partial sun
                     Loamy soil kept constantly moist

The threadlike stems root at the nodes, making this a very easy plant to propagate. However, it's not so easy to grow unless you can keep it by a cool window all winter. Best reserved for sun porches.

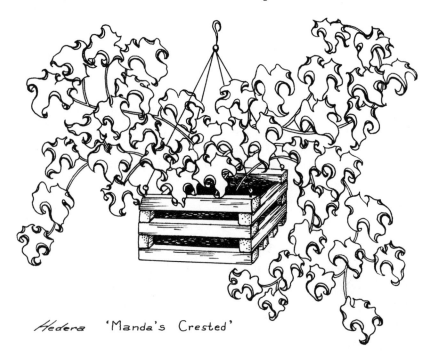

Hedera 'Manda's Crested'

Ficus pumila (Climbing Fig, Creeping Fig)
> MICROCLIMATE: Warm partial sun
> Loamy soil kept constantly moist

When young, small dark leaves less than an inch long growing on freely branching stems make this plant look like anything but a first cousin to *Ficus elastica*, the common parlor rubber tree. A very hardy grower climbing by means of aerial roots at the leaf joints like a true ivy. Trainable either up or down. The roots, if encouraged by daily spraying, will attach themselves to almost anything, including the windowpane, although they prefer something rough-textured like wallpaper, burlap, or bark. Bears figlike fruit on maturation, by which stage the plant has adopted a treelike stance and boasts four-inch leaves.

Glecoma hederacea 'Variegata' (Gill-Over-the-Ground, Variegated Ground Ivy)
> MICROCLIMATE: Temperate partial sun
> Loamy soil kept constantly moist

A lively creeper with leaves not unlike those of some pelargoniums— hairy, light green, variegated in white. Small blue flowers, but these are rarely seen indoors in any profusion.

Hemigraphis colorata (Red Ivy)
> MICROCLIMATE: Warm shade
> Loamy soil kept constantly moist

A very attractive trailer for areas with little or no direct sunlight. The puckered leaves grow up to four inches long and are reddish violet with a metallic sheen. The plant tends to drop leaves if the air is too dry.

Lamium galeobdolon 'Variegatum' (Archangel Vine, Silver Nettle Vine)
> MICROCLIMATE: Cool partial sun
> Loamy soil left to dry between waterings

A positively rampant grower as long as night temperatures are not too warm. The square stems are covered with small nettlelike hairs. The leaves, up to two inches long, are brushed with silver. Very easy to root.

Peperomia fosteri (Vining Peperomia)
    MICROCLIMATE: Warm partial sun
                        Loamy soil left to dry between waterings

Peperomia fosteri, a member of the pepper family like other peperomias, bears thick short leaves in whorls along slender red vining stems. Roots readily at the nodes and can be grown as an epiphyte, or air plant, if sprayed with a nutrient solution occasionally.

Philodendron oxycardium (Cordatum Vine, Heartleaf Philodendron, Parlor Ivy)
    MICROCLIMATE: Warm partial sun
                        Loamy soil kept constantly moist

The size of the heart-shaped leaves depends on the age of the plant and the light conditions under which it is grown. Will thrive in anything from a sunny window to a dark corner lit by no more than twenty footcandles. In a corner, however, leaves will be considerably shorter than their normal five inches or so. At maturity, when the plant enters its flowering stage, the leaves may grow to over a foot. But indoor flowering is rarely reached except in a greenhouse.

Piper ornatum (Celebes Pepper)
    MICROCLIMATE: Warm partial sun
                        Humusy soil kept constantly moist

Another close relative of the pepper in your pepper shaker and another red-stemmed climber. This one has broad, shieldlike, waxy green leaves up to four inches long. The leaves are etched with a silvery pink mottled embroidery that turns white with age. Easily propagated from stem sections having at least two eyes.

Plectranthus australis (Spur flower, Swedish Ivy)
    MICROCLIMATE: Temperate partial sun
                        Loamy soil left to dry between waterings

Although grown a lot in Sweden, Swedish ivy is an example of how popular names don't coincide with botanical reality. The plant is not a real ivy, and it originates about as far from Sweden as it is possible to get geographically, namely, Australia and the surrounding Pacific islands.

The almost round leaves are thick, leathery, and very tough. Excellent for hanging pots. A close relative of coleus, it is capable of withstanding considerable neglect. With good care, on the other hand, there's the bonus of small white spike-borne flowers in summer.

Saxifraga sarmentosa (Mother of Thousands, Strawberry Begonia, Strawberry Geranium)
MICROCLIMATE: Temperate sun
Loamy soil left to dry between waterings

Probably a record holder for false epithets, *Saxifraga sarmentosa* is neither strawberry, begonia, nor geranium. It is a free growing, undemanding plant whose threadlike runners, bearing young plantlets, make it an attractive hanging specimen. The leaves are olive green with silvery vein markings, purplish underneath. Wants good light, but shade from the heat of summer's noonday sun.

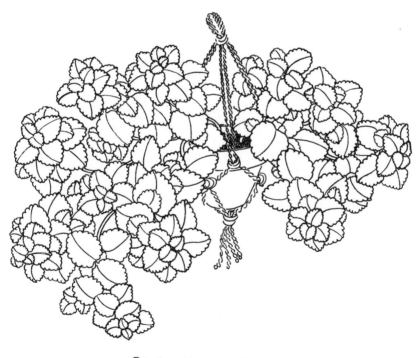

Plectranthus australis

Senecio mikanioides (German Ivy, Ivy Groundsel, Parlor Ivy)
    MICROCLIMATE: Temperate partial sun
                     Loamy soil kept constantly moist

A hardy old-line favorite. However, it predates central heating and should be grown near the window where it can enjoy cool nights. The leaves are very ivylike. The plant remains shrublike while young, climbing as it gets older.

Senecio tropaeolifolius (Nasturtium Groundsel, Succulent
                            Nasturtium)
    MICROCLIMATE: Warm partial sun
                     Loamy soil left to dry between waterings

A small vine rarely growing more than a foot or so in length. The leaves, up to three inches across, are pale green on top, violet underneath, and resemble those of the nasturtium. Propagate from tuberous roots.

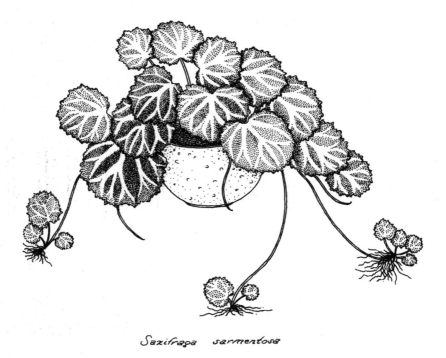

Saxifraga sarmentosa

Syngonium podophyllum (African Evergreen)
    MICROCLIMATE: Warm partial sun
                    Loamy soil kept constantly moist

For a touch of interest in the leaf shapes of your ivy-and-such collection, try this plant with its arrow-shaped foliage. As they age, the leaves become palmate, lobed into five to nine segments per leaf. There are several varieties, of different greens and variegations. They grow readily in water if a little fertilizer is added for extra nourishment. And along the same idea, by the way, there's a whole group of plants that have developed specialized leaves for catching their own fertilizer, since the soil in which they grow doesn't have much more to offer than your *Syngonium podophyllum*'s glass of water. . . .

Not for Vegetarians

We were at about the eight-thousand-foot level of Mount Kinabalu in Borneo when I slipped in the mud and fell headlong into the brush surrounding the steep trail. My hand just missed a monstrous pitcher plant big enough to swallow it past the elbow. Although it was by far the largest of its kind I've ever seen, two flies a day probably would have kept it full and content. And had my fist lunged into its hungry jaws, the pitcher probably would have been smashed to pieces. Even so, I noticed Susan wasn't about to stick her hand down its throat in search of the hidden jewel that folktales commonly credit the carnivorous plants with guarding.

Discounting the hoopla surrounding carnivorous, or more properly insectivorous, plants ever since the 1800s when stories of explorer-eating plants abounded in the popular press, they are interesting curiosities to grow. And although they aren't really suitable houseplants in the normal sense, when raised in terrariums or under other moisture-maximizing conditions they make a fascinating project for children, introducing them in a picturesque way to the adaptive functions of plant survival.

THE LOW-NITROGEN DIET

As with most plant oddities, the peculiar nature of insectivorous plants is a product of evolutionary selection. The plants are survivors, in the Darwinian/Lamarckian sense, of a particular environment lacking sufficient amounts of certain needed nutrients, primarily nitrogen and some of the trace elements. The insect-catching ability is probably more of a backup system than anything else. The plants can grow for a considerable length of time without catching any game, storing scarce nutritional commodities in their bulbs, rhizomes, and roots to tide them over periods of poor hunting.

Carnivorous plants are considered parasitic by some, using the definition of a parasite as an organism subsisting on another, giving nothing in return. However, they are not parasitic in the normal sense, since they do not concentrate on a specific host as does, for instance, *Rafflesia arnoldii*. This marvelous plant from Sumatra, commonly called the Sumatra monster flower, has the world's largest blossom (up to four feet in diameter and fifteen pounds in weight), no real leaves of its own, and the most primitive of root systems that takes hold only on the grapelike vine of *Cissus angustifolia*. If one considers a Venus flytrap, say, a parasite, then man and every other animal around must fall into the same category. After all, the Venus flytrap is about as omnivorous as it can be for its size, eating anything it can catch, from mosquitoes to caterpillars and, as was once recorded, even a small frog.

To grow carnivorous plants successfully, you must starve them, since their insect-snaring talents are there solely for the purpose of gathering nourishment. *Don't* ever fertilize them. Give them only distilled or rain water. Tap water, besides being full of things the plants don't like, has some of the trace elements that would stifle their appetites.

These plants grow in open, unshaded subtropical bogs. They need lots of sunlight and high humidity. They will grow well in a terrarium, but only one supplied with good ventilation and poor soil. Probably the best "poor soil" is a mixture of seven parts sphagnum moss, two parts coarse sand, and one part humus.

A CELL FOR EACH OCCASION

If you stick your nose into a well-developed trap of a *Dionaea muscipula*, the Venus flytrap, you will smell a slightly sweet scent. (Don't worry about your nose. Traps have been timed closing in less than a second, which might mean it will get you. On the other hand, the maximum closing force has been measured at only an ounce, so it shouldn't be hard to extricate the old proboscis.) The fragrance is unusual, since most fly-attracting plants give off a carrionlike odor—mosquitoes really don't go much for sweets. It is also unusual because the trap is not the flower, that part of a plant which normally produces the scent, if any. The flowers come only in spring, and resemble small white daisies.

Besides the perfume cells, or nectaries, located just below the eighteen teeth on the edge of the trap that help imprison the prey, *D. muscipula* has digestive cells and trigger cells. The trigger cells, as their name implies, are the highly specialized mechanism that springs the trap. Other carnivorous plants have mucilage-producing cells, the sticky liquid literally gluing the insects' feet to the plant.

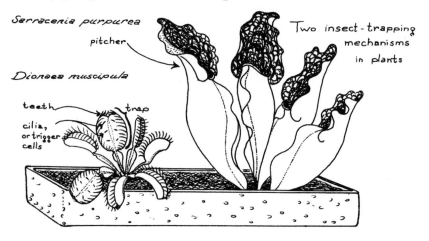

The digestive cells are located toward the bottom of the trap. They manufacture enzymes used in digestion very much in the fashion of your stomach. These cells are activated by the trapped insect's movement. The more it struggles, the more enzymes are released.

Since carnivorous plants may take almost two weeks to digest a good-sized meal, they have a real problem with spoilage. In the warm regions where they thrive, the insects would putrify within a day, attracting all sorts of destructive fungi and bacteria. To counteract this, the digestive cells, besides emitting digestive enzymes, also produce a natural preservative. The plants not only catch insects, they pickle them as well.

Trigger cells have been a mystery to botanists for a long time. It was known that an insect's contact with them was the signal activating the trap. The question was, How did the message get across? After all, plants have no nervous system by which to transmit messages from one part of the body to another.

Recently Stephen E. Williams, a plant physiologist at Cornell University, demonstrated that the tentacles, or trigger cells, of the sundew, *Drosera rotundifolia*, actually do convert physical energy into an electrical impulse, very much, if also very rudimentarily, in the manner of an animal's nervous system. The impulse travels from the sensing cells to the base of the tentacle, setting off a reaction that causes the trap to curl, ensnaring its prey.

Besides its primitive form, this elementary nervous system is differentiated from that of animals by its slowness. The impulse travels some ten thousand times slower than its equivalent in the system of a higher animal. Still, as Dr. Williams noted, it's remarkable that plants utterly unrelated to animals should have developed on their own such similar sense organs.

YOU'VE GOT TO HAVE TURGOR

Apart from the intercellular communication problem, the other long-standing question regarding carnivorous plants was, How do traps close? All plants move in one way or another, turning with the sun like sunflowers, curling grasping tentacles around nearby objects like climbing vines, or just bending toward the light, a factor common to almost all plants. Any of these actions, occurring over a period of hours, is easily explained. But the split-second moves of carnivorous and some sensitive plants, like *Mimosa pudica*, present a real problem. Plants don't have muscles. So how can they move so quickly? The answer lies partly in changes in the cells' turgor, or water content.

In mature plant, as opposed to animal, cells there is a part called the vacuole. It may occupy as much as 90 percent or more of a cell's total volume. The vacuole is filled with water and dissolved material. If the water content is reduced, the cell loses its rigidity. The extra water goes into the space surrounding the cell, however, not out of the plant. This is similar to what happens when a plant wilts from lack of water, or loses its turgor. But, as you no doubt have observed, a wilted plant, provided things have not progressed too far, will pull itself up again if given enough water. The decrease and increase of water in the cells of the trap is the essential "muscle" that causes it to close and open.

A further question still remains unanswered. How can these plants react so quickly?

THE HUNGRY ONES

Darlingtonia californica (California Pitcher Plant, Cobra Plant)
    MICROCLIMATE: Cool partial sun in terrarium
                    Humusy soil kept constantly moist

Looking like a small hooded cobra complete with fangs—its habit of sway-ing back and forth hypnotically in the wind heightens the image—this plant grows to two feet tall outdoors in its native California. It is a one-of-a-kind species, *californica* being the only known *Darlingtonia*. A poor houseplant because it needs cool water around its roots constantly, it is nevertheless often foisted upon the eager and innocent indoor gardener as a real exotic; in point of fact it will grow passably in a cool terrarium. Initially the leaves sprouting up from the rootstock are slender and grass-like. They widen into tubular stalks with maturity, eventually develop-ing their hooded pitchers. The blood red veins marking the leaves lend credence to its malicious reptilian reputation. However, nothing larger than a tiny snake seeking a mistakenly comfortable spot away from the night chills has been known to be devoured by one of these plants.

The trapping mechanism is the quiet, passive kind. Insects are lured into the botanical cobra's mouth by a sweet scent. Lining the trap are slippery ciliary hairs pointing inward and downward. Once past the first of these fringed rows, the insect finds retreat very difficult and is usually forced down the plant's throat. There the insect is drowned in a pool of water. Bacterial action breaks down the slowly dissolving corpse. And in the process the plant extracts the nutrients it needs.

Dionaea muscipula (Venus Flytrap)
    MICROCLIMATE: Cool sun in terrarium
                    Humusy soil kept constantly moist

The most popular and active of all the carnivorous plants is the jaw-snapping Venus flytrap. But it needs a good two- to three-month rest period to be at its best, so keep it cool in winter and don't try feeding it while it's taking its ease. However, the soil should be kept moist during this time as well as when growth is underway. Best method of reproduc-tion is by division of the diminutive bulblets from the mature plant.

You can tease *Dionaea muscipula* by touching the three or four tiny sensitive hairs or bristles on the red inner surface of a fully developed trap with a pencil point. The trap will either snap shut—if the plant is in top form and the trap young—or close slowly enough for a fly to be half-way across the room before the prongs interlock—if the plant is out of shape. A trap that has caught an insect will remain closed for five to fifteen days while it dines. A teased trap will open from a few minutes to an hour after deception. Repeated teasing, however, will frustrate any trap. After a while the plant will simply doze off, refusing to respond.

Drosera rotundifolia (Roundleaf Sundew, Sundew)
     MICROCLIMATE: Cool sun in terrarium
                    Humusy soil kept constantly moist

The least impressive of the droseras, as far as size goes, this is the one most commonly sold, because it's the one most readily available. No more than two inches across at maturity, and usually less, so beware of the mail-order ads used by a few not-so-reputable companies that make them look big enough to swallow the canary and the cat too.

The traps are sticky leaves that lie close to the ground. Their odoriferous mucilage glistens in the sun, hence the common name. Insects, attracted by the aroma, step onto the spoon-shaped tip of the leaf and get stuck as if to flypaper. The more they struggle, the more glue is given off by the plant. Once the fly or ant or what have you is firmly affixed, the leaf rolls up with its meal. It dines about five days on the average-sized meal. Then the leaf uncurls and waits, ready once more. Unlike *Dionaea muscipula*, *Drosera rotundifolia* will rarely be fooled by a pencil or other inedible object, a discriminating trait Darwin describes in some detail in *Insectivorous Plants*.

Drosophyllum lucitanicum (Dew Leaf)
     MICROCLIMATE: Temperate partial sun in terrarium
                    Loamy soil left to dry between waterings

Coming from Spain and Morocco, this close relative of *Drosera rotundifolia* is not available too frequently. However, it is much larger than its kinsman, with thin leaves up to ten inches long, covered entirely by a dense growth of glandular hairs that exude a sticky nectar. Insects are eaten in place. Less action to watch, but nice yellow flowers in summer, and easier to grow than most of the more popular carnivorous plants. Readily grown from seed.

Pinguicula various (Butterwort)
>   MICROCLIMATE: Temperate partial sun in terrarium
>   Humusy soil kept constantly moist

I spent my childhood eating butterwort rather than—not being insect-sized—vice versa. The juice from the leaves when stirred into milk makes it curdle in a somewhat strange and once-popular fashion. The acidity causes the milk to become stringy—hence its Swedish name *longmjölk*, or long milk—a very tasty yogurt-type dish.

As for the plant's diet, it is a passive eater, trapping insects on its sticky leaves and digesting them slowly much in the manner of *Drosera rotundifolia.* You've probably passed a lot of pinguiculas in the woods without really thinking of them as carnivores. And in fact they don't eat very much.

Sarracenia purpurea (Purple Pitcher Plant)
>   MICROCLIMATE: Cool partial sun in terrarium
>   Humusy soil kept constantly moist

A hardy perennial with low-lying ballooning pitchers up to twelve inches long. They aren't hooded like *Darlingtonia californica,* but the ensnaring mechanism works pretty much the same way. Interestingly enough, there are a number of insects that live quite comfortably, thank you, with the sarracenias. The caterpillar of one particular moth, *Papeipemia appassionata,* considers the pitcher plant a delicacy, dines on its leaves, washes down the meal with a good sip of nectar, and never gets caught. Why it doesn't is an unsolved question. There are even some species of mosquitoes and flies that lay their eggs inside the pitcher plants. The larvae swim around in the water with which the pitchers are filled until they mature. Again, how so?

The water in the pitchers, incidentally, for the most part is not collected from rain or dew. The plants actually pump it up from the soil.

OVERFEEDING MAY LEAD TO CAVITIES

If all this talk of carrion makes you think you'd better feed your plant an insect quickly, relax. A carnivorous plant would probably take several years to starve to death if it never had a single fly. And as to that gimmick of feeding it hamburger, don't bother. Hamburger is too heavy and greasy for it to digest. The morsel would only lie there and rot.

The best way to feed, say, a Venus flytrap is to catch a fly—if you're so inclined—and thrust it into the flytrap's gaping jaws with a pair of tweezers. A simpler method is to put a piece of banana in the terrarium to attract some fruit flies, and leave the cover off. But don't tell my college roommate about it. I once had several thousand fruit flies in some jars that broke, and I understand he still has nightmares about the buzzing cloud that settled around his head and on his dinner the day it happened.

Burgeoning
Bulbs

Like the bear that curls up in a cave to sleep away the woes of winter, most plants of the temperate regions go into some type of hibernation. Many tropical varieties also stop growing or die back in order to survive the droughts. And like the bear, many of these plants stock up on great quantities of food beforehand. Some species develop thick underground storage stems, called rhizomes or tubers, depending on their morphology. These storerooms are true stems, not roots, even though they do grow underground.

Besides doing pantry duty, rhizomes and tubers play a handy role in vegetative propagation, for almost any houseplant with one or the other can be divided to give you new plants. By the way, if several shoots are growing from one rhizome, until you make that final cut to separate them it's considered one plant.

Both rhizomes and tubers store enough food to start a new plant growing well. Bulbs go them one better. A bulb is a whole miniaturized plant, complete with embryonic flower, packed neatly into its own self-contained food parcel composed of numerous bulb scales. If you cut a bulb in half—of course that means one less to plant—from tip to bottom, you can see the individual leaves and the embryonic flower stalk and bud tightly compressed in the central cylinder.

To grow, the flower needs only moisture and light, which is how daffodils, tulips, hyacinths, and other bulbs can be forced to bloom out of season, in winter, when their cheerful colors can do the most to brighten up gray days. Comparing the price of even the highest-quality bulb with that of the same flowering plant in bloom, you'll find the bulb is a real bargain for very little extra work.

THE TENDER TOUCH

The easiest of all bulbs to force indoors are the so-called tender varieties, particularly paper-white narcissus, its yellow cousin *soleil d'or*, and the somewhat nomenclaturally confused French Roman hyacinth, which has a more open flower spike than our regular hyacinth. These bulbs, known as tender because they cannot survive the frost of winter, have been brought to a peak of early-blooming cooperation through intensive horticultural selection and are pretreated for forcing. If possible, get the so-called double-necked bulbs; they will give you more flowers for your money.

The catch with forcing tender bulbs—and by now I've learned the plus factor for any plant usually pulls some kind of catch behind it—is that once the specially treated bulbs have been induced to put on their show, there will never be an encore. After they have bloomed you might as well throw them away, or at best chop them up and bury the chunks in the soil of one of your large potted plants, where they will add body and substance to the terrain.

Planting the tender bulbs is simplicity itself. You don't need a special bulb pan or pot. Any decorative container roughly twice as wide as it is high will do fine provided it will hold both water and pebbles. For pebbles and water are all the bulbs need to grow.

Fill the container about a third full of aquarium pebbles. These are usually rounded and unlikely to injure a correctly planted bulb, whereas sharp-edged white marble chips could bruise the bulb and lead to rot. You want to end up with a pebble layer no less than three inches thick if you can. Put as many bulbs in the container as it will hold without the bulbs' actually touching either each other or the pot rim. Then pour tepid water into the pan till it is level with the bulb plates. The plate is the base of the bulb, holding all the bulb scales together by their bottoms, and the area from which the roots will emerge. It's also the piece that always seems to gum up the works when you're trying to dice an onion. The bulbs *should never more than just barely touch* the water. Wet bulbs mean rotten bulbs. As long as there is water available beneath them, the roots will reach down to suck it up. Follow the water with more gravel till the bulbs are about half covered.

Don't try to save time by putting all the gravel down at once and then screwing the bulbs in. Chances are that would injure the basal plate or the outer bulb scale, known as the tunic, inducing rot.

Put the whole shebang in a cool dark place, around sixty degrees—not necessarily the easiest thing to find even in winter, particularly if you live in an apartment where dark closets are often warmed by hot-water pipes between the walls. Yet coolness is essential until the roots are well formed, which generally takes two to three weeks. Without it you'll end up with a great collection of leaves sans flowers. For if the green growth precedes root growth, the flowers will never emerge.

My solution to the cool-dark-place problem is a north windowsill to which I add darkness by covering the pot. Enveloping the pot in a plastic bag in which you have punched ventilation holes, and putting this contraption in turn in the vegetable crisper of your refrigerator for the two or three weeks it takes the roots to develop, also ensures blooms. Of course, a cold cellar or basement is the easiest solution of all.

Any shift in temperature should be gradual. Once the roots have formed, take the bulbs from the refrigerator or the cellar to the next coolest, darkest place in the house, from there to a lighter corner the following day, and then at last a few days later to the sunniest spot available. Even when the plants are growing at their best, however, try not to let the temperature around them get much above seventy degrees. That's a condition easy enough to meet by the window in wintertime, which is when you're most apt to be forcing bulbs and looking forward to their splash of color. Once the bulbs are out in the sun you'll have to check the water level every couple of days, since evaporation will be much more rapid than during the cold-storage period. Again, however, make sure the water level never goes above the basal plate.

COIFFURE FOR MEDUSA

If you grow tender bulbs in gravel and water, you may find that the leaves and flowers tangle and flop like Medusa's hair the day after. They will grow fine this way, but it does make a rather unsightly patch. One solution is to increase the light intensity by growing them under strong artificial illumination, making growth more compact. Another is staking. But stakes don't hold well in gravel.

For this reason, and because less attention need be paid to watering, more and more of the tender bulbs are being grown in something called bulb fiber. It comes from Europe and is not always easy to find. You can make your own, however, by using moist peat moss with about a third as much of activated charcoal mixed in to keep acidity down. The charcoal is readily available at any store that sells tropical fish.

The key to success here is keeping the peat moss merely moist, not wet. Unlike the gravel method, where the water remains mostly below the bulbs, with peat moss moisture will surround them and is easy to oversupply. If the bulb fiber drips when you squeeze it, the bulbs will rot.

Well, why not just use soil? you may ask. It will support stakes even better than fiber. Because these tender forcing bulbs are so high-strung and overbred that if the roots really have to work at digging their way through potting soil, the flowers will not develop to their best advantage.

A CLOSER LOOK AT BULBS

There are several other bulbs that can be brought into beautiful bloom indoors including tulips and daffodils. Since they are not forcing bulbs in the sense of being preconditioned like the paper-white narcissus, however, they must be planted in soil. Many of them can be made to bloom for several years. The reason lies in their design. Besides the bulb scales with their food supply and unexpended flower shoot, they also contain a number of growing points on the basal plate. These produce miniature bulblets which will mature into full-sized bulbs themselves producing flowers as beautiful as the original.

The trick with such bulbs is that they must be buried to the right depth. Nature is well aware of this, and since the new bulbs are often carried too close to the surface by the growth of the mother plant, they develop contractile roots that actually *pull* them down into the ground to their proper depth.

Another protective device designed into certain bulbs is a hardy skin. When you eat an onion, you're eating a laminated bulb. Like the tulip, it has a dry covering encasing the entire bulb and protecting the future growth from drying out or being injured. Scaly bulbs, such as lilies, do not have this protective overcoat. Scaly bulbs are easily damaged and must be kept continuously moist or they will shrivel and dry.

Many bulbs in their dormant stage, so-called, are actually undergoing fantastic internal development: the simple growing point is changing into the complex incipient flower without any external sign. They keep their secret well. One clue, however: here is a place where bigger definitely means better. Not only will really small bulbs not flower, but the bigger the bulb, the bigger and more profuse the flowers.

DUTCH TREAT

If ever there was a country stereotyped by plants, Holland is it. Probably no one who has taken a grade-school course in geography can help but think of the Netherlands as covered from one end to the other by fields of colorful tulips. Well, there's a lot more than meets the eye in that country, but horticulturally speaking it is the foremost producer of bulbs in the world, so much so that Dutch bulbs have become synonymous with tulips, daffodils, hyacinths, and the like.

Let's start with tulips. Originally from the Mongolian steppes, routed by way of Constantinople, where they picked up their name from the Turkish *tulbend*, meaning turban, tulips were hybridized into perfection by a succession of Dutchmen, probably most of all one Conrad Gesner. Tulipomania hit the Low Countries and Germany in the early 1600s. Anybody who didn't raise tulips was simply not in society or even close to it.

Besides, the smell of fortune was in the air. Tulips began being listed on the stock exchanges of Amsterdam, Haarlem, Rotterdam, and Leyden.

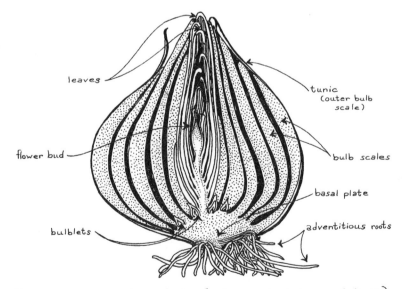

Cross-section of a tulip bulb (a laminated type of bulb)

Every town pub became a bulb-trading hub where future plants exchanged hands at incredible prices. Millionaires were made overnight simply by importing a handful of a rare species. A chronicler of the times, Munting, recorded a barter deal for *one single bulb* of the rare cultivar 'Viceroy': the payment was eight thousand pounds of wheat, sixteen thousand pounds of rye, four fat oxen, eight fat swine, twelve fat sheep, two hogsheads of wine, a thousand gallons of beer, five hundred gallons of butter, a thousand pounds of cheese, a bed, a suit of clothes, and, just to round things off—and perhaps to quaff a congratulatory toast with—a silver drinking cup.

Then in December 1636 came the great tulip crash. The bulb market fell out of bed and never recovered.

So after all that, what about growing tulips without worrying about making a fortune? Well, tulips are fine in the garden, can be forced quite readily in the greenhouse, and are often a disaster indoors. Once you've forced a number of other bulbs, go ahead and try tulips, but why set yourself up for a fall right off?

When you do force tulips, treat them as you do your other soil-planted bulbs, but keep them a bit cooler. And choose what are referred

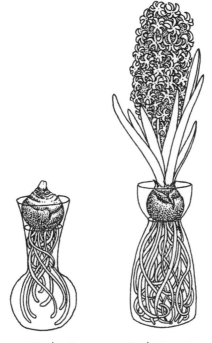

Hyacinth bulbs sprouted in water

to in the catalogs as early singles or early double varieties. They will produce blooms most easily, all at the same time, and on manageably sized plants that barely exceed a foot in height.

On the other end of the difficulty scale from tulips are hyacinths. Members of the lily family, also originally introduced to Europe from Constantinople, they, through the vagaries of horticultural fashion, never sold for more than the price of a good steak. The fragrant flowers are as easy to grow as a child's sweet potato vine, and bulbs pretreated for forcing can be done up the same way, that is, stuck in a glass with water just touching the bottom of the bulb. There are special bulb glasses available, or you can use any clear glass in which the bulb fits without slipping all the way down. Place the bulbs pointed end up. Again keep them in a cool dark spot like your refrigerator, garage, or basement, if there's a room away from the furnace, until a sturdy root system forms. As with the tender bulbs, bring the hyacinths out into full sunlight gradually.

Except for the hyacinths, the so-called Dutch bulbs need good old-fashioned soil to grow. To compensate for this choosiness, however, daffodils (the small-cup varieties are best), tulips, lilies of the valley, and crocuses (which are actually corms, not bulbs) are all hardy, that is, they can be transplanted outside after their indoor bloom is over. If you do set them out, don't cut back the leaves until they have yellowed completely. As long as they are green they will continue to produce food for storage in the bulbs till the next year's flowering.

Start Dutch bulbs around the end of August for Christmas flowers, about October for early spring blooms. Make sure you get varieties expressly designed for forcing. Use bulb pans if available. Squatter than

Planting depth for various bulbs

the normal pot, they will save space and are less expensive. Place some shards over the drainage hole. Then add enough potting mixture, using equal parts of soil, sand, and vermiculite, so that when you put the bulbs in, their tips will reach about an inch from the pot's rim. Don't add any fertilizer, or you'll be forcing greens instead of flowers. Put in as many bulbs as you can for maximum display. There's some debate about whether they should actually touch or whether a small space be left between them. Either method seems to work well. Pour some more potting mix around the bulbs and rap the pot—not too sharply—against the table to help settle the soil. You want it firm, but not packed.

Submerge the planted bulb pan in the sink or a bucket for half an hour with the water up to soil level. Then let it drain overnight. Cover it, allowing for ventilation, put it on the lowest shelf of your refrigerator, or in the vegetable crisper or cool basement, and wait—three to four months.

Come the end of the quarter, knock out the pot and check the roots. They should look like white snakes circling the entire edge of the soil clump. If they don't, put the clump back and wait another month. Often when the bulbs are ready, not only will there be strong roots, but the soil's surface will be broken by the pale ghostlike leaves of the incipient plants. These will turn green, naturally, once they are exposed to light. But again the reminder, expose them gradually. Put them in a cool, light spot, not in the sunlight, for a few days. Then give them more light, and finally as much sun as you can, still keeping them cool.

If all this coolness, particularly the three or four months in the refrigerator, sounds like too much trouble, well, frankly. . . . Susan is threatening to get me a refrigerator of my own for the study come next birthday.

Of course, there are always the tropical bulbs. They don't like it cold.

THE TROPICAL PREPACKS

Tropical bulbs are potted more or less the way their temperate cousins are, but usually only one to a pot. A small pot at that, for a maximum of two inches between pot rim and bulb. You want the plant to be potbound by blooming time.

Eucharis grandiflora (Amazon Lily)
    MICROCLIMATE: Warm partial sun
                      Humusy soil kept constantly moist

One of the trickier tropical bulbs to grow in that it requires high humidity. The flowers look somewhat like large white daffodils, are very fragrant, and make their appearance several times a year, all of which should be enough encouragement to give them a try if you can find the bulbs. Plant one or two in a five-inch-diameter pot, cover with about an inch of soil. Keep moist, but don't water heavily until the first shoot shows itself. A warm location, seventy to eighty degrees, with bottom heat if possible, helps it get going. After flowering, be more chary with the water. A month of relatively dry soil will usually initiate blooming again.

> *Haemanthus katharinae* (Blood Lily)
> MICROCLIMATE: Temperate sun
> Loamy soil kept constantly moist

The best haemanthus because, unlike most bulbs, it keeps its green foliage almost throughout the year. The fleshy leaves are sword shaped, wide and thin, with a depressed midrib. The six-inch-round flower head is composed of up to fifty small starlike salmon flowers with protruding red stamens, and is borne on a separate stalk. Flowering is usually from spring until August. Unlike the hardy bulbs, which can be set outside for rejuvenation, *Haemanthus* needs fertilizing like your other houseplants, particularly in the period before and during flowering. After flowering,

Haemanthus katharinae

until dormancy sets in, a supplement of fertilizer low in nitrogen and high in potash and phosphorus will help the bulb along for the next season. Keep cool, fifty to sixty degrees. At the same time, gradually reduce watering until you've cut back to the point where the soil is kept just a step from being dry for the duration of the rest period, which runs through midwinter.

Haemanthus albiflos, the white blood lily, *H. coccineus*, the scarlet blood lily, and *H. multiflorus*, the salmon blood lily, produce similarly impressive flower balls in various colors. Their foliage, however, dies back completely, the plants taking a more noticeable rest period of six to twelve weeks.

Grow haemanthus plants in five-inch pots and do not repot unless the bulbs become too small, which will take a number of years. When you do repot, new bulbs, or sets, can be removed and planted separately. The bulbs are always potted so that the top third remains above soil level. Once a year scrape away the topsoil, making sure not to disturb the fussy roots, and replace it, including some dried cow manure. This is a substitute for repotting, which the plants really don't like.

Hippeastrum various hybrids (Amaryllis)
    MICROCLIMATE: Temperate sun
        Loamy soil left to dry between waterings

If you want a flower big enough to pass itself off as an antique Victrola trumpet, this is it. Another example of the hopeless confusion in nomenclature, the popular name amaryllis rightly belongs to quite a different plant, *Amaryllis belladonna*, or belladonna lily. *A. belladonna* has a solid flower stalk; hippeastrums have hollow ones. Cut one off sometime and see—if you have the heart.

Good hippeastrum bulbs don't cost as much as tulips did back in their Holland heyday, but they will set you back more than the run-of-the-mill bulbs. General care is about the same as for haemanthus plants, except that hippeastrums like their environment warmer. Bulbs are usually rested from August until October, which is the best time to plant them for Christmas blooms. To force them for the holidays, keep in a warm, seventy to eighty degrees, dark place until they are well rooted and the flower stalk, which develops before the leaves, is six to eight inches tall. Then move them gradually out toward the light, increasing fertilization as you go. The plants prefer lots of sunlight, but wait till the flowers open to give it to them, and the blooms will last longer. After they flower, pinch the plants off at the top. A few days later, cut the scape, or flower stem, near the bottom. Don't worry about the sap that flows out, it will help seal off the wound. Let the leaves grow through the summer; as with other bulbs, don't cut the plant itself back until it has wilted completely. Remember, it is energizing the bulb for the next year's growth.

Sprekelia formosissima (Aztec Lily, Jacobean Lily, Orchid Lily)
    MICROCLIMATE: Warm sun
                            Loamy soil left to dry between waterings

Sprekelia formosissima needs the same care as *Hippeastrum* to produce its crimson flower, with the added attention of alternating moisture and dryness in the soil as for *Eucharis grandiflora*. Again like *E. grandiflora*, it prefers a humid atmosphere.

Vallota speciosa (Scarborough Lily)
    MICROCLIMATE: Temperate sun
                            Loamy soil kept constantly moist

This poor man's amaryllis, besides being less costly than hippeastrums, is also evergreen, which means you don't have to find a place to hide the plant during its bald stage as you do the hippeastrums. The strap-shaped leaves grow up to two feet long and the flower stalk to three. The latter is surmounted by a cluster of long-lasting scarlet flowers, three inches across, that usually bloom from June till fall. Strong, mature bulbs will produce a series of flower stalks in succession. Cut away stalks after flowering. Keep moderately moist even during the plant's cool winter rest period— remember it's an evergreen. If all the foliage does die down, give the plant a month's rest, then water and apply bottom heat.

THOSE BEAUTIFUL SKUNKS

Here's a tropical mixed duo from the Araceae family, which also contains that tasty scout wilderness survival plant, the familiar skunk cabbage. They actually grow from tubers, not bulbs, but I include them here because, for most horticultural purposes, bulbs, tubers, and corms can be treated more or less the same.

Caladium various

    MICROCLIMATE: Warm partial sun

                      Humusy soil kept constantly moist

These plants, available in several varieties, are all hybrids, predominantly with either white or red marble pattern on large thin almost translucent leaves rising on thin stems. The ones you buy already in leafy splendor have been grown under eighty-degree, 80-percent-humidity greenhouse conditions. You'll rarely match their splendor at home.

The plants look frail. In some ways they are, in others not. Direct sun will scorch the leaves. Air conditioning or drafts will send them into a palpitating frenzy that folds up their leaves and kills them. Otherwise they're pretty durable. Plant one or more tubers from February to April in five-inch pots, covering them with about an inch of standard potting mix with a handful of extra peat moss. Keep them at seventy-five degrees with the soil barely moist until growth starts. Once leafing begins, the plants are heavy drinkers. Let foliage die down, and dry out the tubers in winter for a rest period. Come spring, you're all set for a new show. Division of new bulbs gives you extra plants.

Zantedeschia aethiopica

Zantedeschia aethiopica (Calla Lily)
MICROCLIMATE: Warm partial sun
Loamy soil kept constantly moist

Plant the tuber and grow the plant in the same way as a caladium, but give it even more water. Like the skunk cabbage, *Zantedeschia aethiopica* is a swamp plant. It is, in fact, one of the few houseplants that cannot be overwatered. Flowers in winter and spring when the plant is two to four feet tall. Besides the copious supply of water, needs good sunlight, warmth, and fertilizer to produce the familiar waxy white spathes. These are actually leaves, not flowers. In the center of the protective spathe is a long bright yellow spadix on which are mounted numerous tiny true flowers, the males on the top part, the females toward the base.

Summer-blooming *Z. elliottiana*, or the golden calla lily, has deep yellow spathes. Those of *Z. rehmanii*, the rose calla lily, are pink. The summer bloomers are usually potted in late winter or spring. Both like a little less sun than *Z. aethiopica*.

The prime requirements for attractive caladiums and zentedeschias are good humidity and warmth. If you've got those in quantity, there's a whole slew of other tropical plants that would love to join your jungle. . . .

More Plants for Good Measure

So after all that you still don't have enough plants to choose from. Or somebody mailed you a leaf from *Kalanchoë pinnata* and you don't know what to do with it. Well, read on, for here are still more plants to help fill every nook and cranny of your home.

AD INFINITUM

Abutilon hybrids (Flowering Maple)
    MICROCLIMATE: Temperate sun
                     Loamy soil kept constantly moist

Soft-haired, long-stalked, somewhat rangy plants with leaves resembling those of a maple tree—in some cases a good imagination helps. *Abutilon megapotamicum* 'Variegatum,' the variegated Brazilian abutilon, does well in a hanging basket and is cultivated for its attractive leaves as well as flowers. The hybrids are showy only when in bloom. Blossoms are bell-like and range from bright red to salmon yellow to white to two toned. Very easy flowering plants to care for as long as they receive at least four hours of sun a day. Propagate from new growth in spring or fall, also from seeds.

Acalypha hispida (Chenille Copperleaf, Foxtails, Red-hot Cat's Tail)
    MICROCLIMATE: Warm partial sun
                  Loamy soil kept constantly moist

Likes liberal watering, fertilizing, and atmospheric moisture. If the air is dry, the plant will attract red spider mites quite persistently. Grows to fifteen feet in the tropics, making most impressive hedges. Blooms predominantly in summer. The long tassels, often descending a foot outdoors, are composed of a multitude of petalless crimson flowers.

    Acalypha wilkesiana 'Macafeana,' from the New Hebrides, has insignificant flowers, but the leaves match their popular name of painted copperleaf. *A. wilkesiana* 'Obovata' starts out with green leaves, edged in white, that turn to copper with rose orange margins at maturity. Both will grow to six feet indoors, although they usually remain half that size.

Agave miradorensis (Dwarf Agave, Dwarf Century Plant, Mirador
                  Agave)
    MICROCLIMATE: Temperate sun
                  Sandy soil left to dry between waterings

Here's one not to grow for its flowers. It doesn't take a full century for the plants to bloom, but it may take fifty years. If you're lucky and have

Acalypha hispida

a very sunny corner, you might get a cluster of yellowish flowers rising from the rosette of sharp-edged leaves after only a decade or two. This, however, would present a problem. On *Agave americana*, for instance, the blossoms surmount a fifteen- to thirty-foot flower spike. *A. miradorensis* is a bit better: the spike develops sometime in the first decade and is only six to ten feet tall. To boot, all agaves die right after flowering. Propagate from the offsets any time they develop or from adventitious plantlets that form on inflorescence. The plants tolerate air conditioning as long as sun is plentiful.

Aloe vera (Bitter Aloe, First-Aid Plant, Medicine Plant, True Aloe)
    MICROCLIMATE: Temperate sun
                      Loamy soil left to dry between waterings

There are over two hundred known species of *Aloe*, and it's considered one of the earliest of all pot plants, having been under cultivation indoors since Roman times. The species produce rosettes of succulent leaves, making them look superficially somewhat similar to the agaves. The agaves, however, have tough, stiff, dry, fibrous leaves, while the leaves of the aloes are usually thicker, always juicy, and quite crisp. The dagger-shaped leaves of *A. vera* reach a maximum length of two feet. Gray green and plump, toothed along the edges, they are spotted when young, but lose this characteristic at maturity. Numerous suckers form at the base of the plant, making propagation easy.

As to the medicinal qualities of the plant—yes, it actually does soothe burns and cuts. Remove a leaf from the plant. Peel back the leaf's skin and apply the juicy surface to the injured skin area. Not only soothing, but seems to promote healing—I have to say "seems," or I'd be practicing medicine without a license.

Anthurium andraeanum (Flamingo Anthurium, Oilcloth Flower, Tail
                           Flower)
    MICROCLIMATE: Warm shade
                      Humusy soil kept constantly moist

This is the proud bearer of that bright red heart-shaped plasticlike thing with the yellow tail protruding from its middle that is often seen in florists' windows. Its popularity is based on color and long-lasting quality. However, it looks amazingly artificial for being so natural, and you either love it or hate it. I'm in the latter category myself. The red part of the so-called flower is actually a large spathe, or rudimentary leaf, which surrounds and protects the yellow tassel, a spadix or flower cluster. High humidity is an absolute must for this plant. The soil should be very loose, at best composed primarily of leaf mold or sphagnum moss with coarse humus and charcoal. Under good conditions aerial roots will tend to develop; cover them with potting mix. Fertilize every two or three weeks. *Anthurium andraeanum* will bloom all year round.

> *Beloperone guttata* (Rattlesnake Plant, Shrimp Plant)
> MICROCLIMATE: Temperate sun
> Loamy soil left to dry between waterings

Here's a relatively easy-to-grow everblooming plant for the sunny windowsill. The actual flowers are insignificant in size, but they grow at the ends of colorful long pendulous bracts, or elementary leaves. The whole structure is usually referred to as the flower in the trade. It vaguely resembles a boiled shrimp, except perhaps in the cases of the cultivar 'Yellow Queen,' which has chartreuse bracts rather than red ones. The plant will grow to three feet. Needs frequent pruning to keep it from becoming straggly. Will flower most of the year.

Bougainvillea glabra

Bougainvillea glabra (Paper Flower)
> MICROCLIMATE: Warm sun
> Loamy soil left to dry between waterings

Again a plant whose flowers are insignificant, yet surrounded by large brilliant papery bracts. The purplish pink bracts grow in threes. They burst forth into bloom primarily in summertime. *Bougainvillea glabra* is more compact than most. For larger varieties try the numerous hybrids, which can be either trained as climbers or pruned into bush shape.

Bowiea volubilis (Climbing Onion)
> MICROCLIMATE: Temperate partial sun
> Loamy soil left to dry between waterings

The succulent light green bulb of this plant grows halfway out of the ground. Each new year's growth is a twining raveled fresh green string posing as a branched, almost leafless stem. Grown primarily as a curiosity. Use a pot only an inch wider than the bulb. Avoid overwatering, which would quickly induce rot, and dry off well for a rest from July through October. Can be grown from seed as well as offsets.

Bowiea volubilis

Capsicum annuum (Bush Red Pepper, Ornamental Pepper)
MICROCLIMATE: Warm sun
Loamy soil kept constantly moist

A temporary member of your windowsill jungle, *Capsicum annuum* should be disposed of once its chartreuse to scarlet or purple peppers drop. If you're really dedicated, the plant can be held over till the next season, but you'll never get as fine a display as the first. The variety found at the florist's or nursery has been grown outdoors, to set more fruit. But the plant is very sensitive to chills, so be careful if you decide to raise yours via the outdoor route. Yes, the peppers are edible—albeit sometimes *very* hot.

Citrus limonia 'Ponderosa' (American Wonder Lemon, Giant Lemon, Ponderosa Lemon)
MICROCLIMATE: Temperate sun
Loamy soil left to dry between waterings

How about growing a two-pound lemon of your very own—indoors? It will be a little tart for much of anything but pies. On the other hand, you can make a whole lemon meringue pie from a single fruit. Since small trees often bear only one of these five-inch monsters at a time, perhaps it's just as well. *Citrus limonia* 'Ponderosa,' like all indoor citrus, needs all the sun you can give it for good fruit production. Plants propagated from stem cuttings will often flower the first or second year, although some of the pit-grown citruses I've raised indoors have yet to blossom after seven years.

C. aurantifolia bears miniature limes. C. limonia 'Meyeri,' a turn-of-the-century favorite from China, will give you relatively sweet lemons. C. nobilis 'Deliciosa' provides classic mandarin oranges; C. mitis, calamondin oranges; and C. taitensis, plum-sized oval oranges. All are edible except C. taitensis, which might be all right for marmalade if you used a pound of sugar per orange.

Coleus blumei (Flame Nettle, Painted Nettle)
MICROCLIMATE: Warm sun
Loamy soil kept constantly moist

A nontasty member of the mint family, which includes such salivators as marjoram, rosemary, and thyme. *Coleus blumei*, from Indonesia, and its various hybrids grow from one to three feet tall. Multicolored (almost everything, but true blue), plain, serrated, or deeply lobed leaves reach four inches. Keep plants compact by continuous pinching back. The blossoms are insignificant, and the key to lush growth is to pick off all flower buds as soon as they become noticeable.

Cordyline terminalis (Flaming Dragon Tree, Good Luck Plant, Hawaiian Ti, Red Dracena, Tree of Kings)
MICROCLIMATE: Warm partial sun
Loamy soil kept constantly moist

These are the plants from whose leaves hula skirts are made. Little "logs," actually bits of branches a couple of inches long, are frequently sold as "miracle plants." Soak them for a few weeks and a plant will spring forth. By now you know this is no miracle—except as all plants are miracles—but merely an efficient means of vegetative propagation. The miracle is if the plants thrive in your house. They need a minimum of 60 percent humidity at all times. It may be a better idea to buy easy-to-grow dracaenas, which they greatly resemble.

Cyclamen persicum 'Giganteum' (Alpine Violet, Florist's Cyclamen, Sowbread)
MICROCLIMATE: Temperate partial sun
Humusy soil kept constantly moist

A strange backward flower. The blossom has petallike corolla lobes that bend back and up from the center, giving it an inside-out appearance. Blooms in a broad spectrum of color from white through glowing red, including many shades of pastel pink. Profuse flowering in fall and winter. The plant grows from a tuber, like the sinningias, and is cared for more or less the same way during the July-August rest period. When repotting, plant the tuber to the same depth as before, that is, with the tuber about halfway out of the soil. Water the soil, never the protruding tuber, or you may induce rot. May also be grown from seed, usually sown in August. It will take at least eighteen months to flower. As with anything having to do with horticulture, generalized rules are simply that. Last year, for instance, I absentmindedly never gave my cyclamens a rest at all. Yet not only did they bloom lavishly, albeit a bit later than normal, but the silver-veined foliage was perfect, something that doesn't always happen the second time around.

Hydrosme rivieri (*Amorphophallus*, Devil's Tongue, Snake Palm, Voodoo Lily)

MICROCLIMATE: Warm partial sun
Loamy soil kept constantly moist

A real doppelgänger in the plant world. A bulb of *Hydrosme rivieri* planted in February will first produce, by late spring, a bizarre maroon-and-brown-spotted lily-sized spathe with a lighter-colored spadix as long as ten inches, all on top of a two- to three-foot marble green stem. Has the delightful odor of last month's catfood, but you really have to stick your nose into it to notice the smell. After flowering, the plant forms a leafy single-stemmed plant three feet by three feet, looking not at all unlike a small umbrella and in no way hinting at its past behavior. Large tubers will develop a spadix, come spring, just sitting on a windowsill like a bald onion, without water or soil. However, for the plants to grow any further, the tubers must be planted. Should be rested in winter, preferably kept at a temperature range of fifty to fifty-five degrees. Propagated from bulblets that form during parent foliage stage.

Iresine herbstii (Beefsteak Plant, Bloodleaf, Chicken Gizzards)

MICROCLIMATE: Temperate sun
Loamy soil kept constantly moist

The unusual, rich wine-red leaves of *Iresine herbstii* make it a popular plant in formal tropical gardens. For the same reason, color contrast, it is

Cyclamen persicum 'Giganteum'

an excellent addition to your indoor greenery. Plants with colored leaves, incidentally, have their chlorophyll-filled cells buried beneath the other pigmentation and so need lots of sunlight to grow well. *I. herbstii* is no exception. It also needs atmospheric moisture and heavy watering. Once the plant grows over three or four feet tall, staking becomes necessary— either that or you can cut it all up into six-inch lengths and root the collection for new specimens. Plant a dozen or so to a pot for the lushest display.

Kalanchoë pinnata (Air Plant, Bubble Plant, Floppers, Good Luck Leaf, Miracle Leaf)

MICROCLIMATE: Temperate sun
Loamy soil left to dry between waterings

Kalanchoës are untroublesome houseplants. Some, like *Kalanchoë blossfeldiana*, the Christmas kalanchoë, are grown for their profusion of small, bright orange red flowers; others, like *K. pinnata*, for their attractive green foliage and curious method of reproduction. A single leaf of *K. pinnata*, often sold as *Bryophyllum pinnatum*, incidentally, will produce up to half a dozen or more plantlets. They grow from the notches of the leaf and may start doing so while still on the parent plant. A three-foot *K. pinnata* can literally be covered with hundreds of plants falling down and taking root all over. If you are given a single leaf, pin it to a curtain

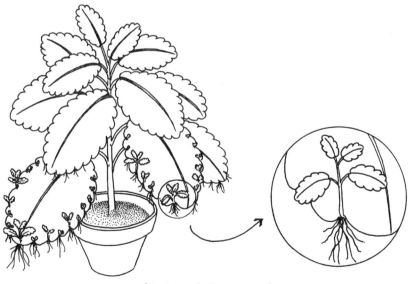

Kalanchoë pinnata

receiving a fair amount of light. Small new plants will begin to form within two to three weeks and will keep on sprouting until the original leaf has shriveled into a yellow blotch. Cut away the new plantlets once they've formed four small leaves of their own and some white roots. Plant right away. If you don't have a curtain handy, simply pin the leaf down on some soil in a pot. New plants will just keep coming up.

> *Maranta leuconeura* 'Kerchoveana' (Banded Arrowroot, Ten Commandments Plant, Prayer Plant, Red-Veined Prayer Plant)
> MICROCLIMATE: Warm partial sun
> Loamy soil kept constantly moist

The colorful leaves of this plant fold upward at night like hands in prayer. If you turn a bright light on, they open up again—no harm done. The six-inch oval leaves are slate green with marked veins and chocolate to dark green patches on either side of the midrib. Let soil become slightly drier in December and keep it that way through February to promote more vigorous growth in spring. Propagate by division when repotting during the beginning of the growing season. Plants are sensitive to cold and to dryness except when resting.

> *Mesembryanthemum crystallinum* (Ice Plant)
> MICROCLIMATE: Temperate sun
> Loamy soil left to dry between waterings

Another curiosity plant, this one has leaves covered by clear bubbles filled with a shimmering liquid turning almost amethyst colored toward the leaf tips. The bubbles give the appearance of an extremely heavy dew or permanent hoarfrost sparkling in the sun. Originally from South Africa, the plant is now naturalized to parts of California. Besides the intriguing leaves, the plant offers one-inch multipetaled white to lavender flowers from July through August. In true California spirit, the flowers always face the sun. Easily grown from seed.

Mimosa pudica (Humble Plant, Live-and-Die, Sensitive Plant,
Touch-Me-Not)
MICROCLIMATE: Warm sun
Loamy soil kept constantly moist

A small compound-leaved plant with no particular attributes to recom-
mend it as a houseplant except the leaves' habit of folding up at the
slightest touch. Children find it fascinating (as did Darwin, who used it a
great deal in his experiments on the power of movement in plants). Easy
to grow, as attested by its weedlike spread from Brazil to Africa to
Southeast Asia.

Ornithogalum caudatum (False Sea Onion, Healing Onion, Whip-
lash Star-of-Bethlehem)
MICROCLIMATE: Temperate sun
Loamy soil left to dry between waterings

An old favorite cold remedy, cauterizer, and curiosity, *Ornithogalum caudatum* is making a comeback. The big green bulb, usually over four inches
in diameter, grows *on top* of the soil, producing half a dozen to a dozen
channeled straplike leaves and a single long-lasting stalked raceme up to
three feet long and bearing more than fifty one-inch flowers. Easy to grow
if you let the plant dry and rest after flowering. Baby onions clamber up
the sides of the main bulb at the end of the growing season and can
easily be used for propagation. In Germany peasants use the *Meerzweibel*,
or sea onion, leaves crushed to cauterize wounds. A sugar syrup, known
as syrup of squill, is also made using the leaves for flavoring. Hardened
into rock candy, it is then used as cough drops.

Since this is the false sea onion, if you're looking for the real one, it's
Urginea maritima, also known as the shore drug squill. A slightly larger
plant whose flower raceme forms after the leaves have died down, it takes
the same care as *O. caudatum*, except that *U. maritima* should be kept
dry between the leaf and flowering stages. Besides being good for coughs,
this one is also an emetic and a cathartic.

Oxalis various (Good Luck Plant)
MICROCLIMATE: Temperate sun
Loamy soil left to dry between waterings

There are several dozen species of oxalis being sold as good luck, or
lucky, plants. They all have three-lobed, cloverlike leaves. (I've yet to find

a four-leaved version.) Flowers range from red to yellow to white. Buy the plants in flower to make sure you get the color you want. Winter-blooming species are dormant in summer, summer-blooming ones take their vacation in winter. Some are everblooming. These should be re-potted yearly in the fall and trimmed back to half their growth or more to give them a chance to recharge their batteries in lieu of a rest period. Flowers open only on sunny days and close at night, as do the leaves.

Primula polyantha (English Primrose, Lady's Fingers, Polyanthus
Primrose)
MICROCLIMATE: Cool partial sun
Loamy soil kept constantly moist

Not far from the house of my childhood there was a field in which yellow primroses bloomed extravagantly. Ever since, the primrose has been one of my favorite flowers, which is why it is included here. Considering the fact that my childhood was spent in Sweden, one might think the flower wanted a cooler environment than most pot plants—which indeed it does. The primulas grown indoors all come from China rather than Europe, but still need a cool sun porch rather than a steam-heated living room. *Primula polyantha* most closely resembles the wild primrose in that the sweetly fragrant yellow, orange, red, maroon, or white floral trumpets grow on stalks extending considerably above the long, obovate leaves. It is grown as a perennial.

A common outdoor annual sometimes grown indoors, *P. obconica* is known as the poison primrose because the hairy leaves cause a skin irri-tation in some people. *P. sinensis*, the Chinese primrose occasionally avail-able at florists', is almost impossible to grow except under greenhouse conditions.

Ruscus hypoglossum (Butcher's Broom, Mouse Thorn)
MICROCLIMATE: Temperate partial sun
Loamy soil left to dry between waterings

A small evergreen shrub grown as a curiosity. The minute yellow flowers are borne on the upper surface at the center of each leathery leaflike branch in early summer. The true leaves are insignificant and pass unno-ticed. Grows to eighteen inches high and is not temperamental.

Solanum pseudocapsicum (Christmas Cherry, Cleveland Cherry,
Jerusalem Cherry)
   MICROCLIMATE: Temperate sun
                   Loamy soil left to dry between waterings

Like *Capsicum annuum*, the ornamental pepper, *Solanum pseudocapsicum* is a relative of our potatoes and tomatoes. It is an old houseplant standby sold throughout the country for its deep green foliage and large round shiny orange to scarlet fruit, which superficially resembles cherries. The fruit hangs on all winter, adding cheer and color to the season of darkness. Although the plant can be grown as a perennial, it is best disposed of once it ceases to be attractive, particularly if it was bought as one of the florist's forced specimens. Before it goes, take some cuttings and start plants for the next season. Also easily grown from seed.

Tolmiea menziesii (Piggyback Plant)
   MICROCLIMATE: Temperate partial sun
                   Loamy soil kept constantly moist

One of the few common houseplants originating in the United States, and the only one I can think of from Alaska, *Tolmiea menziesii* derives its

Ruscus hypoglossum

popular name from the fact that adventitious plants form at the base of the soft, lobed lime green leaves. These plantlets will take root in water, sand, vermiculite, or any other moist medium. However, they don't have to be removed, and a well-developed plant will be a veritable spheroid population explosion of plantlets. The greenish, maroon-lined flowers nodding on slender racemes are an added, if not frequent, plus.

THE DISASTER DOZEN

The following plants are often sold in florist shops, sometimes in plant stores, and not infrequently given as gifts. They can be grown indoors—if conditions are right and you're lucky. A large number of them such as freesias, gardenias, and fuchsias were successful houseplants for decades, until the advent of central heating. They need cooler night temperatures—down in the fifties and even high forties in winter—than most modern homes allow. Others, like the crotons, are tropical in nature—as are most modern houseplants—but they are pest prone to the point of disaster or generally pose problems best avoided. So, if possible, spare yourself the agony and don't grow them. If you absolutely can't resist, or if someone gives you one, well, they may do quite well for a month or two. You can always think of them as long-lasting cut flowers.

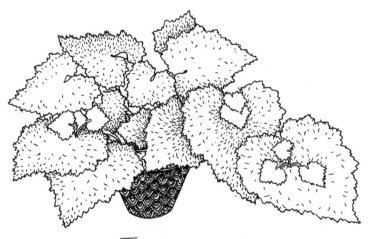

Tolmiea menziesii

Adiantum various (Maidenhair Fern)
 MICROCLIMATE: Warm shade in terrarium
  Humusy soil kept constantly moist

A delightful light airy-looking plant that simply needs more humidity and warmth than the average home can offer. If the soil dries out once, the plant is down for the count. And even grown in the dark recesses of a moist soup kitchen, it can die in a day from the cool draft when you open the refrigerator door. The only place to grow adiantums at home is in a terrarium, where they may do very well.

Anemone coronaria (Lily of the Field, Poppy Anemone)
 MICROCLIMATE: Temperate sun
  Loamy soil kept constantly moist

This one needs things moist and cool. The unimpressive, scraggly plant itself will survive on most windowsills, given sufficient light. But those spectacular poppylike flowers you see pictured in the glowing advertisements for this "giant miracle four-inch bloomer" will never develop except in a cool greenhouse.

Aphelandra squarrosa (Saffron Spike Aphelandra, Zebra Plant)
 MICROCLIMATE: Warm partial sun
  Humusy soil kept constantly moist

A plant that keeps selling and selling because it looks so nice at the store. Yet it seems to fall apart after a few weeks at home, so one goes out and buys a new one. Aphelandras were very popular in Victorian conservatories, where their showy striped foliage and large yellow flower clusters made a good display. And they are easy enough to grow in a warm greenhouse. But in a house with insufficient moisture the plants suffer extensively from leaf drop. Most apartment specimens are lanky-trunked indeed. Actually, they are perfect plants for those who want to practice air layering—twice a year or more. If you do grow them, don't transplant often; usually they do not flower until they have become potbound.

Camellia japonica (Japanese Camellia)
> MICROCLIMATE: Cool partial sun
> Humusy soil kept constantly moist

Another cool-sun-porch plant. The profusion of white, pink, or red blooms will rarely mature unless night temperatures drop into the low forties during autumn and winter. Even then the buds are apt to fall like snow for no discernible reason. Merely looking at the plant the wrong way may cause bud drop. The soil must be rich in organic material, constantly moist but never wet, and always well fertilized. To encourage flowering, disturb the plant as little as possible except for debudding, that is, removing all but a single bud in each cluster, to maximize the size of the remaining flower.

Codiaeum various (Croton, Leaf Croton)
> MICROCLIMATE: Warm sun
> Loamy soil kept constantly moist

Codiaeums are to red spider mites what honey is to flies. Plant pests find them paradise, particularly if the air is dry, which weakens the plants. Also the colorful leaves tend to adopt a plain green hue when light and humidity are not up to the plants' demanding standards—those few leaves that don't drop, that is. In a greenhouse the plants will thrive and grow a bushy foot or more a year.

Euphorbia pulcherrima (Christmas Star, Poinsettia)
> MICROCLIMATE: Warm sun
> Loamy soil left to dry between waterings

Your poinsettia will never again look as it did at the florist's. If you do get one for Christmas and you don't want to get rid of it after the red leaves are gone (the flowers are actually only those tiny yellow dots at the center of the red bracts), cut watering to once a month or so. After the leaf stalks have dried out, cut them back as well, leaving about two inches above soil level. Repot in a pot the same size, but with fresh soil, and place outside in full sun. For blooms, however, you will have to supply some short days. The plants must have less than twelve hours of light— any kind of light at all—during the latter part of September and October if bracts are to form in time for Christmas color. The temperature must be below sixty degrees. All this, of course, can present a problem of some proportions. If the challenge intrigues you, good luck.

Freesia hybrids
> MICROCLIMATE: Cool partial sun
> Loamy soil left to dry between waterings

Now here's a lovely batch of flowers to buy—cut for your vase. They will give you a delightful bouquet of color and fragrance. As pot plants they will give you empty pots in a rather short time. Even if you buy a potted plant in bloom, chances are you won't have any flowers the week after you bring it home. For the cool greenhouse only.

Fuchsia hybrids
> MICROCLIMATE: Temperate partial sun
> Loamy soil kept constantly moist

Could well be known as the white-fly plant, since you rarely see the characteristic tubular bell flowers without a small cloud of the insects hovering around them. No matter how pretty you think fuchsias are, if I were you I wouldn't attempt to grow them unless you have a cool sun porch where you can keep them isolated. On the other hand, if you really like them, maybe you could grow just fuchsias and nothing else.

Gardenia jasminoides (Cape Jasmine)
> MICROCLIMATE: Warm sun
> Humusy soil kept constantly moist

The plant is replete with handsome shiny green leaves, which are probably all you will ever get. Those thick-textured fragrant flowers so much admired by some rarely make it when the plant is grown indoors. Bought in bud from a florist, supposedly to ensure flowering, they will usually simply blast, or drop off, once home, for the buds were forced under greenhouse conditions. If you're not going to give them a greenhouse, chances are they won't give you flowers. As far as pests and diseases go, the particular nemeses of gardenias are root knot nematodes, for which reason the plants must be grown in sterilized soil, and chlorotic yellow leaves, which are counteracted, if at all, by using a chelated iron leaf spray.

Hydrangea macrophylla hybrids (Bigleaf Hydrangea, Snowballs)
    MICROCLIMATE: Temperate sun
                   Loamy soil kept constantly moist

These plants come around every year just like Easter. If you have a yard in which to plant them for the following season, and winter temperatures don't go below freezing, fine. If you don't, leave the hydrangeas sitting on your florist's shelf. They simply are not houseplants by any stretch of the imagination.

Nerium oleander (Oleander, Rosebay)
    MICROCLIMATE: Temperate sun
                   Loamy soil left to dry between waterings

A lovely old tub plant—poisonous every inch of the way from root to flower. A nibble will make you or the pets nauseous; a little more, and. . . . The summer to fall rosy red to white trumpet flowers are nice, but nothing exceptional, and the bush is somewhat scraggly. With all the other plants to choose from, why meddle with this one?

Ranunculus asiaticus (Persian Buttercup, Turban Flower)
    MICROCLIMATE: Temperate sun
                   Loamy soil kept constantly moist

A perennial garden tuber that lately has been sold more and more as a flowering houseplant. Offers a beautiful cut flower—and a scrubby, rarely blooming pot of foliage. Needs, among other things, a very high but also very even light intensity. Only for the humid, cool greenhouse.

*...and
What to Do
with Them*

Making the Plants Feel at Home

So there are several hundred easy-to-grow plants to choose from. But how do you get the ones you want, and what do you do with them once you've got them? A new plant is usually acquired in one of three ways: directly from a plant store or nursery, by mail through a catalog, or as a cutting from a friend. Each way has its benefits and drawbacks.

Buying direct means you get to inspect the plants before you buy. Often it also means the selection is limited and the price relatively high.

Mail-order catalogs display an extensive choice of plants, usually with lower pricing, but you have to put your trust in the shipper, since you have no idea either what size or what condition the plants will be in until they actually arrive. On the whole my personal experience with mail order has been very good, though I do have a couple of horror tales. Because of them I usually send for the minimum order the first time I try a new supplier. If this works out, then I go after what really tempts me.

When it comes to buying orchids, you'll almost certainly do so by mail. They are considered too much of a specialty for most local nurseries and shops to handle. Specify that you want them shipped in their pots. Many growers ship out-of-pot to save you express charges. But what you want is good results quickly, not a lot of potting work before you even become familiar with the plants. For the same reason, don't buy an orchid in a two-inch pot if the species doesn't bloom until it's in a six-inch pot. Orchids are generally sold by pot size, and the two-incher will be a seedling. More often than not the catalogs specify blooming size and season, so you can time your purchase for flowering a couple of months after its arrival.

The third mode of acquisition, trading cuttings or other propagations with friends, is almost all benefit with very little drawback. The price is right, and chances are you'll get healthy plants already acclimated to indoor conditions. About the only negative aspect I've discovered is the selection. As with baseball cards, the other person is apt to be looking for the same plant you are.

There is another, less commonly known way of acquiring choice plant specimens based on a grower's surplus, namely, the plant sales held by local horticultural societies. Usually they accompany the regular meetings, but quite often the general public is invited. It's also a good way to get to know what's going on in the horticultural world. More or less along the same lines are fund-raising sales by botanical gardens. If you live near one, check on this possibility—you may find it most rewarding.

THE PICK OF THE CROP

So there you are in the store, about to buy your first plant. You ask for help in choosing a plant that will be comfortable with the growing conditions you have to offer. Most shopkeepers know their plants. As in any other business, however, there are always a few quick-buck operators out to get your green for theirs. Don't go wild the first time around. Buy a small plant on advice. Take it home and see how it grows. If all is well, then go back for that choice bromeliad or palm you were eyeing. And when buying plants, as with other items, be wary of bargains that seem too good to be true—they usually are.

Once you've selected the plant you want, go over it carefully. You want a full, stocky, lush plant. If the leaves on a stem seem to be spaced farther apart than on similar plants, chances are that specimen has been forced under greenhouse conditions and will take a year or so to get used to your house.

This, incidentally, is an excellent reason to buy young, and therefore smaller, versions of plants such as dracaenas, dieffenbachias, and monsteras. Dealers as a rule like to sell you big ones. But, unless you insist on an instant jungle, it's not only more fun to grow one to size, it also gives you a plant that has acclimated itself to your surroundings as it matured, making it healthier and less susceptible to disease. Furthermore, should mishap occur and for some reason or another that particular plant not make it, you have less to lose, financially if not emotionally.

If you do decide to buy a four- to six-foot decorator-sized plant, hold it firmly by its trunk and rock it back and forth a little. If the plant seems loose, avoid it like the plague, for the shakiness means that a branch was lopped off something down south and stuck in a pot to give the appearance of a plant. This practice is only semifraudulent, since the cutting should take root. But you'll be paying for a supposedly mature plant that could take more than two years to become really established and start sending out new growth.

Pick up a plant and look at it straight on. Looking down on a plant will always make it appear fuller and more lush. This holds true particularly for vertical plants, which are often displayed sitting on the floor to promote the illusion.

In the same vein, many foliage plants are offered grouped three or four of different heights to a pot, to add lushness. Not a bad idea if you do it yourself. The prepacked ones, however, are often sold this way to compensate for the fact that as individual specimens they are rather poor.

Check the leaves of plants carefully. Look *particularly* for insect infestation, especially where new growth is underway. On this score some plant stores and florists are the worst offenders, counting on stock to turn over quickly so no damage will show itself until after the plants have been sold. Leaves should be richly colored and crisp. Although the texture will vary from plant to plant, anyone can tell a wilted head of lettuce from a fresh one, or even from its own unwilted heart. Discerning unhealthy leaves on your future plant is no more difficult. On palms and other large foliage plants, check that the leaf tips haven't been manicured. It's easy enough to cut back brown tips on leaves to make a plant look healthier, but the procedure doesn't improve the plant's condition, nor will the leaf tips regenerate.

Flowering plants should be chosen with some specific characteristics in mind. First of all, most of them should be in flower. This not only gives you an idea of what the color and quality will be, but demonstrates that this particular plant is in fact capable of putting on its pyrotechnic show. The exception is plants bought by mail: shipping them in bud is sometimes acceptable; in bloom they will rarely make it. Compare the blossoms of various specimens, choosing the one with the best texture, color, brilliance, and substance—all fancy flower terms that put together mean the best looking of the lot. Also, it's not the number of flowers that counts, but the number of buds. Ideally you want just one or two flowers showing off what the rest will display for your private viewing. The pedicel, or flower stalk, should be sturdy and erect (unless of course it is a pendulous species). Poor pedicels mean poor flowering.

Roots are a bit harder to check. Good top growth and substantial branching on species that do so are good indications that all is in order below. In any case, turn the pot over and check the drainage hole. You should be able to tell if there are shards over the hole, permitting good drainage. If the hole is jammed up with soil, the plant probably has been machine packed and has little chance for long-term survival. If roots are making their way out of the drainage hole, chances are the plant is pot-bound. This is not necessarily a negative health factor, but it does mean a repotting job in rather short order.

If you're really suspicious about the roots, it wouldn't hurt to ask the store owner to knock the plant out and show you the root ball. Don't expect him to do it with every plant, but if you're ready to make a purchase, there's no harm in asking. If he can't or won't knock it out, I'd buy my plant elsewhere—unless, of course, I happened to be purchasing a six-foot euphorbia.

THE HOMECOMING

Bringing a plant home after you've bought it is always somewhat traumatic—for the plant anyway. Chances are conditions won't be the same as those under which it has just been growing. Changes in light, humidity, temperature, or air circulation—even more likely, a combination of all four—will often put your plant in a temporary state of shock. This is particularly true of the larger, more mature specimens.

To minimize trauma, always try to give the plant conditions better than or at least equal to those to which it was accustomed and don't buy a plant that doesn't suit your home environment. For instance, don't buy a plant from an outdoor nursery in the middle of a summer heat wave and bring it home to a thoroughly air-conditioned apartment. In all probability, the plant will survive—they usually do—but it may take several months to pull itself together again.

Once you've got the plant home, keep it isolated from your other plants for about two weeks. Some people feel it's best to thrust the new-comer into the midst of the established grove, so it will feel cozy immediately. This is a bit of overanthropomorphization. What's more likely to happen is that it will have brought some bugs to pass around. Probably 90 percent of all houseplant pest and disease problems are carried in with new plants. Isn't it worthwhile to keep the newcomer isolated for two weeks if you can reduce your chances for problem plants by 90 percent?

Common trauma signs in new arrivals are dropping of a few leaves, shortened blooming time in flowering plants, a slight leaf pallor, and bud drop, and they may persist for as long as a month. On the other hand, they may never manifest themselves at all, particularly if you keep the moisture around the plant high. The point is, if your plant does go into a slight state of shock, that is precisely the time when insects will attack. One hidden spider mite might raise a family. If you have the plant in isolation, you can more readily convince the mite of the values of planned parenthood.

THE GOOD EARTH NEEDS SOME HELP INDOORS

Eventually you will be faced with either repotting a plant or giving a cutting some terra firma in which to sink its roots. The better the soil, the healthier and more attractive your plants. And unlike conditions in the wilds, where a plant may send its roots out tens of feet in search of the nutrients it needs, in your house it must take potluck.

Basically, soil mixes for houseplants can be divided into three categories: loamy, humusy, and sandy. In all three cases, the texture of the soil is as important as its richness. A good potting soil is, after all, only half solid, the other half being open air spaces. Richness can easily be improved with the addition of fertilizer. Poor soil texture, on the other hand, simply becomes worse with the passing of time.

This can be a real problem with prepacked bags of soil available anywhere from the supermarket to the pet store. In most, if not all, commercial mixes the soil is sterilized, which is a great boon in disease prevention. But city gardeners, who are paying almost as much for a pound of dirt as for a pound of cottage cheese, rebel at the thought of finding lumps, twigs, and other impurities in the soil, so the prepacks are sifted to such a degree they're almost powder. Their rich dark brown color comes from humus, which means their nutritional value is high. But unfortunately, because of its fineness, the soil will compact to such a degree that your plants will be stunted in spite of its richness.

Add one part perlite, vermiculite, or *coarse sharp builder's sand* (beach sand just turns your compacted soil further into cement) to every two parts of prepackaged soil you use, and it will suit most of your plants fine. Prepacked cactus soil can be used as is—for cacti.

Eventually you'll probably want to mix up your own soil. It is less expensive, allows you to experiment, and somehow gives you a feeling you're treating your plants better—which you are. So let's look at some of the possible basic components of soil.

CLAY ordinarily will not be sold as a separate part of your potting mixture, but it is an integral part of good soil and is found to a greater or lesser extent in prepackaged soils. It will almost certainly be found in soil that you dig up in the great outdoors. Of the three natural soil textures—clay, silt, and sand—clay is the finest, with an average particle size of one two-thousandth of an inch. The specks are colloidal in size and flat crystalline in structure. Water as well as fertilizer clings to the relatively large surface area of the individual platelets, acting both as a lubricant and as a glue. The platelets act like a stack of wet dimes at the laundromat, and are what gives clay its squeezability and plasticity. Clay serves a vital function. Its particles, being negatively charged, attract fertilizer ions, which are positively charged, and hold onto them. This is what keeps the fertilizer you give your potted plants hanging around the roots rather than just washing out the drainage holes. Clay is also one of the reasons why jungle soil, which we temperate zone dwellers associate with lush richness, is really so poor. Among other things, jungle soil usually lacks sufficient clay to hold nutrients, so they keep leaching out. What it does contain is great quantities of silt.

HUMUS, as sold commercially, is most often well-decomposed, fine-textured decayed vegetation. In many cases it is extracted from lake bottoms as muck, that is, soil containing between 20 and 65 percent organic material. Even though its black richness might tempt you to use it straight, the fineness of humus particles makes it unsuitable as potting soil without the addition of some larger-chunked substance. Humus tends to look the same wet or dry, so make sure you feel the soil to check on a plant's water needs if it is being grown in a high-humus mix.

LEAF MOLD, where available, is an excellent natural humus. As its name implies, it is partially decayed forest litter, composed primarily of leaves and small twig particles. Should be flaky when used, not powdery fine.

LOAM is a collective term for a sand, clay, and silt mixture. It is what one normally thinks of as soil in the great outdoors. Containing a large quantity of organic matter, it makes good garden earth. But again, it's a bit too heavy for use in pots without the addition of some bulk medium such as perlite, vermiculite, or coarse sand.

PERLITE is volcanic ash that man has heated up and exploded for a second time. It looks almost like shredded Styrofoam and is just as light. Perlite is porous. It attracts and holds some moisture, at the same time adding quality to the soil's texture. However, since it adds almost no weight, it lessens the pot stability of larger plants. It also has a propensity for floating out of the soil and settling on top after you water the plants. Most of the perlite will stay where it belongs, but enough will surface to form a distracting white scum over the soil. Personally I find it un-aesthetic. Sand or vermiculite serves the same function. One advantage of the perlite, though, is that it never really compacts. Vermiculite, unfor-tunately, will squash after a year or two.

SAND is basically stone flour, with particles some fifty to a hundred times the size of clay ones. Primarily quartz, it does not break down or react much chemically. Sand is what gives soil its gritty feel. More impor-tantly, sand particles, because of their size and angular shape, foster aeration and water movement. You want the sharp, large-particled build-er's sand usually available at building supply centers or lumber yards if your nursery doesn't stock it.

SILT is flourlike, feeling silky and smooth when dry. The particles are larger than those of clay, almost like ultrafine sand. They are much less capable of attracting and holding fertilizer. They also don't stick together the way clay particles do, but form an oozy, running mud that is very hard on plant roots, since it allows little aeration. You'll run across silt only if you're digging up your own potting soil from the ground. It will be found in mud deposits or patches of earth that feel floury when dry. Stay away from silt.

SPHAGNUM MOSS goes the sterile-soil additives one better: it has an inherent antibiotic quality that protects young seedlings from damping off. The light brown sphagnum comes in two consistencies, natural and milled. The natural sheets, precut chunky style, are used in some orchid mixes; the fine-milled variety is used straight from the bag for starting seeds. A third grade, with particles between chunky and milled, is sold as sphagnum peat moss or plain peat moss. The plant fibers in this case have already begun to break down, and it is really quite a different thing from sphagnum moss. Contrary to the dark brown black peat moss sold for gardens, it is light brown like sphagnum. The garden variety of peat moss, by the way, is too heavy for pots. If you are using sphagnum or peat moss, don't let it dry out, or you'll have the devil to pay getting it wet again. The best antidote I've found for dry sphagnum is steeping it in boiling water.

VERMICULITE is another heat-expanded potting medium, this one made from mica. Being silverish gray, it is less conspicuous in the soil than perlite. Also its moisture-holding ability is greater. On the other hand, it is more compressible, so you will have to use a proportionately larger quantity in your soil mix. It usually comes in grades of fine, for starting seeds; medium, for general soil mixes; and coarse, used as packing material for bulbs and plants. I save the coarse vermiculite whenever something comes packed in it to use in my potting soil.

SOIL RECIPES

Soil mixing can be almost as complex as synthesizing rubies. A friend of mine, half gardener and half alchemist, has a formula involving no less than thirty-two ingredients. His plants thrive. On the other hand, so do those of another friend who, except for his epiphytic plants, uses only the standard three-part mix. The plants described in this book have soil requirements divided roughly into three categories: loamy, humusy, and sandy. In general, although all plants will do well enough in the loamy soil of the standard three-part mix, those such as the gesneriads with very fine roots will do better in a humusy mix. Cacti and succulents do best in a sandy soil that provides quick drainage and aeration.

The ingredients for the following mixes are all readily available at the local plant store, the florist's, or the five-and-dime, except perhaps for leaf mold. If you have a backyard, the best and cheapest way to get leaf mold is to build a compost pile and make your own. Otherwise, peat moss or chopped sphagnum may be substituted with equally good results.

Does it all sound a bit inexact? Well, it is. Which is really what makes formulating potting soil easy. You can't go wrong as long as the soil has good drainage and nutrients. To this end, when you decide to experiment and make up some mixtures of your own, remember a little extra sand and a tablespoonful of steamed bone meal per pot always help.

LOAMY SOIL MIX (standard all-purpose mix)
    1 part topsoil, garden loam, or prepackaged potting soil
    1 part leaf mold, peat moss, or chopped sphagnum moss
    1 part sharp builder's sand
    1 tablespoon steamed bone meal

HUMUSY SOIL MIX

  1 part topsoil, garden loam, or prepackaged potting soil
  2 parts leaf mold, peat moss, or chopped sphagnum moss
  1 part sharp builder's sand

SANDY SOIL MIX

  1 part topsoil, garden loam, or prepackaged potting soil
  1 part leaf mold, peat moss, or chopped sphagnum moss
  3 parts sharp builder's sand

Assorted special mixes for the puttering potter:

BEGONIA MIX

  2 parts topsoil, garden loam, or prepackaged potting soil
  2 parts leaf mold, peat moss, or chopped sphagnum moss
  1 part sharp builder's sand
  1 part coarse charcoal

EPIPHYTIC MIX (for bromeliads)

  3 parts chopped sphagnum or rough peat moss
  3 parts medium-grade orchid bark, coarse perlite, or vermiculite
  1 part coarse charcoal
  1 part sharp builder's sand

PELARGONIUM MIX

  2 parts topsoil, garden loam, or prepackaged potting soil
  1 part leaf mold, peat moss, or chopped sphagnum moss
  1 part sharp builder's sand

KITCHEN SINK MIX

  6 cups topsoil, garden loam, or prepackaged potting soil
  6 cups leaf mold, peat moss, or chopped sphagnum moss
  6 cups sharp builder's sand
  3 cups coarse vermiculite
  1 cup coarse charcoal
  1/3 cup dried cow manure
  1 tablespoon steamed bone meal
  1 tablespoon limestone

That's a beginning when it comes to possible soil constituents, but only a beginning. Other materials used by growers include: dried cow manure (never fresh, or it will burn your plants' roots), charcoal (use parakeet gravel and you get both sharp sand and charcoal together), bone meal (adds phosphorus, which promotes blooming and strong roots), superphosphate (for the same reason), limestone (to reduce the acidity of the soil), wood ash (for potash and stronger stems), eggshells (for calcium), and dried coffee grounds (to increase acidity and add organic matter). All of which takes me back to the basement chemistry lab I built in grade school. So let me hasten to add that almost all houseplants can be grown in the basic potting soil mix: one part topsoil, one part leaf mold, and one part sharp builder's sand.

Except for orchids, gesneriads, and a few other specialties, I rarely use anything but this standard three-part mix. Going a step further, and giving those specimens that prefer it sandy or humusy soil, your plants should thrive. Of course, in the end, *Gynura aurantiaca* might do even better than it's doing now with a spoonful of bone meal, or maybe one should try a pinch of wood ash, or. . . .

Meanwhile, if you go digging for your own soil, one of the best sources is a long-established hayfield or meadow. It will be heavy in organic material. In any case, wherever you go for it, avoid roadside areas or fields that may have been sprayed with residual-effect herbicides. And don't forget, outdoor soil brought indoors should be sterilized to avoid an invasion of various native creatures that would just love to join your windowsill jungle.

pHORGET ABOUT pH

The pH factor, which measures the alkalinity/acidity variable of soil, is important when growing large-scale crops on the farm or even in the vegetable garden. And if you want to, you can get a soil-testing kit, at about the price of a bushel of apples, and check on conditions in your pots. In order for plants to be able to absorb the nutrients available in soil, the ion balance, of which pH is a measure, must be just right. But the reason I don't own a kit is that any standard potting mix has a pH range that suits the plants fine.

The only general exception is found in areas of the country where the water is extremely alkaline. And even there you don't need a pH kit, since you already know you have very hard water. What you need there is distilled water for your plants.

Of all the plants listed in this book, only pittosporums and *Osmanthus fragrans* really prefer their soil more than normally acidic. Water them with leftover tea once a month and they'll be overjoyed.

THE PERFECT POT

A plant sits in the soil, which in turn must be contained. Usually in a pot. Until recently this was one area of horticulture relatively free from controversy. That is to say, until the advent of the plastic pot, and more recently its Styrofoam counterpart.

Before I go any further, let me say I'm unequivocally biased. As far as I'm concerned there exists only one type of pot for a plant, the one made of unglazed clay. All others—except perhaps the occasional one for a hanging plant—can be described at best as satisfactory and rarely with that much enthusiasm.

Plastic pots are cheap to make and profitable for the manufacturer; handy for the professional grower, since they take up little storage room; and excellent for the shipper, because they are very light. These are their positive qualities. The negative ones include the fact that they tend to be brittle, big ones cracking when picked up, particularly after sitting in the sun for a year or so. They are so lightweight that plants of any substance topple over with the greatest of ease. But most importantly, they don't breathe.

Plastic is nonporous, and so the only way water can leave the pot is through the drainage hole or holes. This is often touted as a great advantage, since it means one has to water the plants less. It may be convenient for you, but by no stretch of the imagination can it be considered better for the plants. Transpiration through pot walls not only reduces chances of overwatering the plants—probably the most common cause of houseplant fatalities—but aerates the soil as well. And aeration can be crucial to the health of a pot plant. It keeps the roots from drowning, supplies them with a constant circulation of nutrients, and just as important, keeps the soil as much as ten to fifteen degrees cooler than the air. Cool roots, warm leaves make for the best growth. The next time you're out in the country on a scorching July day, stick your finger into the soil. It will be surprisingly cool—just the way plants like it.

Don't clay pots have any disadvantages? Certainly. Nothing is perfect, some just less imperfect than others. Clay pots break if dropped—of course, plastic often cracks under the same circumstances. Then too, because of transpiration, clay-potted plants have to be watered more frequently. Also, owing to this water movement, fertilizer salts tend to collect on the outside of the pots. After a couple of years you may have to clean them off if you find the brownish white stains unsightly.

But what if you merely, for some reason, don't like the earthy color of clay pots, or at least would prefer something in a livelier hue? Well, in that case, consider cachepots. These are fancy pots into which you stick the plain Jane. They come in a wide range of shapes and colors, from ultramodern to pseudo-Renaissance, from white to black, ready to fit any decorating scheme.

If you do use cachepots, you'll have to cut back on watering a little bit, since the rate of evaporation will be lower. Otherwise they should pose no problems for your plants, except perhaps for the epiphytic ones, which really do go for first-class root ventilation.

If you don't use cachepots, remember the saucers. Deep ones designed especially for collecting surplus water, available at most plant stores, are your best bet. They're apt to be made of plastic, but for them plastic is fine, since you don't want them to leak. Pebble trays, of course, eliminate the need for saucers.

A TWO-YEAR LEASE

Repotting, or transplanting, is usually necessary when a plant's roots have completely filled a pot. This is apt to occur no more often than every second spring. And spring, when new growth is beginning, is the best time to give a plant new footing. A slow-growing species, like a cactus, citrus, ficus, or palm, sometimes need not be repotted for a decade if well tended and potted in soil whose quality does not deteriorate. You should repot only when it's really needed.

To inspect a plant's subterranean environment, wait until it is ready for watering. Then, spreading your fingers to cover the soil and steadying the plant's stem between your index and middle fingers, invert the specimen. Rap the pot sharply against something hard like the edge of the table. The pot should lift off the somewhat dry root ball easily. If when you turn the pot over a mass of roots is forcing its way out of the drainage hole, you know without going any further that the plant needs transplanting.

If you are repotting a mature plant only because the soil has deteriorated—if, in other words, the mix has lost all its chunky texture and is as smooth as dust—use a pot the same size as the original. On the other hand, if the plant has outgrown its pot, shift to the next larger size.

Plants like their roots fairly snug and close to a pot's edge where they get good air and nutrient circulation. Too much soil can lead to root rot. So don't step up to a pot three or four sizes larger in an attempt to save another repotting later.

Pot sizes go by diameter in inches at the top, starting at thumb pots usually an inch and a half to two inches across and reaching as much as sixteen inches in one-inch increments. Pot shape also varies. The standard pot is as deep as its diameter. An azalea pot is only three-quarters as tall; bulb pans, only half as high as their diameter. Unless you're growing azaleas or bulbs, for simplicity's sake you might as well limit yourself to the standard type.

Old pots may be reused, but don't expect your plants to sleep in beds that are still warm. Wash the pots out in hot water, scrubbing or scraping off any mineral stains with a scouring pad or knife. Then, to reduce chances of transmitting pests and disease, put them to soak overnight in a 10 percent solution of chlorine bleach, that is, one part bleach to nine parts water. Rinse the chlorine off well the next day, and the pot is as good as new.

Speaking of new pots, if you are using such, you may want to let them sit overnight in plain water. You can skip this step; it isn't really necessary. On the other hand, it does soak the pot thoroughly, priming the pump, so to speak, preventing it from too quickly drawing the moisture out of the newly potted soil with which it will be filled. At the same

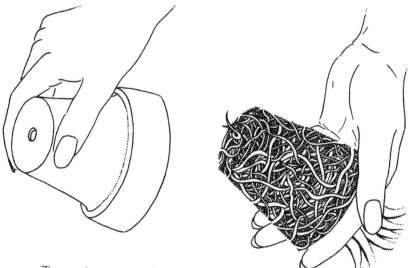

Inspecting a potbound plant

time it will prevent roots from coming in contact with dry absorbent clay and becoming desiccated. It is the root tips that are most essential to a plant's growth, and it's just these that might be damaged.

So you have the pot, the plant, and the dirt—let's put them all together. Remember those textbook pictures of the earth's crust divided into different layers? Well, that's the way a cross section of your pot should look after you're finished. First place some shards or crock over the drainage hole. These are usually chunks of a broken pot. If you're potting your very first plant, though, shards might present a problem, since you probably don't have a broken pot around. I've recycled small can tops for the purpose with great success. Just bend them slightly so that when they cover the hole, concave side down, there's plenty of room for the water to drain out. The purpose of sharding is to prevent the soil from being washed out while at the same time permitting the water free flow. If you use broken pottery, several pieces may be needed to cover the hole adequately.

From here on in you can get as plain or fancy as you want. I've grown numerous plants successfully by merely filling the rest of the pot with a soil mix as I rooted the plant. The opposite extreme is to cover the shards with about a half-inch layer of gravel or pebbles, this in turn with another half an inch of charcoal, and all with a thin layer of sphagnum moss before starting to fill in the pay dirt.

If you are potting on, or in other words moving a plant to a larger pot, put in enough dirt so that when you set the root ball on top, its old soil level is where the new soil level will be. I prefer a level about halfway down the pot's rim. This leaves enough of a reservoir so that when

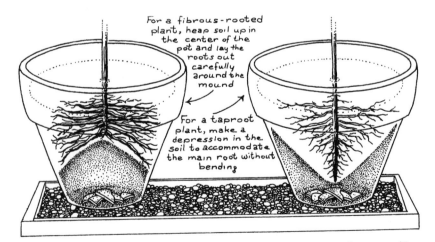

For a fibrous-rooted plant, heap soil up in the center of the pot and lay the roots out carefully around the mound

For a taproot plant, make a depression in the soil to accommodate the main root without bending

Potting bare-root plants to suit their underground growth

I water the plant, usually all I have to do is fill the pot up to the brim once; it holds just the right amount to douse the soil thoroughly, allowing a little excess to run out the drainage hole.

Once the root ball is sitting at the proper level, pour soil around the edge to fill the pot. The new soil must be tamped down to a firmness equivalent to that in the root ball. If it is loose, the roots will tend to avoid it. Not only that, but those that do venture out into the unpleasant sponge will tend to rot.

You can knock the pot against the table a few times if you want, supposedly to settle the soil. It's an old habit everyone recommends and it adds an air of completion to the project. As for settling the soil and filling air pockets, that it won't do if you've packed the soil to any degree at all as you potted it.

Give the newly launched plant a real baptism to settle the soil properly. Don't just water it well. Put the whole affair in the kitchen sink and fill the sink with tepid water to a level equal to or just above that of the soil. Then gently pour water onto the soil itself until it won't take any more. Let the pot sit for ten to fifteen minutes. It's the only way you'll really dissolve the boundary layer between the old and the new soil. When potting plants that have arrived bare root or cuttings that have rooted in water, this is also the one certain way of filling soil in around the tiny hair roots, which would die if they grew into air pockets.

When the plunge is done, don't lift the pot out of the sink, rather pull the plug and leave the pot be for another half hour. An amazing quantity of water will seep out—enough to fill the average saucer to overflowing.

Three more brief tips on potting and repotting. First, if possible, give a newly potted plant a little less than normal light for the first few days after its transfer. Second, never fertilize a freshly potted plant. Chances are you'd just end up burning the roots, doing far more damage than good. Wait about a month. Third, let the soil dry perhaps a little bit longer than usual before resuming normal watering routine. Remember you've given it a real dousing.

HOW'S THE WATER?

Probably no question about houseplants is asked with greater frequency or answered with less definition than, "How often should I water my plant?" Truly one can only reply, "As often as necessary." But there are some basic points to consider that will help you determine what's right for your plant under its given conditions. For instance, a large plant in a small pot needs more water than a small one in a large pot. If the plant has been repotted recently, chances are the root ball is rather small in relation to the pot's volume, which in turn means less water absorption than if the roots filled the pot. Also, sunny, windy, warm weather means transpiration and evaporation going on at a higher rate, so you'll need to increase watering. Lastly, a plant is much thirstier during periods of active growth than at other times. The sprouting of buds and young leaves is a sure indication that more water will be needed.

Yet, after all that, let me repeat that more plants are probably killed by overwatering than by anything else. Sopping soil means there is no room for air in your pot. No air, soon no roots. No roots, no plant.

If the greenery you're growing falls into the constantly moist category, you want to water well whenever the surface feels dry but the soil underneath is still moist to the touch if you wriggle your fingers an inch or so down into it. Moist means just that, not wet. Except right after watering, the soil should not stick to your fingers and water should not drip out when you squeeze a bit of soil into a ball. If it does, it's too wet.

For plants in the drench-then-let-dry category, the soil should feel quite dry even an inch or two below the surface before being watered again. This doesn't mean dust-dry, though; some moisture is needed to keep the roots from drying out. Incidentally, you don't have to bury your fingers every day to check. Visually, dry soil looks lighter than when it's wet. Still, it's a good idea to finger the soil occasionally while you're getting the feel of watering.

You'll find watering really becomes quite automatic once you get to know your plants' needs. Meanwhile, there are a couple of basic rules that require no experience at all. First, use tepid water, never cold. The only possible exceptions to this are miniature roses and cool-loving plants, but even these don't like a frigid root bath. Most indoor plants are tropical. Cold can send them into shock. Second, when you water, do a thorough job. Flood the plant from the top. If this seems to contradict the caution against overwatering, remember that you have potted your plant with good drainage and that you are allowing enough time between waterings. All the water should drain from the top of the soil within a couple of minutes; if it doesn't, the soil is packed too heavily.

The reason you want to flood your plant, to such an extent that some water always drains out into the saucer in which it's sitting, is twofold. For one, percolating down, the flood adds oxygen. For another, it assures good root development. Cautiously sprinkling the top of the soil usually means that only the upper half of the pot gets enough moisture. Main root growth then occurs there, leaving the bottom half bare. The plant grows half as well as it should.

GOOD ENOUGH TO DRINK

An old wives' tale that has grown up with modern technology and the popularity of houseplants is that the best water for your plants is rainwater, since it contains no impurities, like chlorine, to harm the plants. The point about chlorine is all well and good, except that unless your tap water smells like the pool at the YMCA, the chlorine content is not high enough to damage your greens. So letting the water stand overnight in a tub to allow the chlorine to volatilize off doesn't make a bit of difference to the plants—other than raising the humidity in your home.

On the other hand, and quite contrary to the old wives' tale, today's rainwater can be positively lethal in heavily industrialized areas. Its potential for disaster is on a worldwide scale. One harbinger of the many problems man's dirtied rain may cause in the decades to come is the "acid rain" of Scandinavia. It is stunting the lichen on which the reindeer depend for their main nourishment. The reindeer in turn are becoming smaller with each passing generation. Closer to home, the Lincoln Memorial in Washington is literally melting away in the acidic rain. Where once it might have stood for eons, now it and many other monuments will probably crumble in a couple of hundred years. So watch out where you collect rainwater. It's not as pure as you might think.

Another water problem is hardness. Or perhaps I should say the real problem is the cure. Ion-exchange water softeners replace calcium and magnesium, both of which are harmful to your plants in too large quantities, with sodium, which is more harmful. If you have a water softener and your plants are not thriving, chances are the softener is your problem. Fill the watering can from a faucet—one outside the house, for instance—that is not connected to the softener. Houseplant lovers in areas of New Mexico and Arizona with really alkaline water sometimes have to use bottled water, both for their own taste buds and their plants' health.

WICK IT

There are a number of self-watering devices available. Most commercial ranges use one variety or another for at least some of their pot plants. Whether they are worth having in your windowsill garden is a personal decision. I like puttering with my plants and so prefer to water them myself.

Incidentally, if all this is beginning to sound too involved, relax—it's generalization, no more, no less. Plenty of times I've forgotten to water a plant, discovering my omission in the evening when the leaves were drooping from thirst like a panting dog's tongue. You'll do the same occasionally, I imagine, and it's times like these when one really appreciates the marvelous resiliency of plants. But back to self-watering pots.

One of the oldest and most popular systems is the wick. Used on saintpaulias and other plants that prefer constantly moist soil, wicking to be really successful must be installed when the plant is potted. A wick of fiberglass or other low-rot material—make sure it does in fact suck up water—is threaded through the drainage hole. Shards are placed as usual, with the wick extended beyond them into the soil area; the plant is potted; and the wicked affair is then placed in a deep dish of pebbles and water. The wick will draw up water constantly, quenching the plant's thirst. Of course, if you get used to the plant's tending itself and forget to fill the reservoir. . . .

STOCKING UP THE LARDER

Fertilization for houseplants is usually accomplished by one of two methods. The first is to mix a number of naturally nutritional ingredients into the soil when potting the plants. These supply reserve nourishment, dissolving slowly and feeding the plants over an extended period. They also supply a number of trace elements. Dried cow manure is about 4 to 10 percent nitrogen, dried blood about 13 percent, and fish emulsion 5 to 10 percent. A heaping tablespoonful of any one of these for a six- to twelve-inch pot of soil is good. The same holds true for bone meal, which

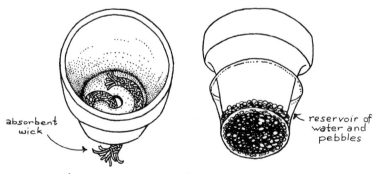

absorbent wick

reservoir of water and pebbles

A wicking device for self-watering

is 20 percent phosphorus, and for wood ash, containing about 5 percent potash. An extra spoonful of dolomitic limestone, oyster shells, or even crushed eggshells from Sunday morning brunch will add a calcium boost to your soil mix. But if all this sounds too troublesome or if you're growing orchids or other epiphytic plants that draw relatively little of their nourishment directly from the soil, you can skip it entirely and just use fertilizer occasionally as per the package's instructions when you water the plants. Combining the two methods, that is, using a well-balanced soil with supplemental fertilization, will give you the healthiest plants of all.

CONVENIENCE FOODS

There are numerous brands of ready-to-use fertilizer available. All of them are convenient. Most of them are synthetic water-soluble compounds. Only the fish meals and fish emulsions are what would be considered "organic" in the gardening sense of the word—that is, derived from once-living organisms.

The advantage of the natural fertilizers is that they tend to add quality to the soil as well as nourishment. Also the availability of trace elements is higher and more certain, since the chemical fertilizers often do not specify which of these elements are included, or indeed if they are. Boron, copper, iron, magnesium, manganese, molybdenum, and zinc are some of the micronutrients needed by your plants and readily available in most organic fertilizers, as also in those chemical ones that specifically state that they contain trace elements as well as the big three, nitrogen, phosphorus, and potassium.

The label numbers identifying a fertilizer, 15-30-15, for instance, or 20-20-20, represent the three major elements and the proportion in which they are available. A 15-30-15 formula would have 15 percent nitrogen and potassium and 30 percent phosphorus, for a total of 60 percent growth elements, with the remaining 40 percent being filler and trace elements. The 20-20-20 formula would have the same 60 percent total supply, but proportionately more nitrogen and potassium and less phosphorus. The questions are, Why not make the formula 100 percent of the big three? and, Why do they vary the percentage?

In organic fertilizers such as bone meal, 0-12-1, the numbers simply represent an analysis of what the material naturally contains. Bone meal has no nitrogen, it has 12 percent phosphorus and 1 percent potassium. That's the way it exists. If you ever need nitrogen and want a natural fertilizer, fish emulsion, 5-1-1, is the solution.

Chemical fertilizers can be tailor-made much more readily. Should you for some reason want a 1-46-3 formula, a manufacturer could easily put it together for you. And while I would not use chemical fertilizers in my vegetable garden any more than I would use chemical pesticides, on the small scale of tending potted houseplants they certainly add a degree of convenience. They are, however, dangerous with children around. Organic fertilizers merely taste unpleasant; the chemical salts can be very poisonous.

As to why the analysis numbers of the manufactured fertilizers vary so, there is a good reason. Nitrogen, represented in the first number, is primarily responsible for leaf growth and photosynthesis. Obviously your plant won't get very far without it. If you are growing orchids in fir bark, which has no available nitrogen, you will want to use a 30-10-10 formula regularly.

Phosphorus, the second number on the label, concentrates its effects primarily in root and stem development and, more importantly for your color display, in flower development. As flowering season approaches, or when a plant is already in bloom, it's a good idea to switch to a fertilizer with a high middle number. At other times you are generally best off using a balanced formula such as 20-20-20. Most fertilizer manufacturers also have booklets showing which of their specific fertilizers to use for what purpose.

Oh yes, and that last number represents potassium or potash. It does a number of things; most importantly for you, it's like a health tonic to your plants, making them more disease-resistant.

So if a plant seems to be sick, give it a good dose of fertilizer to pep it up? *Wrong.* Never fertilize a plant that is sick. It will do more harm than good, for the plant won't be able to avail itself of the nourishment, but instead the rich fertilizer will be a shock to its system. Remember those childhood illnesses during which your mother brought you tea and milk toast, or chicken broth, or whatever other light food was the sick-bay special in your house?

Another time not to fertilize a plant is right after you've gotten it. Give it a month or so to settle down and become used to its new environment before beginning a regular program of fertilization. The same holds true for newly transplanted specimens. A third time not to fertilize is when the plant is in its resting stage.

So when and how often should you fertilize? This question, thank goodness, is a lot easier to answer than its counterpart on watering. Use fertilizer as directed on the label—but at half strength. Overfertilization will burn plant roots. Fertilization at full strength works well most of the time; fertilization at half strength works well all the time—*as long as the plant is growing.* Unless you live in the South, do not fertilize the plants from November to February. Even if you live in a latitude of minimal winter solstice, don't forget to cut back on fertilization when the plant does take its rest. Plants don't eat in their sleep any more than you do.

THREE SQUARES A WEEK

Insects, decaying plants, and leaching minerals supply the soil of an outdoor plant with a constant stream of nutrients. Potted plants that are fertilized about once a month—or less, if you forget to tend them—are on a much more cyclic diet than is natural. This feast-or-famine existence can be improved upon to the plants' benefit. Instead of following the traditional method, fertilize them every time you water the pots. *But use an extremely dilute fertilizer solution,* not the regular strength specified for whatever brand you use. I mix up a quart of fertilizer at about a fourth the recommended strength. Then each time I tend the plants I splash a quarter of a cup or so into my two-quart watering can before filling it. Once a month, however, I water the plants very well, using no fertilizer. This washes out any fertilizer that might accumulate as salts.

DRIVING YOUR BROMELIAD BANANAS

Foliar feeding, that is, spraying diluted fertilizer directly on leaves, was a fad with houseplants a while back. Now avocado-butter night cream may feel pleasant on a human being's face, and it may even do a little something for the skin quality, but it won't nourish you much. Foliar feeding for the most part falls into the same category. There are two exceptions.

One is plants suffering from chlorosis, the plant world's version of iron-deficiency anemia, symptomized by pale and yellowed leaves with veins remaining darker and greenish. An acid fertilizer with chelated iron applied to the soil will remedy the situation. A bit sprayed on the affected leaves will speed the cure.

Bromeliads and orchids constitute the other exception. These epiphytic plants are designed to "eat air," and so are structurally more capable than other plants of absorbing nutrients through their leaves and aerial roots. This is particularly true of the bromeliads. A quarter-strength solution of fertilizer placed in their vases once a month goes a long and appreciated way. By the same token as placing an apple beside your bromeliad to induce flowering, try a banana peel for good leaf growth. Banana peels have an extremely high potassium content. Small cubes of banana skin allowed to age in the bromeliad vase will give the plant a real boost.

While on the subject of spraying leaves, stay away from the various products that are supposed to give your plants shiny lush leaves. In fact, stay away from the stores that use them on their plants as well. Leaf-shining gook does nothing but clog pores, particularly if sprayed on the leaves' undersides, where most of the stomata are located. Clogged pores mean poor growth.

BATHING YOUR PLANTS

One thing a plant's leaves can do with occasionally is a spraying thorough enough to really wash them. An amazing amount of dust and soot can collect on leaf surfaces in no time. A thorough weekly spraying, or sponging off of larger leaves, will help the situation.

Better yet, once every month or two give the plants a bath. Use tepid water and a small hose with a spray attachment to give them a real rain shower. Besides rinsing the leaves, it will help wash away insects and eggs that might be just about to make their presence known. To this end, always tip a plant being showered at an angle of forty-five degrees or more so that the water drips down into the sink or tub, washing the potential problems away rather than into the soil. Small plants can simply be picked up, turned upside down, and dunked completely into the water. Swirl them around gently for best results. Hold the pot with your hand over the soil the way you do when knocking a plant out of its pot, and everything will hold together.

A PINCH IN TIME

Another occasional bit of maintenance is pinching back or pruning your plants to train them into fuller, more aesthetic shapes. Not all plants can be pinched back. On palms, for instance, it's fatal. The main purpose of pinching is to force the plant to branch, which of course excludes from the process all nonbranching plants, like bromeliads, most cacti, orchids, and such common houseplants as *Chlorophytum*. Where the technique is at its best is with vining plants such as ivies and gynuras and bushy ones such as pelargoniums and begonias.

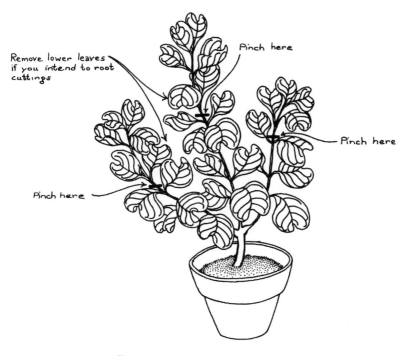

Remove lower leaves if you intend to root cuttings

Pinch here

Pinch here

Pinch here

Pinching back a young plant

Pinching entails removing the soft growing tip of a shoot. The energy that would have been expended on new stem and leaves is then "forced back," to be used in further branching and/or flowering. You get bushier, more floriferous plants by pinching.

WHO'S WHO AND WHO DID WHAT?

Once you've got more than two plants, chances are you're well on the way to a dozen. Labeling each one not only serves as a reminder of what new plants are until their nomenclature becomes second nature, but provides a handy space for a great deal of useful information: the date you got the plant, from whom, when it last flowered, and so on. If you decide to experiment with your plants, you may need the further space that a small notebook affords to keep a record of, say, which ones were grown under round-the-clock illumination, which ones were fertilized with eggshells and which with banana peels. On the other hand, this is certainly not necessary. Simply growing beautiful plants is its own reward.

An Indoor Ecology Guide

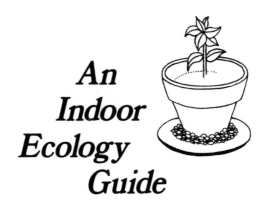

If there is a single key to the successful cultivation of houseplants, it's light. Most plants will grow at the prevailing indoor temperatures; few won't at least survive under the usual interior atmospheric conditions. Light, however, is an entirely different matter.

Civilized man has learned to ignore nature whenever possible. Benjamin Franklin's old observation on Londoners still applies to urban and suburban dwellers, even if their circumstances are more sophisticated: namely, they choose "voluntarily to live much by candle-light, and sleep by sunshine, and yet often complain, a little absurdly, of the duty on candles, and the high price of tallow." And although the diminution of light in the late hours as we switch from natural to artificial illumination goes almost unnoticed, ordinarily our artificial nocturnal illumination is not sufficient for plant growth.

That in itself wouldn't matter so much to the houseplants; they are not late sleepers, and take advantage of the sun as soon as it rises. But since we are used to the somewhat darkened interiors of our dwellings, and since our eyes are such marvelous sensors when it comes to adjusting to reduced light intensity, we rarely notice how dim it actually is inside even by day. The plants, on the other hand, do.

For instance, windows in a city like New York look dirty a week or two after they've been washed. A month or two later, of course, they still look dirty, but not that much dirtier. We've become accustomed to the gloom. Yet a window in New York City that has not been cleaned for six months loses as much as 40 percent of its light-transmitting qualities. The plants will most certainly notice that.

COOKING WITH LIGHT

Unlike animals, plants produce most of their food themselves, and it is light that triggers and energizes the internal process of photosynthesis that makes carbohydrates, the plants' food. Without light, food production ceases, and the plant must survive on stored energy. That's how a seed sprouts in the dark or a bulb beneath the soil. It contains enough energy reserves to push new growth up into the light where it can develop chlorophyll, turn green, and begin manufacturing sugars to try to assuage the plant's insatiable sweet tooth. But the manufacture of food through photosynthesis goes on only when there is enough light to supply the necessary energy.

Photosynthesis in plants utilizes no more than roughly 0.1 percent of all the solar energy that reaches the earth. Yet this process, almost single-handed, has over the millenniums filled up the energy bank account that man is now using: coal, gas, even plain firewood. On a global scale photosynthesis involves some incredible numbers: 470 billion tons of organic matter, absorbing some 690 billion tons of carbon dioxide and 280 billion tons of water, while adding 500 billion tons of oxygen to the air. The oxygen is particularly important in the cycle of life when you consider that plants are the only organisms that *add* oxygen to the air. *Everything else uses it up*—your breathing, the running of a car engine, even the rusting of that old tin can out on the dump.

By a second process, called respiration, a plant itself uses some of the energy it has produced through photosynthesis to grow and make new cells. Unlike photosynthesis, which occurs only during daylight hours, respiration goes on as continuously as our own breathing, whether or not there is light.

When a plant is getting just enough light during a twenty-four-hour period for the process of photosynthesis to manufacture the amount of food that the process of respiration uses up, the plant is in a neutral state.

If it gets more light, the plant can store energy for a cloudy day. Under favorable conditions this photosynthesis/respiration ratio is five or more. That is, the plant is making five times as much food as it is actually using. If, on the other hand, for an extended period the plant receives insufficient light, it literally cannibalizes itself, drawing on all its stored food. Eventually, deprived of light long enough, the plant starves to death.

The intensity of light is measured in several different ways. The most common in horticulture is by footcandles. Since illumination increases logarithmically, the numbers climb rapidly as the light becomes brighter. And vice versa. In a north window on a sunny winter day there are usually one hundred fifty to five hundred footcandles of illumination close to the pane. If at a given time it's, say, three hundred, which is about average, then only two or three feet in from the window the intensity will be one hundred footcandles or less. At the other extreme, the outside reading at the same time could be as high as six thousand footcandles. This is why it's important to put light-loving plants as close to the window as possible.

Footcandles, measured with a footcandle meter or a photographic exposure meter, represent light intensity in terms of the human eye. But a plant doesn't "see" light the same way we do. For instance, the human eye is most sensitive to the green part of the spectrum, whereas the plant's sensitivity is more likely to be toward the red or ultraviolet. In a photographic laboratory, a red safelight is often used because of the film's relative insensitivity to this portion of the spectrum. In plant laboratories pursuing research on the effects of light on plants, a green safelight is used for a parallel purpose.

A LIGHT FOR ALL REASONS

Daylight, or white light, as you probably remember from grade school, is composed of all the colors of the rainbow. If we let sunshine pass through a prism, we get a spectrum of visible light ranging from blue to red.

The problem with measuring light in footcandles is that it doesn't take into account the color composition or color temperature of the light being measured. As long as you're measuring daylight, this doesn't matter too much, since daylight is fairly well balanced at all times. Artificial light, however, is often lacking in certain parts of the spectrum. And although all wavelengths appear to be needed for plant growth, certain of them are more important, playing specific roles without which the plant cannot survive. The wavelengths of blue and a particular red, for instance, control photosynthesis. Ultraviolet, green, and another blue are the activators of phototropism. These, interestingly enough, are absorbed by carotenoid pigments manufactured in the plants—the same pigments that give us our vision. Two different parts of the red spectrum determine the overall size and development of the plant, within the limits of its growth pattern, by activating a blue pigment called phytochrome, presently considered the key enzyme controlling all plant growth.

MOONLIGHT OVER RUSSIA

Recently while perusing the English version of the May 1973 *Doklady Akademii Nauk SSSR*, an obscure Russian scientific journal, I came across a fascinating little article still somewhat out of science fiction. Somewhere in their vast bureaucracy the Russians must have plans to colonize the moon, for here were described the beginnings of research on how to feed the emigrants.

The article, "Growth and Development of Plants with a Lunar Period," discussed the fact that most annual plants, if they even survived being subjected to a period of darkness lasting three or more days, lost not only their photosynthetic pigments, but their reproductive ability as well. Cereals were particularly sensitive to the light deprivation, a two- to three-day period of darkness being sufficient to eliminate development of the grain for which the plants were grown.

The phenomenon would present quite an agricultural problem on the moon, where the days and nights are each fifteen earth days long. Artificial lighting could be used to grow the plants, of course, but the energy demands and cost would be tremendous.

Scientists reasoned, however, that sharply reduced night temperatures might slow down the plant's metabolic rate enough to avoid the disastrous damage to the reproductive system. It worked. So far as lunar wheat harvests went, the particular problems of extra long nights, at least, had been solved.

What I found just as interesting, from a houseplant point of view, was that the plants used in the experiment made up for lost time during the fifteen-day days. Overall the wheat plants grown on a lunar timetable matured as quickly as their more normal earth-environed cousins.

I had never given serious thought to bestowing on plants twenty-four-hour illumination, since, like too much of anything, excessive light can be damaging to them. But trying it at home after reading about the moon wheat, I found that some plants exposed to light around the clock for months on end—with, however, a substantial, twenty degrees plus, drop in night temperatures—seem not only to do better than their day-and-night-cycled siblings, but also to suffer much less from insect problems. Normally plants grown under lights seem to be more prone to attack by white flies and other pests.

I haven't really grown enough plants under no-night conditions to verify the observation beyond doubt. Perhaps it has nothing to do with the plants' being extra healthy; it could be simply that the bugs need sleep and so go elsewhere. Whatever the case, it is an intriguing field of future exploration for the intrepid indoor gardener. Just don't try it with short-day plants, or you'll never have any flowers.

HELIOTROPISM

The ultimate basis of all life, sunlight, not only is responsible for the production of food in plants through photosynthesis, but controls a number of other essential processes in the green world. One of these, phototropism, is of particular interest when it comes to houseplants. In phototropism, the young growing tips of a plant turn toward the sun. Leaves, too, orient themselves so that their broadest part faces the sun. That's why you have to keep turning the plants on the windowsill; otherwise they would always look as if they were trying to lean out the window.

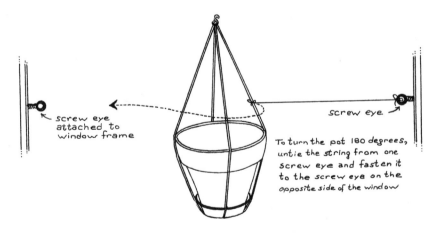

screw eye attached to window frame

screw eye

To turn the pot 180 degrees, untie the string from one screw eye and fasten it to the screw eye on the opposite side of the window

A device for turning a hanging plant to encourage even growth

THE TATTOOED APPLE

Plants grown in insufficient light become spindly. Technically the phenomenon is known as etiolation. If it happens to your plants, pinch them back severely and place what's left in a spot that gets more light. Or, if you want to leave them where they are, supplement the sun's rays with artificial light.

In extreme light deficiencies, plants will become pale and bleached looking due to the lack of chlorophyll. That's how the white asparagus preferred in Europe is achieved; it's simply not given a chance to get aboveground and develop chlorophyll. Blanched celery also is produced by light deprivation; straw is piled up around the celery bunches until they are harvested.

The color pigmentation in fruit is affected by light in the same way. If you happen to have an apple tree in your back yard, an amusing children's project is to let nature tattoo the children's names onto some nice red apples. Cut out the names stencil-fashion on stiff pieces of black paper. Fasten them with small slips of Scotch Magic Transparent Tape onto still-growing apples not quite mature. By the time the apples are ready to harvest, sun and the color pigments will have inscribed the names on the fruit.

THERE'S NOTHING LIKE MORNING SUN

Tradition has it that morning sun is better for plants than afternoon sun. Horticulturally, tradition seems to be borne out by better plants. The question is, Why? Since the morning sun penetrates the earth's atmosphere at a different angle than the midday sun, possibly the difference in spectral composition is responsible.

Personally I think it's a threshold factor: the plants need light of a certain intensity to get photosynthesis going. If the morning light remains below this intensity, the plants don't go to work till the day reaches its maximum brightness sometime around noon or so, in which case they're actually putting in only half a day's work. Less food production, less growth.

Still on the subject of light intensity, many plants that find direct sun in the summer too much for them will thrive on it in winter, when the sun's intensity is considerably less. Yet another variable where sunlight is concerned is the length of the day. Not only is the sun less intense in the wintertime, but it shines on the plants for a shorter period. This brings into effect the rather heavy-sounding law of reciprocity, or law of photochemical equivalence, which simply states that once a light intensity has been reached in which a chemical reaction begins to take place—in the plants' case, photosynthesis—the longer the light shines, the greater the effect. Twenty hours of one hundred footcandles will produce as much photosynthetic reaction as ten hours of two hundred footcandles.

In terms of houseplants, this means that if they don't get bright enough light naturally, you can still make them thrive. Extend the total number of hours they are lit, using artificial light.

SPRING COMES TWICE A YEAR

Consider moving your plants around every few months. It's amazingly easy to overlook a plant that is always in the same spot. The plant is watered and cared for, but only when you move it, actually pick it up, do you notice the new leaves or flower buds.

Move a plant away from a sunny windowsill once the year's initial spring growth is well underway and replace it with another plant that has been sitting further back. Both receive the advantage of the extra spring sun that way and both will grow better. If you don't have a sunny window, the same principle of rotation can be used to the plants' benefit by shifting them from their usual location to an artificial light setup for a few months of supercharging.

Almost all plants will benefit from a summer vacation outdoors. However, you will have to move them there gently. Even if a plant has been sitting in full sun indoors, it should be moved to a relatively shady or dappled-shady spot outdoors for the first week, then to a sunny spot. It's so much brighter outdoors that the leaves will become sun scorched unless given a chance to acclimate slowly.

A SUN OF YOUR OWN

One of the greatest boons to the urban houseplant enthusiast was the development of fluorescent light in 1938. Suddenly the city apartment whose southern exposure consisted of a three-by-three air shaft shared with the gloomy apartment across the way could supply plants with all the light energy they needed. Suburban basements, attics, even dingy old coal cellars could be converted into lush jungle paradises.

Incandescent bulbs have three disadvantages that severely limit their horticultural use. First, they give off a lot of heat. This might be fine as supplemental warmth in winter. But in dark corners that never see natural light even in summer, the heat generated by leaving the light on all day would roast the plants by May, much less August. Second, their light emission is very poorly distributed, being limited to a glowing bulb. This means you practically need one bulb per plant. It also brings up the third point, cost. Photoillumination for plants should be for a period of fourteen to sixteen hours a day. Tally it up. Since one forty-watt fluorescent tube produces as much light as a hundred-watt incandescent bulb with half the energy, the cost savings of fluorescent over incandescent lighting is considerable.

An initial problem with fluorescent light, however, was that it supplied little of the far-red light crucial to activating phytochrome—and flowering. The development of "warm white" or "daylight" bulbs improved things somewhat. Even so, most people growing plants under artificial light continued to use both fluorescent and incandescent, putting incandescents at each end of the fluorescent in order to achieve a balanced spectrum. This is still a good way to grow plants, particularly in the seedling stage.

Recently a host of special plant lights have been developed. Their emission spectrum is more closely attuned to the plants' needs than that of regular fluorescent and eliminates the need for incandescent supplements. There is some debate about whether these lamps are worth their extra cost, however. My personal experience with Gro-Lux wouldn't induce me to invest a lot in them. Twice the tubes have suddenly ceased functioning after less than a month. Flukes, perhaps, but it still left me without recourse. Also their purple-plant-eater aspect left me cold. On the other hand, some people like the purple light because it supposedly makes their plants look lusher.

After my misfortune with Gro-Lux, I switched to Natur-escent tubes, manufactured by Duro-Lite. Originally called Optima, these tubes were developed to approximate natural light for use in the color-finicky textile industry. They not only produce a natural light, but come with a one-year guarantee, which I find comforting. As for results, my plants with their tops four to six inches below the tubes are all thriving. On the whole, growing tops can be no more than ten inches from the bulbs if you expect your plants to do well under fluorescent lights.

Whichever type of fluorescent tube you use, a fixture that holds less than two parallel is generally not worth using. It simply doesn't provide enough light. Four tubes are preferred for growing all but seedlings and the smallest plants.

I replace my Natur-escent bulbs roughly once a year, even though they are operative. Fluorescent lights lose some of their efficiency the day you begin to use them. After a year, or more than five thousand hours of use, they may have lost 25 to 50 percent of their efficiency, particularly at the ends of the tubes. Fluorescent lights expire slowly from the ends, the middle always remaining the brightest. This creeping shadow will progress about as rapidly in a tube forty-eight inches long as in, say, one twenty-four inches. So the longer one is much more efficient, which is why commercial establishments always use tubes forty-eight inches or longer. You should too if you have the room.

BOTTOM LIGHT FOR BETTER GROWTH

Another interesting observation that has recently come to light concerns the underside of the leaf. The majority of the stomata are located there, and it's the area that does most of the plant's "breathing." Interestingly enough, if this area is supplied with extra light—a quite unnatural proposition—the plant grows much better. Take soybeans, for instance. Using wide-spectrum fluorescent lights for twelve hours a day and white polyethylene reflective strips between the rows, Dr. J. W. Pendelton increased the yield of a batch of beans by as much as 30 percent. In similar tests on corn, using aluminum strips between the rows, yields were doubled.

This has caused me to switch to white quartz chips in the moisture trays beneath my lights. They are much more reflective than regular gravel. Incidentally, the quartz chips have also been shown to be inhospitable to fungi spores, which means they help reduce chances of disease. If you have pebble trays on your windowsill, using white chips instead of brown ones would similarly aid the plants' growth.

Another way to take advantage of plants' appreciation of bottom light is to place fluorescent bulbs vertically rather than in the traditional horizontal manner. Not only will this illuminate the undersides of the leaves as well as the tops, but it permits you to grow tall plants under lights—or should one say next to lights? Four four-foot tubes in a floor-to-ceiling formation can change a dark, unnoticed corner into a lush little paradise. Just remember, unlike plants grown under lights, plants grown beside them will have to be rotated, or they will always lean toward the corner.

timer Senecio
tropaeolifolius

Rhapis humilis

Dicksonia squarrosa

A vertical fluorescent light arrangement

THEY'RE HUNGRIER

All this accelerated growth through light optimization brings up another consideration, a ravenous appetite—meaning you should fertilize a bit more. As light levels are increased, the rate of photosynthesis will increase. Actually a single leaf cannot utilize light above some fifteen hundred footcandles, but some leaves are always shaded by others, which is why a plant as a whole thrives in a higher light intensity.

While it needs, and makes, more food, the plant will also utilize additional water. The stomata will be open longer, increasing transpiration, and in turn absorption of water by the roots. At the same time, if you're growing a number of plants under lights, the moisture in the atmosphere will increase, making the environment more beneficial for your plants—and you.

IN THE COLD OF THE NIGHT

The worldwide range of recorded temperatures goes from minus ninety-six degrees at Verkhoyansk, USSR, to one hundred thirty-six degrees at Azizia, Libya, a variation of over two hundred thirty degrees Fahrenheit. The minimum/maximum range of temperature that supports most plant growth is much smaller, less than sixty degrees, in fact, and is usually considered to fall between forty and ninety-eight degrees. That doesn't mean plants can't live outside this range, but to all intents and purposes they cease growing.

Most of a plant's growth processes show a quantitative relationship to the surrounding temperature. As it increases, so do the plant's respiration, photosynthesis, and even, in some cases, flowering and seed maturation. Optimum growth of a plant in relation to temperature depends on its place of origin. Plants from the tropics usually do well in the centrally overheated home, with an average daytime temperature of seventy-two degrees—usually, please note, but not always. There is a decrease of roughly three or four degrees in preferred temperature for every thousand feet in elevation to which the plants are accustomed. There may be a steamy ninety-degree jungle at sea level somewhere, yet at eleven thousand feet a few miles away the daytime temperature would be in the fifties, the nighttime temperature much lower. And for the plants living in the hill country, as, in fact, for most plants to some degree, the variation between night and day is crucial.

In general, plants grown under uniform temperature conditions develop neither as well nor as fast as those grown under alternating day and night temperatures. Looking back at the photosynthesis/respiration ratio, the reason becomes quite clear. On a warm day, photosynthesis is speeded up; the plant produces lots of food. During the cooler night, respiration slows down; the plant uses less of the energy it has stored up than it would otherwise. On balance, this leaves more food with which to build a bigger, healthier plant. Even plants such as dieffenbachias, philodendrons, and caladiums, that come from the steamy, almost equitemperatured lowlands of South America, will do better with a ten-degree drop in night temperatures. For instance, it's rare to see a dieffenbachia in bloom indoors, yet several people I know have coaxed theirs into flowering. My mother's bloomed some months after it spent a summer sitting in the backyard with night temperatures dropping by twenty degrees or more. From the other cases I've heard of, the drop in night temperature seems to be the decisive factor in flowering.

Then too, indoor temperatures in winter can vary as much as twenty degrees or more in the same room at the same time, from near the windowpanes to near the radiators. Get to know the cold and warm spots in your rooms—best learned with the aid of a thermometer—and place your plants according to their preferences.

ITCHY TRIGGER FINGERS AND LEAFY CACTI

Humidity is the amount of actual moisture per cubic foot of air—if you want to get really technical about it, it's expressed in grains of water, there being seven thousand grains to a pound. However, the amount of water that the air is capable of holding is not constant. It is directly related to the air temperature. The warmer the temperature, the more moisture the air can hold. Morning dew is caused by falling night temperatures. As the air cools, it is capable of holding less and less moisture. The excess precipitates out and falls to the ground.

What we and the plants are most interested in is relative humidity: the amount of water vapor in the air as a percentage of what the air could actually hold at that temperature. It can be measured with an inexpensive hygrometer. This instrument is usually composed of two thermometers; the bulb of one is covered by a wet cloth. The dry bulb gives you one reading, let's say seventy-six degrees. The wet bulb gives you a different reading, because as the water on the cloth evaporates, it cools the sensing bulb much as waving a wet washcloth in front of your face stirs up a cool breeze. Say the wet bulb gives you a reading of seventy-one degrees. Well, there's a chart that comes with the hygrometer, and by looking up the difference, five degrees, on the chart, you see that the relative humidity is 78 percent. On the other hand, if the wet bulb gives you a reading of fifty-eight degrees, the difference is eighteen degrees, indicating a relative humidity of 30 percent. Time to get out the old spray gun.

What you want to do is maintain around 50 percent relative humidity or better in your house. This usually means misting several times a day, placing your plants on pebble trays, and/or getting a humidifier. If it all sounds like too much work, remember it will not only give you more beautiful houseplants, but keep you healthier and make your belongings last longer as well.

Lack of moisture is not a problem solely of overheated winter rooms, as one might first think. Come summer and rising temperatures, the air is capable of holding that much more moisture. So although there might be as much water vapor as ever in the atmosphere, the relative humidity drops sharply.

The converse—the drop in the air's moisture-holding ability with lowered temperatures—means that if you keep your house at 50 to 70 percent relative humidity, you'll get frost on the *inside* of your windows come cold winter nights. Don't panic. It's not as chilly as it looks in the room when you peer out from under the blankets in the morning.

But what about my cacti? you ask. They're desert plants. Do I have to keep them in a separate, dry room? Well, yes and no. There really are no fixed rules when it comes to raising plants. The key is to be flexible in your thinking and care. Not only are plants quite adaptable, but they

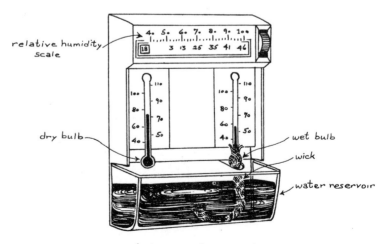

A typical hygrometer

sometimes react in the most unexpected ways. If one thing doesn't work, even if it's just the opposite of what you tried unsuccessfully before, all is not lost. Take Dr. De Werth's cacti, for instance. He's at Texas A & M University, which is exactly where an easterner would think of cacti growing naturally. So how does Dr. De Werth raise his cacti? In a green-house with close to constant 100 percent humidity. And how do they do? Swingingly. Not only are they thriving, but some of his cacti are even growing true leaves!

So get out that old spray gun and spray, spray, spray. When I had just a few plants, I used an old rinsed-out Windex bottle for spraying. It worked fine for cleaning the leaves and keeping moisture high in the one room the plants inhabited. When the forest expanded, I purchased a one-quart plastic sprayer made specifically for the purpose, and it served admirably for a while. (Those cute brass sprayers, incidentally, don't have enough water capacity to humidify a child's dollhouse.) Now I own a two-quart pump-up model—which is just as well, since these days I usually add a full quart of water to each room's atmosphere every day.

WATER BEDS

Another way of adding moisture to the air is with pebble trays. Radiators, almost invariably placed beneath the windows and thus perfect staging platforms for plants, are also too warm and dry for the purpose. However, by using moisture trays—many plant suppliers sell them—filled with an inch or so of quartz chips or gravel and water, on top of the radiators, you give the plants a double boost. A little of the heat pene-

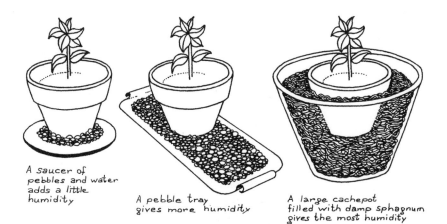

A saucer of pebbles and water adds a little humidity

A pebble tray gives more humidity

A large cachepot filled with damp sphagnum gives the most humidity

Raising the humidity for potted plants

trates into the pots; and plants with warm roots grow best. At the same time the warm water evaporates quickly, surrounding your green growth in a little cloud all its own.

While pebble trays are particularly efficient when placed on radiators, they will give the humidity a boost no matter where they are placed. The key to success in their use is to raise the water level to the point where it barely touches the pots—but only if evaporation will drop the level away from the pots within a few hours. If your air is so humid that the pot is touching the water for a whole day, put in less water the next time. Moisture trays are a good way to water plants from the bottom, but roots should never be exposed to standing water for a long time, or they will rot and kill the plants.

THOUGHTS ON TALKING TO YOUR PLANTS

There seems to be no doubt about the fact that being involved with your plants means they grow better. After all, if you make sure the humidity is high enough, never forget to water them, fertilize them well, and are constantly on the lookout for insect invasions, the plants are certainly going to do better than if you don't do these things. But what about talking to your plants, will that really help? Well, since you exhale carbon dioxide when you talk, and since the plants use carbon dioxide in the process of photosynthesis, as I'm sure you've figured out by now, yes, it will. Only, of course, if you converse with them during the daylight hours, when the process of photosynthesis is underway. Also it helps to get very intimate. At best you should be only six inches or so away from your leafy friend. And, oh yes, for real results, the monologue should proceed uninterrupted for four hours or more a day.

Pets, Pests, and Other Problems

If anybody ever finds a way to keep the household cat away from a plant he really likes, please let me know. And I don't mean with mothballs in the pot, or stone mulch, or growing some grass especially for the friendly feline, or tying dog hairs around the stem—I mean something that really works. My only solution to the problem so far consists of growing particularly spiny species of cacti on the sunny ledge that Adolphus used to prefer for sunbaths, and keeping all the more succulent—in the gourmet sense of the word—plants behind a closed door in my study. Hanging baskets also seem catproof until whatever's growing in them becomes really lush and long, and Adolphus particularly frisky.

Actually, plant pruning by pets—which is not unique to cats, but is undertaken by almost all domesticated animals from free-flying parakeets to sober Saint Bernards—is nowhere near as damaging as the preference of certain zoologic species for a twelve-inch pot containing *Phoenix roebelenii* over their regular unadorned litter box. Two or three binges are sometimes enough to cause the plant to expire. Remember, overfertilization is fatal.

THE CANNIBALS

Fungi, which are responsible for the majority of plant diseases, are themselves simple multicelled plants. However, these primarily microscopic, threadlike organisms lack chlorophyll, found in the higher plants, and thus cannot manufacture their own food. Except for mushrooms, perhaps, if you have a dark cool basement, fungi do not make good houseplants, since they tend to devour your more choice specimens of the larger variety.

Fortunately, most fungi seem to attack only plants grown outdoors: witness such problems as Dutch elm disease. Generally they prefer conditions more moist than human habitations usually offer. On the other hand, if you're bringing the relative moisture of your home up to the level plants love best, some fungi may decide to join the party.

ANTHRACNOSE is sometimes mentioned in discussions of houseplant afflictions. I just mention it here to cheer you up, because it's very unlikely that your plants will ever get it. Manifested on leaves by black to tan depressed spots with thin, darker margins. Sometimes the bottom of a spot falls out, so to speak, creating a Swiss-cheese effect. CURE: The same as for botrytis infestation.

BOTRYTIS infestation, not to be confused with brucitis, although humidity is a factor contributing to both, is a fungous disease that develops among poorly ventilated and overcrowded plants. It usually appears as a grayish mold and begins, contrary to what you might expect, on the top leaves of the plants rather than the more crowded lower ones. It spreads rapidly to all leaves and stems. One way to tell *Botrytis* infestation from other mildews is that it emigrates quickly to other plants. CURE: Isolate suspect specimens at once; pick off all infected leaves; cut back on water and fertilization; keep all water off the leaves; and make sure to wash your hands well before handling any other plants. *Botrytis* is particularly fond of gesneriads.

DAMPING OFF is a fungous disease that can be very common or almost unknown among your plants. It all depends on how you treat them. Basically, it affects only a young seedling. The plant develops a waist, or pinched stem, at soil level, then keels over and dies. CURE: There is none. Once the disease has hit a seedling, dispose of the plant. To avoid damping off, use sterilized soil when planting seedlings. Don't reuse the soil for a second batch, although you can use it to pot mature plants—and even then it wouldn't hurt to resterilize it.

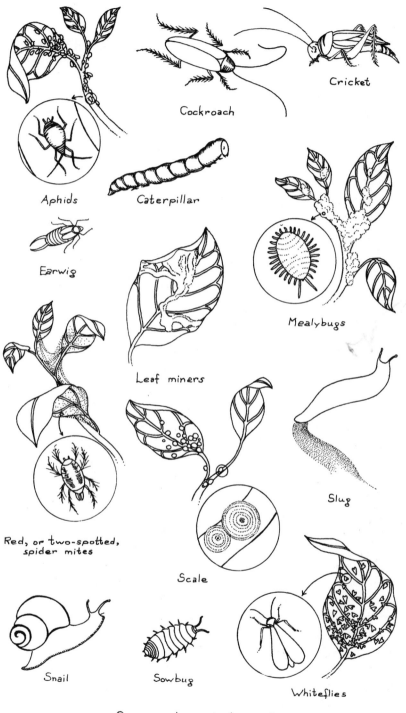

Aphids

Cockroach

Cricket

Caterpillar

Earwig

Mealybugs

Leaf miners

Red, or two-spotted, spider mites

Slug

Scale

Snail

Sowbug

Whiteflies

Common houseplant pests

POWDERY MILDEW is the most likely guest. It looks like bread mold ranging from white to black in color. It doesn't smell quite as strongly as the mildew normally found on, say, a pair of jeans left in the bilge of the sailboat for the better part of a month, simply because the leaf won't let it—remember chlorophyll toothpaste? CURE: The best for mildew is to cut off the infected part of the plant and discard it, then increase ventilation around your plants. And if you've been using plastic pots, consider switching to clay ones; plastic pots foster mildew. Even at 100 percent humidity, mildew should not develop if air circulation is good.

Various molds and mildews are often spread by insects. If you should be visited with an aphid infestation, for instance, check for fungi as a second wave of attackers after the first are dispersed.

Fungi are much more easily avoided than eliminated. Most of them, in fact, will remain dormant on "cured" plants, waiting for conditions to improve for them. Give the plants good ventilation, clear away dead and dying leaves, and you should have no problems. The best treatment for a severely infected plant, however, is to dispose of it, and quickly. There are fungicides on the market, but frankly I don't think they are worth their potential hazard to yourself or your family or even pets. If you do want to try them, the manufacturers supply instructions. I'd rather not.

NEMATODE MACRAME

Nematodes are nonsegmented worms, as opposed to earthworms, which are segmented. They are also a lot smaller than even your run-of-the-mill night crawler, being barely macroscopic. Usually they range in length from a sixteenth to an eighth of an inch, and their presence is often spotted only as a result of their damage.

Most common indoor nematode problems arise from root knot nematodes, which make the roots of your plants look like a macrame kit after the cat got hold of it. The root tissue, particularly those cells involved in water transportation, becomes disorganized. Large gall-like growths, or knots, develop. Sometimes supersized cells are formed, but in all cases the roots' ability to supply water to the plant is impaired. The aboveground symptoms of root knot nematodes therefore are similar to those of underwatering: excessive wilting, weak droopy growth, a yellowed look.

In all probability your plants will never acquire nematodes. Which is good, since there's no cure for them. Also they are as infectious as a sixth-grader's cold. Merely brushing the soil of one pot with the tip of the watering can and then grazing the next pot with it can spread the worms. The best policy is to avoid nematodes altogether by using only sterilized soil in your pots.

INSECT INVADERS FRIENDLY AND NOT SO

The amazing thing about raising plants on a sixteenth-story windowsill is the number of six-legged visitors that are continuously streaming in and out. An aphid invasion is one thing; after all, they can arrive easily on a newly bought plant, even with the best of screening. But what about the ladybugs? I mean, sixteen floors, that's wing power. Yet every spring a few of them drop by my plants to check out the aphid situation—and leave for greener pastures.

Not all insects are bad for your plants. The ladybugs, for instance, eat up smaller sucking insects drawn to your lush plantation. And fungus gnats, those diminutive but slightly lighter-looking fruit-fly-like insects that like to hang around particularly moist pots, are mostly neutral. They really do nothing for or against your plants except spread the disease of their name if it's already present. Springtails, minute wingless insects that jump about by means of a snapping jackknife-like tail, come to the surface of the soil when watered. They hop about a lot, but rarely harm anything besides seedlings, whose roots they may weaken. Other insects, however, are not so benign. In alphabetical order follow the most common malefactors.

APHIDS like to hang around together on the tender new growing shoots of plants. They are pear-shaped insects, either with or without wings, in a variety of colors including green, black, yellow, and even pink. If you have a magnifying glass, they are somewhat amusing to watch, since they stand on their heads as they suck the juice out of the plants. Unfortunately, the effect of their imbibing on the plants is less amusing. Leaves curl, the younger ones drop off, and buds are often malformed. The key to recognizing aphids is the honeydew, or shiny, sticky secretion they deposit on the leaves that remain. Aphids find cooler-habitat plants such as pelargoniums and ivies particularly tasty, and usually do not affect tropical varieties to any great extent. CURE: Wash off affected areas with soapy water. Don't use detergents. Hold the plant on its side or upside down, so the insects won't be washed into the soil. Rubbing alcohol in a small mister also works well.

The alcohol literally desiccates the aphids on contact. Make sure you spray the undersides of the leaves and leaf joints well. Rinse with a plain-water spraying after half an hour.

CATERPILLARS add a nice lush look to the plants, I told myself when I first spotted one crawling across my windowsill plantation. The next morning I noticed a number of chewed-over leaves on the plants and remembered those high-school stories about the silk industry being dependent on mulberry leaves to feed the caterpillars. Obviously my caterpillar was less choosy. CURE: Pick the caterpillars off by hand as soon as you spot them.

COCKROACHES are primarily an urban problem. Although not discussed in polite society, many of even the ritziest apartments in New York, for instance, have them. They prefer succulent plants, nibbling around the juicy edges of the leaves. When we first moved into our apartment they were quite a nuisance. Then our chatty window cleaner mentioned an old home remedy. CURE: Boric acid solution (one tablespoonful dissolved in a quart of boiling water) in little dishes on top of cupboards where neither pets nor children can reach them. Haven't seen a roach since. Problem is, you have to keep filling up the dishes.

CRICKETS are country cousins of the cockroaches, although socially much more acceptable—so much more so, in fact, that I've known people who catch crickets for their terrariums to supply evening serenades. An innocent enough project until you realize that crickets eat the plants, particularly new growth. CURE: Don't bring any home unless you feel like keeping them in Chinese cricket cages. If by chance a few stray nocturnal fiddlers invade your territory, eject them by hand.

EARWIGS are rarely attracted to houseplants. Even then they are a problem primarily along the Coastal South. On the other hand, I received a range-grown orchid shipment from a reputable Florida grower whose color catalog is the fanciest in the industry that was jumping with not only earwigs, but assorted millipedes, centipedes, and other insects not normally associated with indoor plants. CURE: Handpicking is the best solution, even for earwigs with those pincerlike rear ends. They are best caught by turning on the lights at night when they're frolicking about. Or by submerging the pot in water, which drives any hidden ones into the lifeboats.

LEAF MINERS are the larvae of certain flies, moths, and beetles that all manifest themselves in the same way on your plants, digging long slender winding trails and tunnels between the upper and lower parts of the leaves by eating their way along. Not really a major problem.

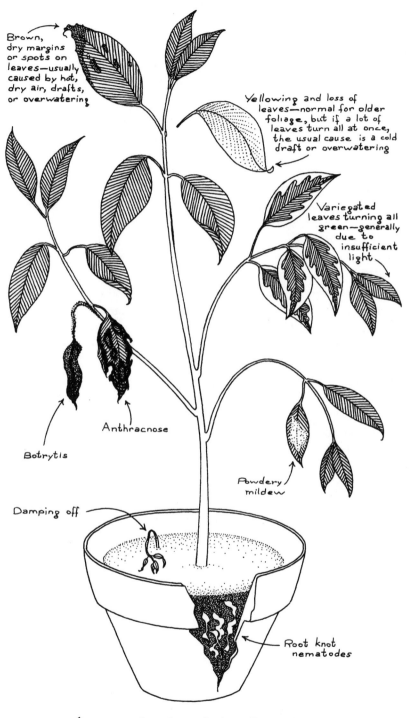

Brown, dry margins or spots on leaves—usually caused by hot, dry air, drafts, or overwatering

Yellowing and loss of leaves—normal for older foliage, but if a lot of leaves turn all at once, the usual cause is a cold draft or overwatering

Variegated leaves turning all green—generally due to insufficient light

Anthracnose

Botrytis

Powdery mildew

Damping off

Root knot nematodes

A composite of a plant with problems

Nevertheless, they sometimes go after the gesneriads. CURE: Pick off affected leaves.

MEALYBUGS are a classic indoor pest. Look like tiny fuzzy pieces of white cotton wool. Found usually at the nodes and leaf axils, these insects live by sucking plant sap. The plant becomes stunted, leaves yellow and wither. CURE: Swab away, using a cotton puff soaked in alcohol. The insects' white fuzz is alcohol-soluble wax, making this treatment more efficient than soap and water. Severely infested plants should be washed completely in soap and water afterward as well, however. A commercial spray I've found effective is Ced-o-flora. Made from a petroleum suspension of cedar and hemlock, it is quite poisonous. However, its action is short-lived and ceases with the insects, and the mixture is truly poisonous only when swallowed. Still, I never use it in a room where the kids or pets will be that day. As a rule I save it for my most stubborn cases of mites.

MITES are probably the greatest insect problem for houseplants—only they aren't really insects. Insects belong to the class Hexapoda and all have six jointed legs. Mites are eight-legged, making them members of the Arachnida, or spider class. However, since they are less than a hundredth of an inch long, that may be leg picking. You'll never really see the mites, just their handiwork, a fine misty cobweb. Usually it starts on the leaves' undersides and spreads to the joints. Mildly infected leaves get small yellow spots; eventually they turn dry and brown, and drop. Plants with severe, although still not necessarily highly visible, infections become stunted, with leaves curled, stems twisted, and generally malformed. There are several varieties of mites: the broad and cyclamen mites are the most common under cool, moist growing conditions; the two-spotted, or red, spider mites go for a dry, hot climate. I'm sure there are some that like it cool and dry, some that like it moist and hot as well, but I haven't discovered which they are yet. CURE: Ced-o-flora spray works fine on smooth-leaved plants. The fuzzy-leaved gesneriads, which are very popular with mites, present another problem: the spray often forms a thin film on the fine hairs and does not penetrate onto the leaf surface itself. Recently *African Violet Magazine* has suggested dipping the plants in a one-hundred-ten-degree solution of three tablespoons Fels Naphtha per gallon of water. Just to show you there's nothing like home cooking, it works.

SCALE insects are number two on the most-unpopular-pest list, with a strong preference for leathery-leaved plants. They cling to stems or the undersides of leaves and are protected by a scalelike shield. This waxy shield, about an eighth of an inch long, is similar to the fuzz of the mealybug except that in this case the wax forms a hard coat, making it more difficult to dislodge. Leaves become stunted and very often sticky to the touch. CURE: Hard-leaved plants can be brushed off with an old soft toothbrush and soapy water. Alcohol or Ced-o-flora works well on the softer ones.

SLUGS, slimy snails without shells, and SNAILS, slimy slugs with calcareous shells into which they withdraw when disturbed, are both relatively rare on houseplants except in the South. When they appear, however, their appetites make up for lost time. Like most insects, these mollusks are particularly fond of tender new leaves. They are midnight raiders and sometimes hard to spot during the day, when they hide between pot and saucer, buried among damp pebbles, etc. CURE: Stale beer. Pour out a saucerful and let it stand next to the plants for a few nights. Slugs and snails are inveterate tipplers, with the benefit to you that they get soused quickly, topple right into the saucer, and drown. Dry instant mashed potatoes also work if the mollusks' appetite is so inclined. They gorge themselves, the mash swells up in their gullets, rupturing them and killing the pests.

SOW BUGS are crustaceans, which puts them in the same category as lobsters and crabs. Unfortunately, they lack the same culinary advantages. Not really harmful, since their main interest lies in dead organic matter. However, they sometimes get carried away and devour roots and stems of seedlings as well. CURE: Handpick or spray with Ced-o-flora.

WHITEFLIES are the last of the big three when it comes to pests. Only a sixteenth of an inch long, these tropical insects can be very persistent. As soon as you approach the plant, they take flight, forming a thin white haze around your greenery. This makes spraying a task even Annie Oakley would find difficult. The young nymphs suck plant juices from the underside of the leaves, leaving a sticky honeydew in exchange. This in turn attracts various fungi, and sooty mold in particular. Leaves on infected plants turn yellow and drop off. CURE: Soapy-water dip for the whole plant. Spraying with rotenone or pyrethrum, both plant derivatives that act as contact insecticides, yet are of relatively low toxicity to humans and pets, may be necessary as a follow-up in extreme cases. Both are deadly for fish, however, and very water-soluble. Do not spray in a room with an aquarium.

SO WHAT'S REALLY BUGGING MY PLANTS?

Notice a certain similarity among the symptoms of various pests: leaves turning yellow and dropping off, stunted growth, sticky surfaces? Well, how do you know for sure which is which? Frankly, even experienced horticulturists sometimes come up with the wrong diagnosis, so why shouldn't you? And in many cases a plant weakened enough to have one pest has a second as well. What you can do is tell that there's definitely something infecting it. Well then, if you're not sure what, spray with alcohol, then give the plant a good dip in a soap solution. Nine times out of ten this combination will cure the plant.

If it doesn't, there are two other solutions: As hard as it may be to do, dispose of the infected plant. Or, the other solution, use a systemic poison—which is rather like hunting rabbits by placing a dynamite stick in every hole the meadow has.

SYSTEMICS ARE FOR SUCKERS

Systemics poison an entire plant from roots to buds. Any part any bug or pet or child may ingest for six months or more after application can be fatal. What more can one say? When trying to maintain the only two known specimens of a species in a conservatory, using systemic poisons may be justified. But in no way can the same be said for keeping a saintpaulia in the home.

Interestingly enough, many of the new superpesticides are not only extremely dangerous, but in the long range self-defeating. Take, for instance, Benlate, a popular systemic fungicide. The manufacturer, in a letter to *The Avant Gardener,* states: "We are aware that there are tolerant strains that exist in natural populations of several fungi. It appears that some compounds may have the capacity for modifying strain patterns in the population and in some cases these tolerant strains have become dominant in the population." * In other words, the poison worked for a while, but now the bugs love it. We'll try to come up with something else to sell you for next season. As a last thought on systemics, they will kill all ferns and most bromeliads on contact.

---

* Letter from E.I. du Pont de Nemours & Co., *The Avant Gardener,* Vol. V, No. 18 (July 1, 1973), p. 141.

A HEALTHY PLANT IS THE BEST REVENGE

Plants growing under good conditions, given the right amount of water and fertilizers, will thrive. And it is very rare that a thriving plant becomes infested. When it does, usually the new growth, the most weak and tender, is the part afflicted.

For this reason, assuming that your plants are healthy, always isolate newly acquired plants for at least a couple of weeks. This serves two functions. First, it gives them a bit of time to adjust to their new environment. Like the New York executive who flies to Tokyo and suffers from time lag, newly moved plants are a bit exhausted, making them that much more susceptible to insect problems. Second, and more obviously, it gives you a chance to investigate the plants closely for any signs of infestation.

Healthy plants also means clean plants. Pick off dead leaves, remove any decaying organic matter. Use only sterilized soil—you can sterilize your own by baking it on cookie sheets for three or four hours at two hundred degrees Fahrenheit. When you reuse pots, be sure to disinfect them by first scrubbing well with soap and water, then soaking for half an hour in a solution of a fourth of a cup of Clorox to each quart of water.

As a last thought, join your local botanical garden association. Not only will you be supporting a very worthwhile cause, but you won't feel you're imposing when you call them up about the lavender spots on your aspidistra.

Long
May They
Multiply

One of the most enjoyable facets of growing houseplants is growing more of them. What I have in mind is not going out and purchasing *Iresine herbstii* to add some red to your foliage group or *Exacum affine* to perfume your boudoir, but starting from scratch, so to speak. Most houseplants propagate readily, with or without sex. The new plants so bred are usually better adapted to the culture in your home than any others. They also, at least for me, provide the most pleasure. As an extra plus, not only are they about as inexpensive a way to build up a collection as imaginable, particularly if you trade specimens with friends, but in most cases they are simplicity itself.

Given a chance, houseplants multiply with a vengeance. A single orchid flower may produce over a million seeds, all technically capable of becoming mature plants. As for vegetative reproduction, the numbers can be equally mind boggling. In nature the majority of new plants do not survive; it is in order to assure continuation of the species that there are so many of them. Another reason why they are so much more prolific than, say, cats or people, is that reproduction affords the immobile plants a way to disperse their numbers over a larger geographic area.

Take *Iresine herbstii*, for instance. For one reason or another it was not available in New York City stores for a couple of years. Yet almost everyone I know in the city is growing it. I received mine as a cutting from a friend. One day after dinner he cut two six-inch pieces off and handed them to me as I was walking out the door. At home I plopped them unceremoniously into a glass of water with some charcoal in the bottom. Two weeks later, the roots had developed enough to be planted and I potted them. A couple of months after that, I gave some cuttings of mine to a friend. She in turn later gave some cuttings to one of her friends. The clincher came a few years later when I met my *I. herbstii* at a party thrown by a stranger living at the other end of town. Seems he'd been given a cutting by a friend who'd received hers from a friend who'd . . . and so on, until when I was through inquiring about who got what where it turned out that about ten cuttings back the plant had sat comfortably in our dining room window. Ours, as you know, had come from. . . .

IT ONLY TAKES ONE TO TANGO

Although the vast majority of plant species growing throughout the world today are of the flowering variety, which reproduce sexually, this form of propagation is a relatively recent development in botanical evolution. All the primitive plants multiplied vegetatively. Many of the more complex plants still retain this ability as a backup system. Although it does not permit the genetic mixing that is the basis of evolutionary development, vegetative reproduction is a simpler, more certain way of assuring continuation of a species. It is also the easiest way to multiply your houseplants.

All houseplants are either gymnosperms or angiosperms, except for ferns, which reproduce by spores instead of seeds. (Until you become a fairly experienced indoor gardener, propagate your ferns vegetatively; it's much easier.) Gymnosperms produce seeds that one could consider poorly packaged, since they have no protective coating. Only conifers, rarely grown indoors except as bonsai, and cycads belong to the gymnosperm group. Neither is usually propagated at home.

This leaves angiosperms, plants whose seeds are protected by a hard outer armor permitting them temporarily to survive conditions unsuitable for germination. Angiosperms are once more divided into two large groups: monocotyledons and dicotyledons.

The most advanced plants, in the sense of being the most highly specialized, are monocots. Roughly fifty thousand species in number, monocots have a single seed leaf, *the leaf veins are typically parallel,* and they do not reproduce well from cuttings. Asexual reproduction of these is usually limited to division and root propagation of one kind or another. Houseplants of the monocot variety include primarily orchids, palms, and bamboos, as well as the various bulbs.

Dicots, of which there are roughly two hundred thousand species, including most houseplants, have two seed leaves and true leaves more complex in shape with *veins forming fanlike networks* or herringbone. Almost all dicots can be propagated from cuttings in one fashion or another.

The difference in propagative abilities between monocots and dicots is dependent on several factors. Primarily it is due to the difference in stem structure. Dicots have a central core surrounded by a woody portion in which the plant's vascular tubes, or "plumbing" system, are concentrated. In woody plants the outer layer forms a bark; on herbaceous plants it is less distinct. But its convenient location on the outside means that when you stick a cutting in water or a rooting medium, the growing surface is continuously in contact with the "soil" and prone to turn its energies into roots. Monocotyledons, on the other hand, have a much more uniform stem structure, with the vascular bundles scattered throughout the stem in what appears to be a random fashion. Since adventitious roots usually develop near vascular bundles close to the stem's outer surface, and since there are fewer of these in monocots, they are much less likely to root. But—just to prove there are no absolute rules in horticulture—the bamboo *Bambusa multiplex,* a monocot, will root cuttings like there's no tomorrow. This is also the primary commercial method of propagating the vanilla orchid.

PARDON ME, YOUR SLIP IS SHOWING

All of us, at one time or another, have seen a rooting or slip cutting from a plant sitting in a glass of water on someone's windowsill. Or we have placed willow or forsythia in a vase and watched it take root. Propagation by cuttings is one of the earliest and most important methods of plant reproduction developed by man. It is inexpensive, simple, and rapid, requires no special techniques or tools, and, most important economically, means the offspring are always true to parentage.

Cuttings are usually divided into three types: hardwood, softwood, and herbaceous. Most tropical houseplants fall into the herbaceous category, being plants without noticeable bark. The difference between herbaceous and softwood plants is relatively unimportant to the indoor gardener, since both types will propagate readily. The point to keep in mind, however, is that the thin-walled herbaceous cuttings are more prone to dehydration damage, so care must be taken that they do not dry out.

Desiccation is one of the few things that can go wrong with rooting slips—which is why grandma rooted hers in a glass of water. Lately that technique has fallen out of favor because when the plants are transferred to soil, after having developed half a dozen or more roots about an inch long, they take awhile to get a new footing. Supposedly this is because roots that develop in water are different from those sprouting in soil. From my own observations, I think it's not so much a difference in root structure itself as the relative absence of hair roots in water-started plants. In any case, being a very successful method of rooting for some people, if not so for others, slips in water are well worth a try. Begonias, cissus, coleus, crassulas, dracaenas, gardenias, hederas, iresines, pelargoniums, philodendrons, scindapsus, syngoniums, and tolmieas are a few of the many houseplants that will root in water almost as readily as willows.

Speaking of willows, recent experimentation by Dr. Makoto Kawase at the Ohio Agricultural Research and Development Center in Wooster has shown that willows release a strong rooting agent into the water. The substance is as yet unidentified, but appears to be more powerful than indoleacetic acid, the traditional rooting hormone sold under such brand names as Hormodin and Rootone. So don't empty the vase in which you've been keeping your spring willows into the sink. Save the water for slips.

An important factor in a cutting's ability to root is the nutritional status of the donor plant. If you take your cutting from a healthy plant in vigorous growth, its chances are much greater than if you take one from a stunted plant in dormancy. That's certainly simple enough to arrange. The master key to successful slip rooting, be it in water, soil, or other medium, is to take cuttings in the spring while the parent plant is literally bursting out all over. Cuttings taken early in the morning will do better than those taken later in the day, when the stomata are fully open, leaving the slip more susceptible to wilting. Also,

CUTTINGS FOR EASY ROOTING

Achimenes	*Monstera*
Begonia	*Nautilocalyx*
Capsicum	*Pelargonium*
Cissus	*Peperomia*
Coleus	*Philodendron*
Columnea	*Pilea*
Crassula	*Pittosporum*
Dieffenbachia	*Plectranthus*
Dizygotheca	*Podocarpus*
Dracaena	*Rhoeo*
Ficus	*Saintpaulia*
Fittonia	*Schefflera*
Gesneria	*Scindapsus*
Gynura	*Sedum*
Hedera	*Sinningia*
Hoya	*Smithiantha*
Iresine	*Tradescantia*
Kalanchoë	*Zebrina*
Kohleria	

it's interesting to note that a cutting's propensity for rooting is affected by its prior location on the donor plant: lateral shoots, those branching off a growing stem, tend to take better than a terminal one or the growing stem itself. At the same time, vegetative shoots will do better than flowering ones. And those that snap off crisply will set better roots than their more flexible siblings. All of these facets are interrelated by the hormonal and nutritional flow within the plant itself. A crisp stem, for instance, indicates a higher concentration of carbohydrates, which means the cutting has more self-contained nourishment and can thus devote its energies to rooting rather than staying alive. What such factors mean to you and your plant propagation is that if you do all the right things your chances of success are probably about nine out of ten; if for some reason you decide to do them all wrong, the odds are still at least better than fifty-fifty. Propagation by stem cuttings is an easy-to-do, fun-to-watch project for everyone, including the children. To be almost assured of success, just remember to take two cuttings.

Rooting an angel-wing begonia cutting in water

THE PROLIFIC CUT

To take a cutting, select a healthy shoot with good growth, preferably one that is developing well but not yet fully matured. Cut it off four to five inches from the tip and just below a node, or joint. Ideally the cut should be made with a sterile knife—scissors tend to pinch the stem closed a bit more when you are dealing with soft plants—but for two or three cuttings sterility is far from necessary. No one has ever accused my pocketknife of being sterile. Sharp, yes, but sterile. . . . However, sterilizing is an extra precaution you might want to take. Dipping in alcohol is totally ineffective; the blade must be flame sterilized if you are going to do it at all.

A cutting is essentially a plant without roots. Transpiration, or water loss, will be much greater than water absorption. After all, the missing root system is what absorbs water. To put the new plant more in balance, remove the lowest pair of leaves. This will reduce transpiration proportionately. It will also keep leaves away from the damp rooting medium, where they might rot.

BE CALLOUS WITH CACTI AND PELARGONIUMS

When a cutting is taken from a plant, a callus forms over the wound if it is left exposed to air. This callus is composed of undifferentiated cells that grow after the cut is made. Since the earliest root formation frequently occurs at the callus growth, the latter has come to be assumed somehow necessary for rooting. It is not. But permitting a callus to form before planting slow-growing succulents such as cacti and pelargoniums, or any other species that exude a heavy sap after cutting, is in fact a good idea, for quite another reason. It helps avoid rotting.

The time it takes for calluses to develop on cuttings left lying unplanted varies from overnight, in the case of pelargoniums, to three or four days, in cacti. You want the cut to be dry before planting.

Herbaceous plants, on the other hand, must be stuck into the rooting medium immediately. If they dry out, *c'est fini.*

THE FOOTING

A rooting medium must provide sufficient moisture and oxygen. Since sterility is an advantage and because nutrients are not so necessary until roots are established, cuttings, except those from deciduous hardwoods, are not normally stuck straight into soil. On the other hand, as with everything else in horticulture, it doesn't hurt to try doing things a different way. I tend to root a lot of herbaceous cuttings directly into small soil-filled pots. When I do so, I've found that placing a slip close to the pot's edge, rather than in the middle of the pot where it aesthetically belongs, seems to give root growth a boost. Probably this is due to the freer flow of oxygen at the pot's perimeter.

Sand, the sharp builder's variety, is probably the oldest and still most common rooting medium. It provides excellent aeration and drainage. However, its moisture-retaining quality is poor; cuttings rooting in sand need more frequent watering than those in other media. To counteract this, 30 to 50 percent of milled sphagnum moss is often added to act as a sponge.

Perhaps the easiest of the rooting media are perlite and vermiculite. Both hold water in sufficient quantities to ensure rooting. Both are sterile, at least to horticultural tolerances, and both are readily available. While I'm at the "both" stage, vermiculite and particularly perlite dust are quite irritating. Avoid inhaling them. On an overall basis, I prefer vermiculite to perlite as a rooting medium, mostly because the glaring whiteness of perlite offends my aesthetic sense. If you use vermiculite, however, try not to handle it too much. It is compressible, and as it compacts its water-holding quality is reduced.

THE JELL-O MOLD

There are several options open when it comes to containers for rooting plants. For easy-to-root species, the simplest procedure is to wrap the bottom of the cutting along with some moist vermiculite or moss in a plastic bag. Prop the bundle up in a bright but not sunny spot and wait till roots form. Then pot as you would a transplant.

The bag method will give you even moisture, but scores low on aeration. A propagation setup that scores high on both counts, and is more or less self-tending besides, is the old clay-pot Jell-O mold. Take a small pot, plug up the bottom with a cork. Put it in the middle of a large three-quarters pot filled with rooting medium. The little pot is your storage reservoir. Fill it with water, and it will keep the potting medium, say vermiculite or sand, moist to just the right degree. Pre-

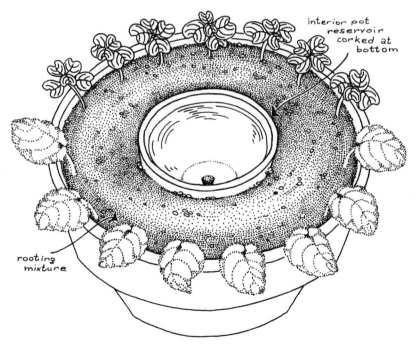

A self-tending propagation pot

moisten the whole affair before you plant the cuttings. The double-pot setup works well with thick-leaved waxy plants like begonias, hederas, peperomias, philodendrons, and scindapsus, as well as the succulents. Juicier plants may run into dehydration problems.

THE BREADBOX GREENHOUSE

Most soft cuttings and thin-leaved plants, even with their lower leaves removed to cut down on transpiration, still lose considerably more water than their rootless stems can absorb. It is important to keep them from wilting, because in extreme cases they will never recover.

Commercial growers use a misting system to keep humidity at 100 percent in their cutting rooms. You can keep your slips at full humidity by putting them in a clear plastic box with a top. There are even inexpensive special propagation boxes made for the purpose. These have small twist ventilators on top. Since stale, mold-fostering air is the major problem with propagation enclosures, the ventilators can be a great aid. Another way of aiding circulation is to remove the top for a few minutes in the morning and evening. But if you do, make sure to check that your cutting medium doesn't dry out.

If you use a propagation box, and besides the professional model, this might be anything from a breadbox to a shoe storage box to a refrigerator crisper as long as it is clear, you must use a sterile growing medium—and use it only once. Also, since there will be no drainage from the box, the degree to which you initially moisten the mix becomes crucial.

Pour in about two inches worth of, say, vermiculite. Then spray with water, and spray and spray until the water starts collecting in puddles on the bottom. Pick up the pan and look up at it from underneath. Tip the box in all four directions till the water comes close to spilling out. Once you're sure the vermiculite is thoroughly wet, drain off the excess water. Stick your cuttings, the more the merrier as long as they are not actually touching each other, about an inch deep into the rooting medium, and for best rooting results put the propagation box in a bright but not sunny spot where the temperature hovers around seventy-five degrees. You can pull the slips up in about a week and check for roots. If they are less than an inch long, just wriggle the stems back in. Vermiculite is so light the plant roots won't incur any damage from your dipstick checking.

An even simpler way to utilize a propagation box is to use a Jiffy-7 for each individual cutting. The Jiffy-7s are compressed peat wafers that expand into pellets seven times as thick as the original when exposed to water. Soak one, squeeze the pellet to remove excess water, then poke a hole with a pencil and insert the cutting. The wafers are sterile and easy to use, and they give each cutting an individual growing plug that is transferred whole to a pot once growth is well underway, thus eliminating transplant shock. Like any other convenience item, they can run into money, but not that much, and if you buy them in thousand-unit lots with friends or through a plant club, the cost is insignificant. Don't let that number, a thousand, scare you either. Usually you can buy a thousand in bulk for the same price as two hundred a handful at a time, and two hundred really don't last that long.

HUFF AND PUFF

A convenient, individual propagation box for each cutting in a Jiffy-7 pellet can be made from a plastic bag. I put the pelletized cutting in the bag; then I blow up the bag—this adds a little carbon dioxide as well—twirl and fold the top, and seal it with a wire twist. A self-supporting minigreenhouse in the best modern air-structure architecture.

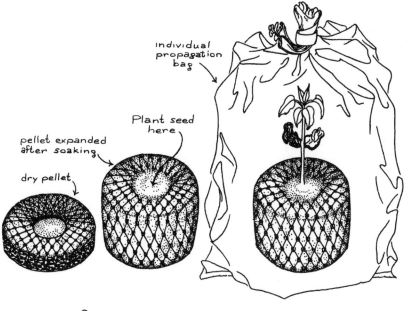

Individual propagation bag

Plant seed here

pellet expanded after soaking

dry pellet

Germinating seeds in expanding pellets

Whether you use the small single-occupancy or the multifamily propagation box, be sure not to place it in direct sun for more than a few minutes a day, or you will have steamed vegetables instead of new plants. Fluorescent lighting is ideal for rooting cuttings. Avoiding heat, it still produces enough light for good development if the cuttings are placed only a few inches below the tubes.

THE PROLIFIC PETIOLE

The leaf petiole is the stem that holds the leaf to the plant. Almost all herbaceous houseplants can be forced to grow new plantlets from the point where petiole and leaf join, or in some cases from the petiole itself.

Cut off a healthy leaf in its prime. Trim the petiole if necessary so it is no longer than an inch. Then bury it in the rooting medium just deep enough so that the leaf itself does not quite touch the surface. Whole new plants, several of them, will form on the petiole near the cut or at the juncture in less than a month. Most gesneriads will propagate readily this way, as will *Begonia rex*, crassulas, hoyas, peperomias, and tolmieas.

If you cut the petiole off almost entirely and halfway bury the leaf, results may be quicker. Also, using short petioles, which forces the plantlets to develop right at the petiole-leaf junction, is supposed to increase the chances of mutation. I haven't propagated enough plants by petiole cuttings to find any notable mutants yet.

VARIATIONS ON A LEAF

Propagating by leaf sections is a lot of fun. It's on the same principle as using a whole leaf, but somehow it's hard to believe it works, so when it does—and that's most of the time—I get a big kick out of it.

The easiest plant of all to propagate by bits of leaves is sansevieria. Cut a leaf off and chop it into two- to four-inch sections. Let them lie overnight until the sap has dried, forming calluses. Then bury the sections halfway in a rooting medium. New plants develop from the chopped pieces usually in less than a month. The cuttings themselves do not become part of the new plants, but merely hang on during development like a placenta. Other succulents easily propagated from individual leaves include crassulas, kalanchoës, and sedums. All succu-

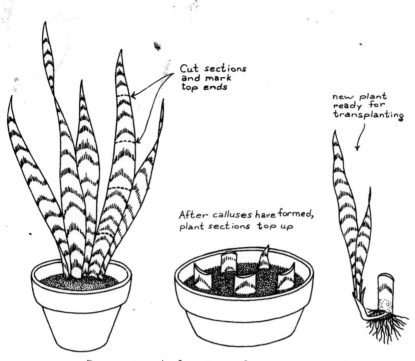

Cut sections and mark top ends

new plant ready for transplanting

After calluses have formed, plant sections top up

Propagating leaf sections of sansevieria

lents root best in relatively dry sand and an uncovered propagation box or pot. Covered succulents tend to rot.

Thick fleshy leaves such as those of sinningias, streptocarpus, and rhizomatous begonias can also be propagated by wound cuttings. Turn a big healthy leaf upside down and make small cuts through the large veins at several points just below where they branch. Then turn the leaf back over and lay it down on some wet rooting medium. I find a sand and sphagnum moss mix works best because it's easier to pin the leaf down to it firmly. Pinning is done with ordinary straight pins, serving merely to anchor the leaf. New plants will form at most of the cuts. But keep the propagating leaves closed off under 90 to 100 percent humidity and give them bright, though not direct, sunlight.

Carving further, you can slice these leaves up as you did the sansevieria, except that in this case, since you're dealing with rounded leaves rather than oblong ones, you'll be making pie-shaped, or wedge, cuts. Be sure each wedge has at least one major vein running through it. Bury the tips of the wedges and cover the box. Some will take root, some will shrivel and die. Still, it's possible to get as many as half a dozen plants or more from a single leaf, so you shouldn't lack for plants even if all of them don't take.

WHICH END UP?

Lest you forget which end of the leaf, particularly the sansevieria, was "up" on the parent plant, mark it somehow. For the plant knows. The phenomenon, called polarity, affects stem as well as leaf cuttings, though you're not so apt to make a mistake with the stems. Pieces of a plant will consistently form roots at the end that was nearest the crown of the plant and shoots at the end nearest the tip. Stems show the greatest polarity, that of leaves is considerably weaker. Also, if the new roots and leaves emerge from more or less the same region of a cutting, the influence of polarity will be minimized. Even so, sansevieria, for one, roots better if it's not standing on its head.

CHIMERA

Variegated peperomias and sansevierias will produce plain green plantlets when propagated from leaf cuttings. The plants are chimeric. I used to think chimeras were limited to Greek goats with heads of lions and tails of dragons. But these plants really are composite, a mutation of two genetically distinct types. Specifically, they are known as periclinal chimeras. They have the skin, several cell layers thick, of one plant and the interior of quite a different one. Some of the cells in the outer skin lack the ability to produce chlorophyll, and this gives the plants their variegated appearance. However, since the adventitious shoots and roots that develop to form new plants in leaf cuttings arise only from the inner tissue, you end up with plain green plants—ones that have literally jumped out of their skin.

OUT IN THE CRUEL CRUEL WORLD

Young plantlets that have been coddled within high-humidity propagation boxes or poly bags do not take well to being thrust out into the more hostile environment of your home. What they need is an acclimation period. If they don't get it, they will usually keel over and die the first day they are removed from their protected surroundings.

Like a diver coming up from the depths slowly to avoid the bends, a plantlet is removed from a covered propagation box in stages. I usually put the top on crooked for a day, leaving an eighth to a quarter of an inch crack. The second day I make the chink half an inch or so; the third, a full inch; the fifth day I take the new plants out and pot them properly.

RUNNING AWAY WITH IT

Some plants that develop crowns have the ability to send out aerial stems from the leaf axis at this base. The aerial stems are called runners, and they produce plantlets. The most familiar and tasty representative of this phenomenon is the strawberry. Several common houseplants have the same characteristic, making their propagation very simple. Either you can cut the young plants off and root them the same way you would cuttings, or you can let nature take its course, which is what I usually do. Put a pot under the plantlet and anchor the plantlet down lightly with a hairpin, leaving the runner attached until the new roots are well established. Only then cut the runner, close to the plantlet. It will give you sturdier plants more quickly. *Chlorophytum elatum, Nephrolepis exaltata, Saxifraga sarmentosa*, and assorted episcias are examples of houseplants easily and commonly propagated from runners.

The initiation of runners is often photoperiodically controlled. If

Propagating runners of episcia

your plants refuse to run, check to be sure they get less than twelve hours of daylight in winter and more than fourteen in spring.

Offsets, also variously known as suckers, ratoons, and crown divisions, are more or less the same thing as runners, except that the young plant-lets don't travel as far from mother and usually are attached underground. Some crop up right at the base of the original plant, forming, as in the case of the saintpaulias, multiple crowns. Common houseplants that can be propagated by offsets are agaves, aloes, fibrous begonias, haworthias, pandanuses, platyceriums, saintpaulias, sempervivums, and many bulbs such as amaryllis hybrids, bowieas, and urgineas. Bromeliads also offset, although in their case it's not so much a matter of propagation as of survival, since the pups, as they are often called, don't form until after the parent plant has flowered, following which it dies.

Offsets can be removed simply by breaking them away from the parent plant. However, the preferred method is to free them with a sharp knife or a pair of shears. If they are well rooted, which is the best stage for separation, pot as you would a regular plant. If not, root them like cuttings in an open propagation box. To remove an offset bulb, scrape the soil away from around it. Then gently turn the bulblet, first one way, then the other. Continue until it is detached. Usually there are no roots or, if they exist, they are too short to be tangled with the much lower ones of

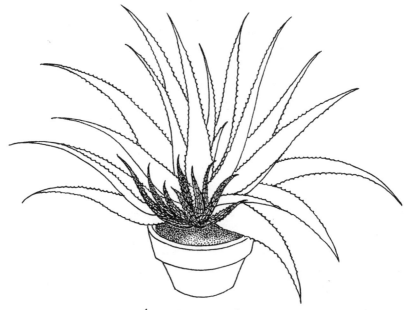

A suckering aloe.

the mother plant. But if you must cut some roots to free the bulblet, cut those of the mature bulb.

LONG DIVISION

Almost any plant with more than one growing stem emerging from the soil—aspidistra, bamboo, cane-stemmed begonia, clivia, many ferns, ginger, sansevieria, and spathyphyllum—can be propagated by division. The sansevieria, by the way, will not be affected by chimera if this means of propagation is used.

There are two ways of dividing. You can remove a plant from its pot and, with a sharp, long-bladed knife, cut through roots and soil as if you were dealing with a loaf of bread. Or, once you have the plant out of its pot, you can gently pry the roots apart, trying to separate the tangled spaghettilike strands as much as possible, and perhaps not cutting at all. Although the bread-slice method sounds ruthless, if the roots are really tangled, in the long run the plants will probably suffer less shock from it than from the other technique. Dip the cut root ends in charcoal dust to help minimize infection.

WALKING CANES

Aglaonemas, bamboos, cordylines, dieffenbachias, dracaenas, and some philodendrons can be propagated from cane sections. A good time to take propagation canes is when you are air layering a plant. Cut a section four or five inches long from the mature growth. Dust the ends of the section with powdered charcoal to dry them off and prevent rot. Lay the section down on the rooting medium in a propagation box and cover the box. New plants will develop from the eyes, or undeveloped buds, on the cane. You can also plant a cane section upright directly in a pot to sprout a single plant. In either case, cover the cane loosely but entirely with plastic to ensure high humidity around it.

NEW HEADS FOR OLD

Grafting is usually associated with fruit and vegetable crops grown outdoors in orchards or gardens, where a species that is a superior bearer but susceptible to root-associated problems is grafted onto the rootstock of a very hardy but not particularly fruitful species. Grafting is also the technique by which dwarf fruit trees are achieved: for some reason as yet not fully understood, certain rootstocks will dwarf the scion, or top piece, even if it comes from a tree normally full sized.

In the case of most indoor plants, grafting is simply a gimmick. On the whole I find the colored-head cacti, in which various brightly hued globular varieties are grafted onto plain rootstock, merely in bad taste. For the avid cactus collector, however, they do serve a function. Much in the way that some fancy-fruiting hybrid apples are too insect-prone to be grown without grafting onto heartier rootstock, certain cactus varieties can only be cultivated with extreme difficulty unless grafted onto more vigorous stock. The practice also gives you faster-growing cacti, and some of the fancy-colored ones normally develop with all the speed of a sleeping snail, since they have relatively little food-producing chlorophyll.

If you want to try grafting—and it's an interesting project for kids—there are four basic rootstocks you can use: any columnar-type cereus, myrtillocactus, pereskia, or selenicereus. The best time to do grafting is in

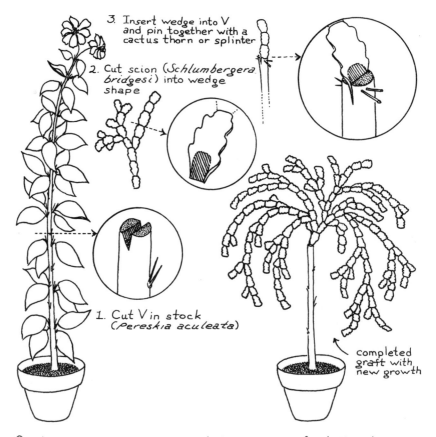

3. Insert wedge into V and pin together with a cactus thorn or splinter

2. Cut scion (*Schlumbergera bridgesi*) into wedge shape

1. Cut V in stock (*Pereskia aculeata*)

completed graft with new growth

Grafting schlumbergera onto taller pereskia for better display

spring and summer when the plants' growth is well under way. Schlumbergeras make good scions, in that the graft usually takes. The scion should be cut to form a wedge that will fit snugly into a matching V cut into the rootstock. Pin the two together at once before calluses can form. Cactus needles are good for the purpose—and you thought those cactus needles that broke off in your finger were of no use. Regular pins may interfere with development. If the graft takes, you'll have new shoots in a month or six weeks.

TOPPING THE TALL ONES

Air layering, known variously as Chinese layering, circumposition, gootee, marcottage, and pot layering, has been used as a means of propagation throughout the agricultural world for over a thousand years. No doubt one of the reasons it acquired the name Chinese layering is that until the advent of plastic film only the Chinese were supposed to have been patient enough to use it. Another analogy is between the old Chinese method of water torture and the method used for keeping the layering wet, the key to success. A tree was girdled, that is, a strip of bark was cut away all around the branch to be layered, and a ball of clay and moss was wrapped around the wound. Above this was fastened a water container of some sort from which a wick led down to the ball and was tied around it. Water dripped down the string, keeping the ball constantly moist while roots grew out of the wound into the ball. All in all a very messy procedure for the living room, particularly the part about trying to get the wick to drip just the right amount.

But enter polyethylene film, which has two qualities admirably suiting it to air layering. First, it transmits very little water vapor. If you wet the ball and then wrap it in polyethylene, it will remain moist until you remove the bandage. Still, the moss would probably rot were it not for polyethylene's second useful quality. It has a surprisingly high permeability to gases such as carbon dioxide and oxygen. An air-layered wound covered with polyethylene gets a fair amount of air circulation.

Air layering, incidentally, is used not only in propagation of indoor plants, but to shorten leggy ones as well. If you have, say, a ficus or a dracaena that of late has acquired the appearance of a flagpole, you can lower the flag and throw out the pole if you wish. The procedure is usually very successful, though normally it can be employed only on what are generally called woody plants.

That doesn't limit it to the obvious ones, like croton and ficus. The woody plants include almost all dicots. The adventitious roots that form at the layering wound are, after all, the same ones that form when cuttings are taken. So what is needed for air layering is any plant with the vascular bundles, close to which these roots form, concentrated near the outer part of the stem—exactly what we have in dicots. Although there's no practical reason to do it, out of curiosity I've even air layered a coleus, whose squishy stem certainly wouldn't be considered woody in the ordinary sense of the word. Generally, a plant's ability to root cuttings is a good indicator of its ability to be air layered.

Let's look a little closer at that ficus that's five feet tall and has all the grace of a retired witch's broom. Bringing its feather-duster top down to soil level would make it a much more attractive, though smaller, specimen. The plant would also be healthier, producing lusher new growth. So we air layer it.

Air layering is usually done in spring on the previous year's growth, although older wood will also take layering. The highest rate of success in tropical species is on plants treated soon after several new leaves have formed.

The first step is to deliberately injure the plant at a spot where you want the future soil level to be. Make the wound right beneath, in fact almost touching, a node. It's where the damage is done that the new growth will take place. You have two choices in technique, and the decision about which to use is best based on the particular specimen involved. On a soft, relatively thin plant, you can pierce the stem with a penknife so that it passes all the way through the stalk, twist the knife sideways a bit so the slit opens, insert a matchsticklike sliver of wood a quarter of an inch or so thick into the wound to keep it from closing, and withdraw the knife. (Don't use a real matchstick; its chemical treatment could interfere with the plant's development.) Then scrape away some of the outer bark and the cambium layer below it on both sides around the wound. On larger, older specimens you may prefer to girdle a branch.

In the wilds, girdling a tree, or cutting off a ring of bark all the way around the trunk or a branch, will kill the growth above it. When you are air layering, however, because of the protective moss ball adventitious roots form before any damage is done overhead.

Whichever method you choose, the next step is to fill or plaster the wound with moistened sphagnum moss. If you've made an incision, jam the sphagnum moss right in. On a girdled specimen, wrap it on well. The more succulent the plant, the moister the sphagnum moss should be. Under no circumstances, however, should it be wringing wet, or the stem tissue will decay. Spreading a rooting hormone on the wound before applying the moss is beneficial but not necessary. Keep wrapping moss completely around the layered area until you have a large fist-sized lump. Cover this in turn with polyethylene so that the whole ball of moss is enclosed, and close off the ends of the film with florist's ties, Twist-'Ems, electrician's tape, or any other means you can think of that stays tight. That's it, you've air layered your first plant.

Now sit down with a good book—say, like the *Encyclopaedia Britannica*. It will take somewhere between three weeks and five months for the plant to send out new roots. All you have to do during this period is check that your two seals are tight enough that the moss remains moist. If it dries out, you will have to water it and reseal. Callus formation is

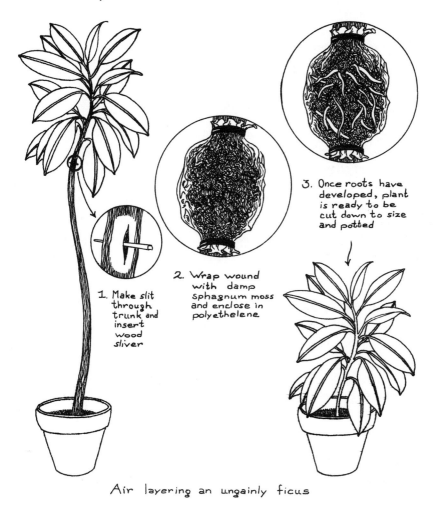

3. Once roots have developed, plant is ready to be cut down to size and potted

2. Wrap wound with damp sphagnum moss and enclose in polyethelene

1. Make slit through trunk and insert wood sliver

Air layering an ungainly ficus

most effective at eighty degrees, so if possible keep the plant where the temperature is relatively high.

Once you see good root formation—don't worry, you'll be so excited you'll have no difficulty telling the roots from the tangled web of moss—gently remove the plastic and cut the stem just below the lowest root sprout. You can leave the moss among the roots if you want to, but removing it will help ensure that the roots are not exposed to air pockets when planted. Then dip the cut in charcoal dust, and plant your new top in the regular fashion.

In the case of a plant shortened by air layering, if you want to you can cut back the broomstick that's left even more, leaving only three or four nodes on the stem. Treat the stump like a plant and in a while you may have one.

A newly planted top will have a small root system compared with its upper growth. To encourage more root formation than leafy development, keep the atmosphere around the plant moist and a bit cooler than normal.

THE HEART OF THE MATTER

Seeds are truly the heart of the matter, horticulturally. They carry a species on into further generations. But more than that, usually being a chromosomal composite of two plants, they add genetic variability to the process. Whole new species, besides modifications of the parental one, become feasible. And seeds are not only a natural miracle, but one of the pocketbook as well. For the cost of one large decorator-sized dracaena bought at the plant store, you could fill a room with a couple of dozen plants—pots and soil included—by growing them from seed. The catch, of course, is that time is money, too, and if it takes less money, it takes more time to raise plants from scratch. Still, provided you don't get carried away with it, for sheer pleasure and a feeling of horticultural accomplishment, there's nothing quite like growing your own plants from seed. Your choice of greenery is greater, as well, since most nurseries tend to fall into a rut as far as their selection goes.

A seed consists of a plant embryo and enough stored food to get growth well under way. The whole affair is usually packaged in a protective covering known as the seed coat. A seed, by the time it is separated from the fruit, and the plant on which it developed, is semidesiccated. It remains in a state of suspended animation, or quiescence, until moisture penetrates the seed coat and germination occurs.

There are a few species whose seeds are viviparous, that is, the seed germinates within the fruit still on the tree. Environmental propagative problems are usually responsible for this type of development. Mangroves, for instance, not only grow into seedlings while still attached to the parent tree, but develop a spearlike root as much as a foot long before they drop. The root embeds itself in the mud below, preventing the seedling from drifting out with the tide.

Seed germination is influenced by a number of factors, but primarily water and oxygen supply, temperature, and light—in other words, more or less the same conditions that affect the growth of plants—plus seed freshness. With certain notable temperate zone exceptions not grown as houseplants, the more recently the seeds have been harvested, the higher the percentage of germination. Seeds of some species remain viable only a few days.

A GROWING SEED GATHERS LITTLE MOSS

The initial step in germination is absorption of water by the seed. Large seeds with hard seed coats, like *Manilkara achras*, the sapodilla, must be scarified in order for the water to penetrate—unless, like nature, you are in no hurry at all. *M. achras*, the tree from which the chicle latex used in manufacturing chewing gum is drawn, is not ordinarily considered a houseplant. I've been growing a lot of odd plants from seed to satisfy my own curiosity, however, and just in case you come across some big seeds you don't know quite what to do with, I thought I'd better mention the process of scarification. Stubborn seeds both large and small can also often be coaxed to yield their bounty by an overnight soak before planting.

Scarification means cracking the whole outer coat gently, nicking it deeply—but without cutting the embryo, or a malformed plant will develop—or rubbing the seed against sandpaper or the edge of a file. The sanding method is the one usually chosen. In nature such a rupture of the seed coat occurs only with great rarity. The seeds germinate without it, but several years of imbibition may be necessary. Too much water, on the other hand, will cause the seed to rot.

To give seeds just the right amount of moisture for germination, you can provide them with a seed bed. One that, besides supplying the proper moisture, is relatively sterile as well gives them a healthy start.

Don't let the idea of sterility scare you away, incidentally. You're not about to convert your living room into a hospital operating theater. Like all things, sterility is relative, and horticultural sterility is nowhere near as strict as the word's everyday connotation implies. Essentially it means starting out with a presterilized rooting medium—or sterilizing your own. As soon as the seeds are sown, sterility decreases rapidly. But usually the seeds have germinated by the time fungi invade, particularly before *Pythium ultimum* and *Rhizoctonia solani*, the primary pathogens of damping off, rear their ugly mycelia. Plants affected by damping off pinch in at the stem near soil level. A few hours later they topple over. There are even cases of preemergence damping off, in which the seedling rots before it breaks through the surface. And there's nothing you can do about it—except avoid the problem.

Fill a well-crocked pot with your standard potting mix. I use one part commercial potting soil, one part sphagnum, and one part sharp sand. Firm it down well. Then you can sprinkle a quarter of an inch to an inch of milled sphagnum moss on top. Besides being sterile, it has a mild fungicidal action. But it has no nourishment, which is why you can't raise seedlings in plain sphagnum moss. The thickness of the layer you want will depend on seed size. For dustlike seed a quarter of an inch is plenty; for something like coffee seeds, themselves a quarter of an inch thick, half an inch of sphagnum moss is more like it; and so on for larger seeds. On the other hand, I may add, I've sprouted numerous seeds without the sphagnum layer, using plain sterilized potting mix. It's all a matter of how careful you want to be. Coconuts, in any case, do not need a foot-thick layer, since the shoot reaches a stage of maturity within the husk such that it does not seem bothered by damping off. Finally, sprinkle your seeds on top. Don't use too many, and keep them spaced so that if they all take there will still be some space between the seedlings.

Set the whole pot, once sown, in a basin of water as deep as the soil level. Once it's thoroughly soaked, lift it out again; then, as you let the pot drain, the receding tide will settle the seeds in cozily. Alternatively, you can water the soil profusely *before* you put down the milled sphagnum moss layer and the seed. Once it is thoroughly soaked, put down the moss and soak it by misting. Then sprinkle the seed and mist again. If you were to try to water the whole affair from the top, the moss layer would wash into the soil and you would lose your antiseptic layer, not to mention probably ending up with all the seeds in one spot.

BOUNTIFUL BUNTING

What about covering the seeds, you ask? Well, that depends. . . . With fine dustlike seeds such as those of begonias or gesneriads, the answer is no. They don't need the protection to stay moist, and light will help them germinate. Once you get past pinhead-sized seeds, however, the answer is usually yes. A covering of dampened milled sphagnum moss will keep the seeds evenly moist and speed germination. The recommended average thickness of the covering is one equivalent to the diameter of the seed. This depth of moss will allow some light through while at the same time maintaining even moisture.

Another way of retaining moisture—and if a seed dries out just once after its initial bath, chances are it will not germinate—is to cover the pot with plastic. You can either invert a plastic bag completely over the pot or cover the pot with Saran Wrap, holding the film in place with a rubber band around the rim of the pot and letting the excess drape down to cover most of the rest, thereby further reducing evaporation.

This is an excellent way to make a self-tending seed starter. Since it is a relatively closed system, there is little water loss, while at the same time air can circulate through the plastic sufficiently for the seeds. After germination takes place, remove the plastic in stages, as you did the cover over your cuttings. When you do remove it completely, be sure to continue keeping the soil surface moist.

One additional hint: droplets tend to collect on the inside of a plastic top. Then they fall down on the seeds, soaking them. Sometimes the seeds become more than moist this way, they become downright soggy, maybe even rotten. To avoid this chance occurrence, I tip the pots slightly during germination. By setting one edge down on a pencil, the whole pot is tipped enough so that the water, rather than dropping on the seeds, tends to run to the edge of the pot.

HOT FOOT

Plants do best with cool roots and warm top growth. Seedlings do best with exactly the opposite conditions. This is because they have an initial food supply stored in the cotyledons, or seed leaves, so they can live on their own fat for a while, concentrating their initial growth belowground rather than on food-producing leaves. Sound roots mean better plants.

There are waterproof soil-heating cables available for indoor gardening. I use one in combination with a pebble tray. The submersible cable runs beneath the pebbles and water. The pots stand on top. The soil temperature is kept around seventy-five degrees constantly; at the same time the cable increases evaporation to such a degree that I don't need to bother covering the pots with plastic for most seeds.

To complete the growth chamber, I have a fluorescent light above and aluminum foil surrounding three sides. Pretty it's not, particularly with an assortment of various-sized cuttings and seedlings growing helter-skelter. Things never seem to look as neat as a *House & Garden* photograph. But I hide the eyesore in the study where no one else has to look at it, and personally I find it a real beauty. Its lushness makes me think of a diorama by Rousseau, had he been up to things like dioramas. Air circulation is good, so I never have problems with damping off. (What never? Well hardly ever.) And the germinating seeds, and the seedlings that follow them, get plenty of light. The light not only accelerates germination of many seeds, but advances the development of the seedlings. For although initially you want root development at the expense of leafy expanses, at the same time you want the plants to remain full and compact. Seedlings pick up bad habits. One that has etiolated, or developed a lean and lanky, bleached-out look from lack of light, will never become really lush and dense.

I've also used a radiator for heating seedlings' roots. It has advantages and disadvantages. The one close to the window yet out of the sun keeps the tops of the plants cool, the roots warm. At night, however, the radiators go off in our building and the base heat is lost. Actually the seedlings seem to thrive on this drop of night temperatures—as long as it is not too severe. But more than one winter cold snap has wreaked havoc with my seedling overflow on the radiator. Also, without adequate insulation the soil can get too hot. The upper heat limit for most seeds is a soil temperature of eighty-six to one hundred eight degrees, depending on the species. Hardly any can tolerate a soil temperature above one hundred thirteen degrees for more than a few hours. And you'd be surprised how hot a radiator cover can become.

LIFT THE LEAF

Most houseplant seeds germinate in between two days and two months. Some palms may take two years, but that's a rarity. The variation within a single species can be quite amazing if you're not prepared for it. Recently an opuntia of mine sprouted in a week while another opuntia seed in exactly the same circumstances took two and a half months.

Anyhow, once the seed germinates, move it into good light if it isn't already there. But don't give it any direct sunlight until it has true leaves, as opposed to the cotyledons, or seed leaves. Once the first couple of true leaves do develop, prepare to transplant. You can graduate the seedlings to either a community pot or small individual pots two and a half to three inches in size. Community pots save space, but except for very slow-growing species, like orchids, in my opinion, since it means one less case of transplant shock, you're better off putting a seedling directly into its own pot.

A young seedling can be easily picked up between the tines of a fork. Hold the plant by a leaf to steady it. Never pick it up or steady it by the stem. Although the stalk is what one naturally reaches for, the leaf is actually stronger; the stem is apt to squash, and that would be the end of your seedling.

Poke a hole in the soil with a pencil and drop the seedling in. Then either tamp the soil down around the seedling or submerge the pot in a basin of water to soil level as when transplanting mature plants. Both methods will fill the soil in around the roots, although dunking does the better job. What you want to avoid is air spaces around the roots that would let them dry out, the number one cause of transplant failure. Needless to say by this point in the book, you will have provided the pot with excellent drainage so that the roots won't drown after their dunking.

That's it, you've just raised a plant from seed. Two reminders on its early care: don't put the new transplant in the sun for the first three or four days, and wait at least a week to let it settle in comfortably before you fertilize the seedling.

OPENING A BANK ACCOUNT

One of the great advantages of raising plants from seeds, besides the sheer pleasure of it, is that you can escape the philodendron-saintpaulia-begonia syndrome that seems to affect most houseplant stores. Send away for some of the catalogs listed in the back of the book, and you'll soon have one of the most exotic indoor house gardens in the neighborhood.

Another excellent source of seeds, particularly unusual ones, is one of the various plant societies. Most of them have active seed banks. By joining such a society, you gain the right to draw from its bank at a nominal charge. Besides access to the excellent periodicals, of which the *American*

Orchid Society Bulletin and *Principes*, the quarterly of the Palm Society, are probably the best, membership in the societies will enable you to get seeds not only of rare and unusual species, but in many cases of the latest rage in hybrids as well.

Bottling Your Plants

Many years ago, during my childhood, an uncle showed me a Swiss brandy bottle with a whole pear inside. It wasn't just any old bottle. It had a long narrow neck and no seams. There simply was no way to get a pear inside the bottle without mashing it. And since the glass was seamless, you couldn't have put the bottom on last, or glued two halves together to enclose the pear. I spent a week staring at the tantalizing puzzle. Finally, one day after dinner, I capitulated. "I give up. The only way to do it would be to *grow* the pear inside. And obviously you can't do that."

"But that's exactly how it was done," my uncle replied. Then he went on to explain. Just after the flower had been pollinated and the fruit set, the spur bearing the incipient pear, still attached to the tree, was slipped carefully through the bottleneck. Then the bottle was attached to the spur and a forked stick used to prop it up until the pear grew to maturity. At harvest time you picked the bottle, pear and all.

I was reflecting on that particular incident one evening as the conversation turned to the South Pacific islands while we were sipping a postprandial Père Williams. A half-gallon jug of Almadén sat next to the remains of our roast goose. Any South Pacific sailor worth his salt would have built a three-masted schooner in that bottle. On the other hand, I'd just been thinking of setting up a terrarium for my daughter Genevieve like the one I filled with newts when I was a kid. Why not do it in the bottle?

EMPTYING AND FILLING THE RIGHT BOTTLE

Clear or very lightly tinted containers of any size or shape will do for a bottle garden. Some plastic ones, however, fog up or discolor after a few months, so where possible stay with glass. Deeply tinted bottles will not allow enough light to support plant growth—which in some cases is precisely why they are tinted; for instance, beer in brown bottles has a much longer shelf life than that in clear containers. The trick is to pick a bottle to fit the plants you want to grow, or vice versa. Don't try to plant a rex begonia in a perfume bottle, or mosses in a five-gallon jug whose floor they will cover with a lovely verdant carpet, leaving the rest of the minienvironment empty. Fitting the plant to the bottle is not only fun, it's an aesthetic art like flower arranging.

But first the bottle. Antique decanters, milk bottles, gallon wine and cider jugs, even old patent-medicine bottles, all make fine glass gardens. If you want to start out the easy way, you can use mason jars or wide-mouthed glass canisters. But I'm sure it won't be long before you progress to the more challenging narrow-mouthed varieties.

Whichever you choose, it has to be clean—very clean. Rinse it out several times with hot water. Then fill it with a mixture of one part Clorox to nine parts hot water. This helps eliminate bacteria and spores that might decide to feast on your garden, turning it into an interesting but not exactly decorative collection of mold. Let the mixture sit for half an hour. Then empty and rinse the bottle a few more times, turn it upside down, and let it dry thoroughly, preferably in the sun.

SIMPLIFIED SERVOMATION

Four simple bottle-gardening tools you can make from household gear are a shovel, leaf duster, pruner, and glass cleaner. Their common denominator is that they have to be long, so you can manipulate them by remote control from outside the bottle. Pick up some quarter-inch doweling at your local hardware store. Or use chopsticks—they work fine if they're long enough for the bottle you are landscaping.

To make a shovel, attach an old fork to the end of a dowel with electrician's tape. Make sure it is securely taped, though, or you will spend a bit of time trying to fish a loose fork out of the bottle. Fasten a soft watercolor or makeup brush to another dowel, and you have the leaf duster. The pruner is a bit more work, but not much. Split one end of a dowel about an inch. Then insert an X-acto or injector-razor blade. If you choose the razor blade, it should be glued in place in the dowel, since the sharp edge would cut the tape.

For the handle of the glass cleaner, use a wire clothes hanger rather than a dowel. You can bend the hanger to get around corners by the neck of the bottle that you couldn't reach with a straight stick. Attach a wad of soft lint-free cloth to one end and you're all set.

One last tool, which isn't easily made but is inexpensive enough to buy, is the pickup. It is available at any automotive supply store, and consists of a small three-pronged claw at one end of a flexible cable and a thumb-activated plunger at the other end. Designed for extracting dropped bolts and the like from inaccessible corners in a car engine, it is equally handy for manipulating plants around inaccessible spots in your bottle garden. However, living plants being a little more tender than nuts and bolts, it's a good idea to bind off the sharp edges of the claws with some masking or electrician's tape. Also, when you use it, never release the thumb plunger quickly or completely. Be gentle when you lower the plants into their new bed of bottled soil.

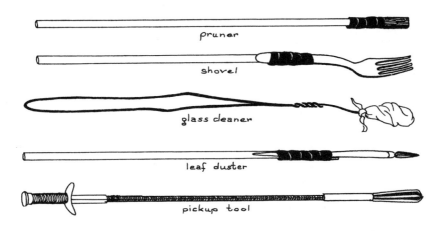

Bottle-gardening tools

THE SEDIMENT

The standard three-part soil mix works well, but below it you should have a one- or two-inch layer of small stones or aquarium gravel and charcoal. Your glass garden won't have any drainage. So, to keep the soil from rotting, you have to provide drainage in the bottle by laying down a layer of material loose enough to let the water seep out of the soil.

Make a funnel out of lightweight cardboard and pour the gravel into your bottle. Follow this with an additional quarter- to half-inch layer of charcoal and two to three inches of soil, depending on how big a bottle you are working with. Tap the bottle after each layer to help settle it. And if two inches of soil doesn't seem like much for a plant to grow on, consider that a cubic inch of soil can support as much as a hundred miles of roots and hair roots—that's right, *miles*.

MARVELOUS MINIATURES

After the soil is in place, you're ready for the actual planting. But what should you grow? Well, unless you're using a fifty-gallon jug—and some people do—you are almost forced to stick with miniatures. However, there are countless specimens of these to choose from. Begonias, cissus, pelargoniums, peperomias, saintpaulias, sinningias, and the like all come in diminutive versions. A simple plant in a small bottle can be very decorative. Peperomias alone supply enough variety and beauty to fill numerous jugs. Then, of course, there are ferns with their lovely lacy appearance. And Venus flytraps that thrive in bottle gardens exposed to good light.

You can buy miniatures in plant stores, mail-order nurseries, sometimes even the five-and-ten. *Be sure to get plants labeled miniatures*, however, not just very young regular plants.

If you want to be very thorough about planning the layout of your garden, cut a piece of paper to match the size of the bottom of your container, and do your landscaping to scale beforehand. Merely arrange and rearrange the plants on the paper till you get a pattern that you think suits the bottle. On the other hand, if you feel a wild jungly look is sufficient in itself, you can skip this step. Just remember to place the tallest and fastest-growing specimens in the center, so they won't block the light for the other plants.

Wash the leaves of all plants in tepid water and soap before you submerge them in their bottle. As a final antipest precaution, spray them with rubbing alcohol. Let the leaves dry off before you bottle them or they will pick up a great deal of dirt while being planted. It's a lot more work to clean the leaves once the plants are in their new home.

To pass the plants through a narrow bottleneck, you will have to gently relieve the root systems of most of their soil. Use your fingers or a carefully manipulated pencil point. Then, after digging a suitable hole with your miniature shovel, lower each plant through the neck roots first. Large leaves can be rolled up. If they still won't fit, prune them off—new ones will grow quickly. And since the root system will suffer some damage, no matter how careful you are, removing a few leaves actually balances the loss and is an aid in getting the plant to take well in its new

---

A TERRARIUM PLANT SAMPLER

The following plants are some that do well in a terrarium. Those preceded by an asterisk do best in the high humidity of a closed terrarium; the rest should thrive in either open or closed containers. Where only the genus is listed, followed by the word "species," all species of that particular genus should give you a good display as long as they are miniatures or very small specimens. The carnivorous plants are not included here, since as a group they all should be grown in terrariums.

Adiantum species	*Haworthia* species
Allophyton mexicanum	*Helxine soleirolii*
Aloe aristata	*Hoya bella*
Bambusa nana	*Kalanchoë* species
Begonia species	*Kohleria amabilis*
Bryophyllum species	*Kohleria lindeniana*
Caladium humboldtii	*Maranta* species
Chlorophytum bichetii	*Oxalis* species
Cissus striata	*Peperomia* species
Collinia elegans	*Philodendron* species
Cryptanthus species	*Pilea* species
Dracaena godseffiana	*Saintpaulia* species
Episcia species	*Sinningia pusilla*
Ficus radicans	*Streptocarpus rimicola*
Ficus repens	*Tradescantia* species
Fittonia species	

surroundings. Once through the neck, hold the plant upright in place with the pickup tool or a long blunt stick, and cover the roots, using your shovel. Then invert the shovel and tamp the soil down with the back end of the dowel. Repeat the process until all the plants are in place.

Use the glass cleaner to remove any dirt that may have become stuck to the inside of your jug. Now add about a quarter of a cup of tepid water for each gallon capacity of your container. But don't just pour the water in. Tip the container and let a little run down the side. Tip it in the opposite direction, and do it again. Then put the cap on the bottle and let it stand overnight.

TENDING THE BOTTLE

Don't put a bottle garden in direct sunlight, or you'll end up with nothing but wilted lettuce. Other than that, any spot with fairly good light, either natural or artificial, is fine.

Check the garden after the first day. There should be no heavy condensation. That is to say, the glass shouldn't be misted over on the inside to the point where you can't see the plants. If it is, leave the cap off for a day, then close the bottle again. If you see no droplets at all after the first day, add a little more water. What you are striving for is a mini-environment of such a nature that just a few drops of water condense toward the top of the bottle each day and then fall down like dew at night. Once you have that, you have the easiest-to-care-for of all houseplant arrangements. Every six months or so, trim the plants where necessary, using the razor stick. Remove any dead leaves with your pickup. Fertilize lightly. You want these plants to remain stunted and small. Watering for your bottles of greenery consists of adding a tablespoonful per gallon capacity of the bottle every three or four months. How simple can indoor gardening get?

TETRAGONAL TERRARIUMS

One of the drawbacks of bottle gardens is that you can't get any large-sized rocks down through the narrow neck. And rocky cliffs mimicking nature at its most primordial are visually quite exciting. To this end a large old aquarium is excellent. If you can get one the right size for a fluorescent fixture, so much the better, but remember two things. First, many of your plants will be as much as a foot away from the light source. which means the artificial sun should be on for sixteen hours or so a day to compensate. Second, you must put a pane of glass between the top of the fish tank and the light fixture. If you don't, the high humidity will erode the fixture within a year or so. Take the glass off for a couple of hours once a week to change the weather in your tank. Or don't do it. People have had success and failure with both methods.

Using an aquarium means you can dispense with the special mini-tools, and some of the challenge will be gone. On the other hand, you can use your imagination much more freely. Build not only cliffs, but caves, and contour the soil with hills and valleys. Chip a depression in a flat rock to make a natural-looking pool. And once you have that, can you resist putting in a newt or other small lizard to strut regally beneath the miniature palms of his domain? Kids certainly can't.

Whatever you put in to create your special terrarium, once it's done, sit back and stare into it for a while. It will be like stepping

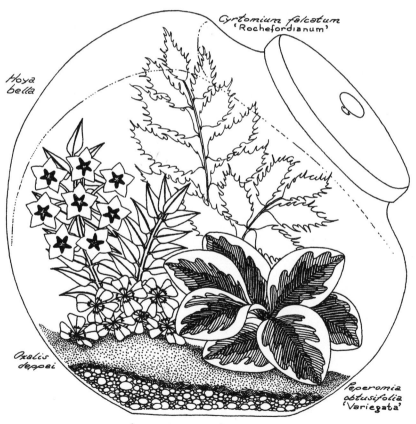

A candy jar terrarium

into a private world of peace and quiet away from the everyday cares of life. And that's what houseplants as a whole are all about—a bit of nature's tranquil mystery all your own, and one to share with friends as well.

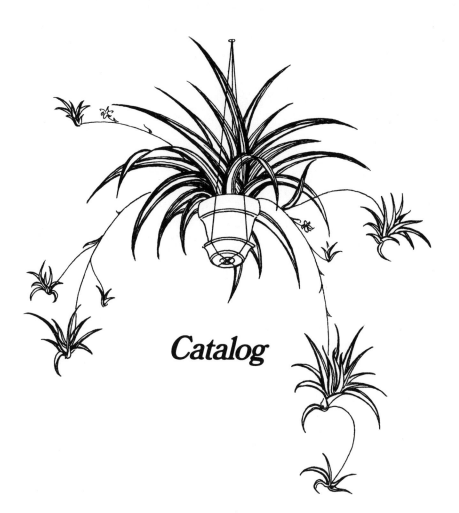

Catalog

What's in a Name?

My education was of a somewhat classical nature—I struggled through Caesar's "Garlic Wars" astride a red pony. Yet now, after all these years, I find Mrs. Stewart's tolerant tutelage was not all useless. Latin may be a dead language in our day-to-day existence, but it's still alive and well in the plant world.

Popular names for plants are fine. Many of them are in fact nothing but an anglicization of the Latin genus name. Thus *Begonia* became begonia; *Caladium,* caladium; and *Cyclamen,* cyclamen. Unfortunately, however, begonias range from the brilliantly color-splashed, large-leaved *Begonia rex* to the delicate *B. scandens,* with tiny ovate trailing greenery, to *B. sunderbruchii,* boasting large six-pointed jagged leaves, or to the small, holly-leaved *B. cubensis.* The family even includes the typically begonia-looking *B. semperflorens.* And that is only the beginning. Most plants don't have a common name at all.

If you've read this far you've already learned your first rule of botanical Latin, perhaps without even realizing it. When you list several members of the same genus, that is, related plants in the same group, you don't keep repeating the genus, but simply use the first letter—in the case of begonias, for instance, the letter *B*.

But you need not learn Latin to raise plants indoors. If you did, your windowsill—and mine—probably would be bare, and in all of New York City there probably would not be a single plant store. You can have beautiful houseplants without knowing a single one of those italicized words. Still, as your green universe expands, you're apt to get curious and want to familiarize yourself with some of the formal names, particularly since buying plants by mail or starting them from seed can be like looking up "Fitch" once you get to Los Angeles—which Fitch? Richard Fitch, Richard H. Fitch, or was it maybe Harry Fitch?

Just as man sorted out the Fitch, Brown, and Smith families by adding given names to individual members, and in many cases middle names as well, plants have been given multiple botanical names. And in the same way that a man's surname, say Bullock, at one time reflected his work or some special characteristic, for example, one who worked with bullocks or one strong as a bullock, so plant names too are descriptive nomenclature. *Semperflorens*, for instance, means "always flowering," which should give you a key to what to expect if you grow *Begonia semperflorens*.

Most plant designations are binomial, consisting of two distinct parts. The genus name, for instance, *Cocos*, is the equivalent of a family name, for instance, Fitch. Add *nucifera* and you get Fitch, Richard. If that's still not enough to differentiate the plant from its kin, you might add 'Dwarf Golden Malay,' giving you Fitch, Richard H. *Cocos nucifera* 'Dwarf Golden Malay' is a diminutive version of the well-known coconut palm seen in Florida or California. The small tree, which originated in the Andaman islands, is less than half as tall and bears twice as many coconuts as the regular coconut tree, making it quite a different fellow.

Binomial nomenclature predates Carolus Linnaeus, the eighteenth-century Swedish botanist usually associated with it. However, he was the one who introduced sex into the matter. Linnaeus, or Linné in Swedish, classified plants by variants in their reproductive organs—not a modest task in an era when even the birds and the bees weren't discussed. One bishop in fact cried out, "Nothing could equal the gross prurience of Linné's mind." A bit overstated, no doubt, but a likely clerical reaction at the time to a botanist humorously describing the reproductive parts of a poppy flower as "twenty or thirty males in the same bed with a female."

A second and perhaps more important facet differentiating Linnaeus's classification from its predecessors was that it indeed constituted a system, rather than just a random collection of names. His system not only designated the plant by a particular name, but in so doing placed it in a position relative to all other plants, giving an overview of kinships close and not so.

That was quite an accomplishment, even back in the 1750s when there were only eighty-five thousand known species. (Today there are almost four hundred thousand recognized species in some twelve thousand five hundred genera.) As a world-renowned botanist he had considerable help, of course, and was able to send expeditions to Arabia and South America in search of more plants to classify.

What Linnaeus lacked, however, was the concept of evolution. Darwin's conceptual discovery, postdating Linnaeus by a hundred years, added a new twist to botanical nomenclature. In Linnaeus's time all things were considered products of instantaneous divine creation. As such, everything that would ever be already existed. All one had to do was label it. Then along came hybridization and vegetative reproduction of spontaneous variants. Totally new plants were created. A place had to be found for them in the taxonomic system.

Specific names of hybrids derived from two species are usually separated from the genus name by an x, indicating a crossbreed. The x-brand is particularly predominant among the more popular houseplants, where a lot of breeding for new and hopefully better plants has occurred. Thus you might have *Begonia* x *cheimantha*, which is a cross between *B. socotrana* and *B. dregei*. A crossbreed can often be crossbred again. But enough for now—when you get a labeled plant, you'll be able to understand what the label is all about. The terminology may prove handy, since some hybrids are better suited to your environment than others. Or you might want to try to build up as complete a collection of begonia varieties as possible. There's something of the collector's instinct in all of us. Besides, if you come up with a new cultivar, you may get to add your name in single quotes. A pair of single quotation marks enclosing the name directly following the genus, as in, for instance, *Begonia* 'Dancing Girl,' indicates a cultivar, a variety that has originated under cultivation. It is again a subdivision, this time for a man-made variety.

Knowing some botanical nomenclature will help you further if you decide to start looking up information on your plants in such incomparable sources as Graf's *Exotica*, or, for the lexicographer at heart, the

1969 *International Code of Botanical Nomenclature.* This has close to fifty articles and rules and makes excellent reading for anyone who has plants—and insomnia. Also, the very names of plants themselves will give you further information about them. To this end there follows a brief Greek-Latin/English word list. It includes only the most common terms used in nomenclature, and although you might guess that a species named *brevis* would be short, how about the species *sanguinalis?*

A BRIEF INDEX OF DESCRIPTIVE GREEK AND LATIN NOMENCLATURE

abbreviatus—shortened
acris—acrid
acuminatus—tapering, long and pointed
aestivalis—of summer
aggregatus—clustered or bunched
agrarius—on the fields
alatus—winged
albostriatus—white-striped
albus—white
alpinus—alpine
anceps—two-edged, two-headed
andrus—stamen
angulatus—angled
angustifolius—narrow-leaved
angustus—narrow
annuus—annual
anthus—flower
aquaticus—aquatic
arenarius—on sandy places
argenteostriatus—silver-tipped
argenteus—silvered
aristatus—barleylike awns
atro—dark
aureus—golden yellow
auricomus—golden-haired
australis—southern
autumnalis—of autumn
azureus—sky blue, azure

baccatus—berried
borealis—northern
breviglumis—having small bractlike scales
brevis—short

calvus—hairless
campanulatus—bell-shaped
campestris—from the open fields
candidus—white
capillaris—hairlike
cardinalis—red
carneus—flesh-colored
carpus—fruit
caulescens—with stem
caulis—stem
cernuus—drooping
chinensis—from China
chrysanthus—yellow-flowered
ciliaris—hairy-fringed
circinatus—coiled
citrinus—citruslike
coccineus—scarlet
coeruleus—dark blue
communis—common
complexus—encircled
complicatus—folded over
cordatus—heart-shaped
cornutus—horned
crassus—thick
crenatus—scalloped
cuneatus—wedge-shaped
cuspidatus—sharply pointed
cyaneus—dark blue
cyme—broad, flattened growth
cymosus—flowers in cymes

deciduus—leaves falling annually
decumbens—reclining at base with upright tips
dendroideus—treelike
dentatus—toothlike
dichotomus—forked
digitatus—fingerlike
discolor—of two different colors

edulis—edible
elatus—tall
erectus—upright, perpendicular
esculentus—edible
eximius—very unusual
exoticus—foreign

falcatus—sickle-shaped
fastigiate—parallel, erect and clustered

fastuosus—bountiful
ferox—very thorny
fertilis—fruitful
ferus—bearing
filamentosus—threadlike
flavus—yellow
flexosus—zigzagging
floribundus—flowering abundantly
florus—flower
folium—leaf
forma minor—dwarf form
fruticosus—bushy
fulvus—tawny orange

giganteus—larger than usual type
glabrus—smooth
gracilis—slender, graceful
gramineus—grasslike
grandis—large
guttatus—spotted

heterocyclus—having unequal round joints
hibernalis—of winter
hirsutus—hairy
hispidus—bristly
holochrysus—entirely yellow
hortensis—of the garden
humilis—low-growing

imbricans—overlapping
incisus—cut
inermis—thornless
intermedius—between two forms
inversus—opposite to
involucratus—a group of small leaves or bracts

japonicus—of Japan

kurilensis—of the Kurile islands

labiatus—lipped
lactatus—milky
laevis—smooth
lanatus—woolly
lanceus—pointed
latus—broad
linearis—narrow

lineatus—striped
lobus—lobe
longus—long
lucidus—bright
luteus—yellow

macro—large
macrospermus—bearing long seeds
marginatus—with margins
maritimus—of the sea or shore
marmoreus—marblelike
metallicus—with metallike luster
micro—small
microcarpus—bearing small fruit
minimus—very small
minor—small
mitis—defenseless, without spines
mollis—soft
montanus—of mountainous regions
mucronatus—sharp-tipped
mutatus—changed

nanus—dwarf
nebulosus—clouded
niger—black
nipponicus—of Japan
nitidus—shining, smooth
nivalis—growing near snow
nobilis—noble, stately
nocturnus—of night
normalis—according to type
nudus—bare

occidentalis—western
oceanicus—of the sea
odorus—fragrant
officinalis—medicinal
oides—like
oleraceus—of the vegetable garden
orientalis—eastern
ornatus—showy

pachy—thick
palmatus—divided or lobed
paniculatus—having tufts of flowers
parcus—small
patens—spreading

pedatus–foot
pedunculatus–stalked
perennis–perennial
petalus–petal
phyllus–leaf
pictus–variegated
pineus–of pines
pinnatus–with leaflets on the side of the main axis
planus–flat
platy–broad
plumosus–feathery
praecox–very early
puberulus–somewhat downy
pubescens–covered with hair or downy
pulcher–handsome
pumilus–dwarfish
punctatus–spotted, dotted
pungens–sharp-pointed, pungent
purpurascens–becoming purple
purpureus–purple

quadrangularis–four-cornered

racemosus–in the form of a raceme
radicans–rooting along stem
ramosus–having many branches
repens–creeping
reticulatus–netted
riparius–of riverbanks
roseus–rosy
rubrus–red
rugosus–wrinkled
ruscifolius–resembling butcher's broom

sanguinalis–blood red
sarmentosus–with runners
saxatilis–of rocks
scandens–climbing
semper–always
serratus–saw-toothed
sessilis–stalkless
silvestris–of the woods
simplex–unbranched
spathiflorus–bearing a flower or flowers in a bract
spicatus–bearing flower spikes
spiculosus–bearing small spikes
spinosus–with many spines

splendens—showy
stoloniferus—producing rooting runners
strepto—twisted
striatus—marked with fine lines or grooves
sub—somewhat
suffruticosus—shrublike
sulphureus—sulphur-colored, yellow

tardus—late
tectus—rooflike
terminalis—at stem end
tristis—dull

ulus—somewhat
umbellatus—with clusters of flowers from a common point

vagans—wandering
vaginatus—sheathlike
vegetus—vigorous
vernalis—of spring
violaceus—violet
violescens—becoming violet
virdiglaucescens—bluish green
virdistriatus—scored or striped with green
virens—greenish
viridus—green
viscosus—sticky
vittatus—striped longitudinally
vulgaris—common

xanthinus—yellow

zonatus—banded

Further Reading

The following is a brief list of more specialized books for the curious. Those preceded by an asterisk are fairly technical in nature, and it is helpful to have had some college-level physics and chemistry to aid in plowing through them. The others are much less technical in nature and just as interesting.

BAILEY, L. H. and ETHEL ZOE. *Hortus Second: A Concise Dictionary of Gardening, General Horticulture and Cultivated Plants in North America.* New York: The Macmillan Co., 1941.

CHIDAMIAN, CLAUDE. *The Book of Cacti and Other Succulents.* Garden City, New York: Doubleday & Co., Inc., 1958.

DARWIN, CHARLES. *The Power of Movement in Plants.* New York: D. Appleton & Co., 1881 (Da Capo reprint ed.).

DE WIT, H. C. D. *Plants of the World.* 3 vols. New York: E. P. Dutton & Co., Inc., 1966.

DODSON, CALAWAY H., and ROBERT J. GILLESPIE. *The Biology of Orchids.* Nashville: The Mid-American Orchid Congress, Inc., 1967.

ELBERT, GEORGE A. *The Indoor Light Gardening Book.* New York: Crown Publishers, 1973.

ESAU, KATHERINE. *Anatomy of Seed Plants.* New York: John Wiley & Sons, Inc., 1960.

FAEGRI, K., and L. VAN DER PIJL. *The Principles of Pollination Ecology.* 2nd rev. ed. Braunschweig, Germany: Pergamon Press, 1971.

FOSTER, GORDON F. *The Gardener's Fern Book.* Princeton: D. Van Nostrand Co., Inc., 1964.

FREE, MONTAGUE. *All About African Violets.* Garden City, New York: American Garden Guild/Doubleday & Co., 1949.

GRAF, ALFRED BYRD. *Exotica Series 3: A Pictorial Cyclopedia of Exotic Plants from Tropical and Near-tropic Regions.* 6th ed. E. Rutherford, New Jersey: Roehrs Co., Inc., 1973.

HARTMANN, HUDSON T., and DALE E. KESTER. *Plant Propagation.* 2nd ed. Englewood Cliffs, New Jersey: Prentice-Hall, 1968.

JANICK, JULES. *Horticultural Science.* 2nd ed. San Francisco: W. H. Freeman & Co., 1972.

JENSEN, WILLIAM A., and FRANK B. SALISBURY. *Botany: An Ecological Approach.* Belmont, California: Wadsworth Publishing Co., Inc., 1972.

KRANZ, FREDERICK H. and JACQUELINE L. *Gardening Indoors Under Lights.* Rev. ed. New York: The Viking Press, 1971.

LAWSON, ALEXANDER HIGH. *Bamboos.* New York: Taplinger Publishing Co., 1968.

°MAYER, A. M., and A. POLJAKOFF-MAYBER. *The Germination of Seeds.* New York: Pergamon Press, 1963.

MCCURRACH, JAMES C. *Palms of the World.* New York: Harper & Brothers, 1960.

NORTHEN, REBECCA T. *Home Orchid Growing.* 3rd rev. ed. New York: Van Nostrand Reinhold Co., 1970

PIEROT, SUZANNE W. *The Ivy Book.* New York: Macmillan Publishing Co., 1974.

PINNEY, MARGARET E. *The Miniature Rose Book.* Princeton: D. Van Nostrand Co., Inc., 1964.

°RUTTER, A. J., ed. *The Water Relation of Plants.* New York: John Wiley & Sons, Inc., 1963.

°SALISBURY, FRANK B. *The Biology of Flowering.* Garden City, New York: The Natural History Press, 1971.

SCHWARTZ, RANDALL. *Carnivorous Plants.* New York: Praeger Publishers, 1974.

°SOLBRIG, OTTO T. *Principles and Methods of Plant Biosystematics.* London: Collier-Macmillan, Ltd., 1970.

VAN DER PIJL, L., and CALAWAY H. DODSON. *Orchid Flowers: Their Pollination and Evolution.* Coral Gables, Florida: University of Miami Press, 1966.

VAN NESS, MARTHA. *Cacti and Succulents Indoors and Outdoors.* New York: Van Nostrand Reinhold Co., 1971.

°WENT, FRITS W. *The Experimental Control of Plant Growth.* New York: The Ronald Press Co., 1957.

°WILKINS, MALCOLM B., ed. *The Physiology of Plant Growth and Development.* New York: McGraw-Hill, 1969.

WILSON, HELEN VAN PELT. *The Joy of Geraniums.* New York: William Morrow & Co., 1972.

WITHNER, CARL L., ed. *The Orchids: A Scientific Survey.* New York: The Ronald Press Co., 1959.

Plant Societies

If you become particularly enamored of one special group of plants, joining a society will put you in touch with people of like mind. Most societies also publish a journal of special-interest topics that keeps you up-to-date and usually offers hard-to-get items through the advertisers. Perhaps the most professional magazine of the lot, and certainly the most mouth-watering with its lavish display of color photographs, is the *American Orchid Society Bulletin*.

Since these societies are nonprofit services usually staffed by dedicated nonpaid plant lovers, it's always a good idea to include a couple of stamps for return postage when making inquiries.

African Violet Society of America
P.O. Box 1326
Knoxville, Tennessee 37901
   Publishes monthly magazine

American Begonia Society
10331 South Colima Road
Whittier, California 90604
   Publishes monthly magazine

American Fern Society
Department of Botany
University of Tennessee
Knoxville, Tennessee 37916
    Publishes quarterly journal

American Gesneria Society
Box 91192
Worldway Postal Center
Los Angeles, California 90009
    Publishes bimonthly magazine

American Gloxinia and Gesneriad Society
Mrs. Charlotte Rowe, Membership Secretary
P.O. Box 174
New Milford, Connecticut 06776
    Publishes bimonthly magazine

The American Ivy Society
128 West 58th Street
New York, New York 10019
    Publishes newsletter

American Orchid Society
Botanical Museum of Harvard University
Cambridge, Massachusetts 02138
    Publishes monthly magazine

The Bromeliad Society
6153 Hayter Avenue
Lakewood, California 90712
    Publishes bimonthly magazine

Cactus and Succulent Society of America
Box 167
Reseda, California 91335
    Publishes bimonthly magazine

Indoor Light Gardening Society of America
1316 Warren Road
Lakewood, Ohio 44107
    Publishes bimonthly magazine

International Geranium Society
Mr. Arthur Thiede
11960 Pascal Avenue
Colton, California 92324
    Publishes quarterly magazine

Los Angeles International Fern Society
13715 Corday Avenue
Hawthorne, California 90250
    Publishes monthly sheet of fern lessons

The Palm Society
Mrs. T.C. Buhler, Secretary
1320 South Venetian Way
Miami, Florida 33139
    Publishes quarterly magazine

Saintpaulia International
P.O. Box 549
Knoxville, Tennessee 37901
    Copublishes monthly magazine with American Gesneriad Society

Additionally there are several good magazines, not affiliated with societies, that deal primarily with indoor plants. These include:

The Avant Gardener
P.O. Box 489
New York, New York 10028

The Orchid Digest
Mrs. Donald D. Dirks, Secretary
1429 Graffigna Avenue
Lodi, California 95240

Plants Alive
2100 North 45th
Seattle, Washington 98103

Plant and Equipment Sources

The suppliers listed below will be able to fulfill your indoor gardening wishes. If a self-addressed stamped envelope is requested, it's best to use the long business size. All companies listed will send a catalog and/or price list.

Alberts & Merkle, Inc.
2210 South Federal Highway
Boynton Beach, Florida 33435

Tropical plants. Large mimeographed catalog 50¢

Allgrove, Arthur Eames
North Wilmington, Massachusetts 01887

Terrarium supplies

Armacost & Royston, Inc.
11920 La Grange Avenue
P.O. Box 25576
West Los Angeles, California

Orchids and some ferns

Armstrong Associates
Box 127
Basking Ridge, New Jersey 07920

Carnivorous plants

Beahm Gardens
2686 Paloma Street
Pasadena, California 91107

Epiphyllums. Send stamp for catalog

The Beall Co. Vashon Island, Washington 98070	Orchid hybrids
Black Copper Kits 266 Kipp Street Hackensack, New Jersey 07601	Carnivorous plants
Black River Orchids P.O. Box 110 South Haven, Michigan 49090	Orchid species
Buell's Greenhouse Eastford, Connecticut 06242	African violets and other gesneriads. Send 25¢ and self-addressed stamped envelope
W. Atlee Burpee Co. Philadelphia, Pennsylvania 19132	Outdoor plants primarily, but some houseplants and seeds
Carobil Farms Church Road Brunswick, Maine 04011	Pelargoniums and fuchsias
Channelview Nurseries 16501 Market Street Road Channelview, Texas 77530	Bromeliads. Send self-addressed stamped envelope
Chester Hills Orchids RD #2 Catfish Lane Pottstown, Pennsylvania 19464	Orchid species and hybrids
Coastal Gardens 137 Tropical Lane Corpus Christi, Texas 78408	Orchid seedlings
Cooks Geranium Nursery Lyons, Kansas 67554	Pelargoniums
Davis Cactus Garden 1522 Jefferson Street Kerrville, Texas 78028	Cacti, large selection. Catalog 50¢
Clark Day, Jr. 19311 South Bloomfield Cerritos, California 90701	Orchids
de Jager's 188 Asbury Street South Hamilton, Massachusetts 01982	Bulbs
De Sylva Seed Co. 21994 Tanager Street Colton, California 92324	Exotic seeds

Edelweiss Gardens
Box 66H
Robbinsville, New Jersey 08691

Begonias, bromeliads, ferns, and other tropicals. Catalog 35¢

Environment One Corp.
2773 Balltown Road
Schenectady, New York 12309

Forced CO_2, controlled light terrariums

John Ewing Orchids
P.O. Box 613
Chatsworth, California 91311

Phalaenopsis novelties

Fennel Orchid Co.
26715 S.W. 157th Avenue
Homestead, Florida 33030

Orchids and supplies

Fink Floral Co.
9849 Kimker Lane
St. Louis, Missouri 63127

Orchids

Fisher Greenhouses
Linwood, New Jersey 08221

African violets. Extensive supply catalog 25¢

Floralite Co.
4124 East Oakwood Road
Oak Creek, Wisconsin 53154

Plant light supplies

Fox Orchids
6615 West Markham
Little Rock, Arkansas 72205

Orchids and supplies, including those for making corsages

G & S Laboratories
645 Stoddard Lane
Santa Barbara, California 93103

Meristemming and embryo culture supplies

Green Hills Nursery
2131 Vallejo Street
St. Helena, California 94574

Ferns primarily

Greenland Flower Shop
Wholesale Division
Route 1
Port Matilda, Pennsylvania 16870

Basic houseplants

Bernard D. Greeson
Horticultural Supplies
3548 North Cramer Street
Milwaukee, Wisconsin 53211

Supplies and growing aids. Catalog 25¢

Growers Supply Co.
33 North Staebler Road
P.O. Box 1132
Ann Arbor, Michigan 48106

Lights and display stands

Herb Hager Orchids
Box 544
Santa Cruz, California 95060

Phalaenopsis primarily

Happy Greenhouses
Box 793
Union, New Jersey 07083

Basic small houseplants

Hausermann's Orchids, Inc.
P.O. Box 363
Elmhurst, Illinois 60128

Orchid species. Beautiful color catalog $1.00

House of Orchids
10 Bailey Avenue
Oakland, New Jersey 07436

Anthuriums and orchids

The House Plant Corner
P.O. Box 810
Oxford, Maryland 21654

Supplies. Extensive list 25¢

Spencer M. Howard
Orchid Imports
11802 Huston Street
North Hollywood, California 91607

Orchid species

J. L. Hudson, Seedsman
P.O. Box 1058
Redwood City, California 94064

Hard-to-get seeds, some for houseplants. Large list 50¢

Hurov's Tropical Tree Nursery
Box 10387
Oahu, Honolulu, Hawaii 96816

Tropical seeds. Extensive list of hard-to-get varieties

Margaret Ilgenfritz Orchids
End of Blossom Lane
Box 665
Monroe, Michigan 48161

Orchid species, extensive collection. Color catalog $2.00

Jones & Scully Orchids
2200 N.W. 33rd Avenue
Miami, Florida 33142

Color catalog $3.00

K & L Cactus Nursery
12712 Stockton Boulevard
Galt, California 95632

Cacti. Illustrated catalog 50¢

Kartuz Greenhouses
92 Chestnut Street
Wilmington, Massachusetts 01887

Gesneriads, begonias, succulents, and other exotics. Catalog 50¢

Kensington Orchids, Inc.
3301 Plyers Mill Road
Kensington, Maryland 20795

Orchids and supplies

Wm. Kirch Orchids, Ltd. *2630 Waiomao Road* *Honolulu, Hawaii 96816*	Orchid hybrids
Lager & Hurrell *426 Morris Avenue* *Summit, New Jersey 07901*	Orchids. Catalog $2.00
Lauray of Salisbury *Undermountain Road (Route 41)* *Salisbury, Connecticut 06068*	Gesneriads, succulents, begonias, and exotics. Catalog 50¢
Lehua Anthurium Nursery *80 Kokea Street* *Hilo, Hawaii 96720*	Exotics
Lilly's Garden *510 South Fulton Avenue* *Mt. Vernon, N.Y. 10550*	Pots & supplies
Logee's Greenhouses *Danielson, Connecticut 06239*	Begonias, pelargoniums, ferns, and exotics. Extensive illustrated catalog $1.00
Paul P. Lowe *23045 S.W. 123rd Road* *Goulds, Florida 33170*	Begonias and bromeliads. Price list 10¢
Loyce's Flowers *Route 2* *Granbury, Texas 76048*	Hoyas and other exotics
McClain's Orchid Range *6237 Blanding Boulevard* *Jacksonville, Florida 32210*	Cymbidiums and other orchids. Color catalog $1.00
Merry Gardens *Camden, Maine 04843*	Exotics. Price list 25¢
Mini-Roses *P.O. Box 4255, Station A.* *Dallas, Texas 75208*	Miniature roses
Nature's Way Products *3505 Mozart Avenue* *Cincinnati, Ohio 45211*	Soil and organic fertilizer. Self-addressed stamped envelope for price list
Walter F. Nicke *Box 71* *Hudson, New York 12534*	Supplies, extensive list of unusuals. Catalog 25¢

Nor'east Miniature Roses *58 Hammond Street* *Box H* *Rowley, Massachusetts 01969*	Miniature roses
Norvell Greenhouses *318 South Greenacres Road* *Greenacres, Washington 99016*	Gesneriads, begonias, and exotics, very large selection. Catalog $1.00
Oakhill Gardens *Route 3* *Box 87* *Dallas, Oregon 97338*	Sedums and sempervivums, large selection. List 10¢
Orinda Nursery *Bridgeville, Delaware 19933*	Camellias
Pacific Bamboo Gardens *P.O. Box 16145* *San Diego, California 92116*	Bamboos, very large selection. Catalog 50¢
George W. Park Seed Co., Inc. *Greenwood, South Carolina 29646*	Houseplants and seeds, supplies
Peter Pauls Nurseries *Darcy Road* *Canandaigua, New York 14424*	Carnivorous plants. Catalog 25¢
Penn Valley Orchids *239 Old Gulph Road* *Wynnewood, Pennsylvania 19056*	Paphiopedilums primarily
Robert B. Peters Co. *2833 Pennsylvania Street* *Allentown, Pennsylvania 18104*	Chemical fertilizers
Pixie Treasures Miniature Roses *4121 Prospect Avenue* *Yorba Linda, California 92686*	Miniature roses
Plantsmith *P.O. Box 2224* *Menlo Park, California 94025*	Chemical fertilizers
Royal Dutch Gardens *#3 Eliot Hills Road* *South Natick, Massachusetts 01760*	Bulbs and tropicals
Santa Barbara Orchid Estates *1250 Orchid Drive* *Santa Barbara, California 93111*	Cymbidiums and paphiopedilums

John Scheepers, Inc.   Bulbs
63 Wall Street
New York, New York 10005

Shoplite Co., Inc.   Plant lights and equipment.
650 Franklin Avenue   Catalog 25¢
Nutley, New Jersey 07110

Fred A. Stewart Orchids   Phalaenopsis and other
1212 East Las Tunas Drive   orchids
San Gabriel, California 91778

Sun Face Products   Pots
Box 87
Cambridge Springs, Pennsylvania 16403

Talnadge's Fern Gardens   Bromeliads (no ferns)
354 "G" Street
Chula Vista, California 92010

Tinari Greenhouses   African violets. Catalog 25¢
2325 Valley Road
Huntington Valley, Pennsylvania 19006

Trader Horn   Palms, cycads, and basic
Box 381675   houseplants
Miami, Florida 33138

Van Bourgondien's   Bulbs
P.O. Box A
245 Farmingdale Road, Route 109
Babylon, New York 11702

West Coast Orchids   Orchids
4905 Cherryvale Avenue
Soquel, California 95073

Westover Greenhouse   Fuchsias
1317 North 175th Street
Seattle, Washington 98133

Index

fertilizer salts, 248, 257
ficus, air layering of, *305*
Ficus elastica, 155
F. pumila, 191
fiery costus (*Costus igneus*), 172
finger aralia (*Dizygotheca elegantissima*), 152-153, *153*
firecracker plant (*Manettia inflata*), *184*, 185
first-aid plant (*Aloe vera*), 219
fish-pole bamboo (*Phyllostachys aurea*), 168, *169*
fishtail palm (*Caryota mitis*), 6, 10
flame nettle (*Coleus blumei*), 222-223
flame violet (*Episcia reptans*), 181
flaming dragon tree (*Cordyline terminalis*), 223
flamingo anthurium (*Anthurium andraeanum*), 219-220
floppers (*Kalanchoë pinnata*), 225-226, *225*
florist's cyclamen (*Cyclamen persicum* 'Giganteum'), 223, *224*
flowering maple (*Abutilon* hybrids), 217-218
flowering seasons:
    of fragrant plants, 37, 38, 39, 41, 43
    light as factor in, 36, 37, 39, 46-47
    of nocturnal flowers, 50, 51, 53, 54
    of orchids, 64, 65, 66, 68, 69, 70, 71
    temperature as factor in, 271
fluorescent light, 266-268
    for African violets, 74
    for cacti, 115, 129
    for cuttings, 296
    durability of fixtures, 268
    incandescent combined with, 267
    number to use, 267
    for orchids, 64, 70
    for palms, 9, 47
    for pelargoniums, 95
    for rose miniatures, 105
    for seedlings, 310
    special plant, 105, 115, 129, 267
    vertical placing of, 268, *269*
    see also light, artificial
foliage plants, 149-161, 217
    air conditioning and, 151, 154, 158, 160
    hardiness of, 149, 150, 152
    hybridization of, 158
    light for, 149, 151-152, 154, 155, 156, 158, 160, 161
    origins of, 152, 155
    pots/potting for, 153, 156
    propagation of, 150, 152, 153, 159
    water for, 150, 152, 155, 156, 160
    water culture of, 150
foliar feeding:
    with chelated iron, 257
    for leaf shininess, prohibited, 258
forcing:
    of bulbs, 205, 208-209, 210-211
    in buying of plants, 238

of orchids, 59, 61, 71
types of plants for, 258
fountain bush (*Russelia equisetiformis*), 185
foxglove gloxinia (*Rehmannia angulata*), 83
foxtails (*Acalypha hispida*), 218, *218*
fragrant olive (*Osmanthus fragrans*), 44
fragrant plants, 33-44
    flowering and growing seasons of, 37, 38, 39, 41, 43
    herbs, 34, 37
    nocturnal, 50, 51, 52, 53, 54
    oils in, 34, 35, 40
    outdoor cultivation of, 38, 39, 51, 52
    perfume-producing glands (osmophores) in, 33-34, 35, 40
    pollinators of, 34, 35, 42-43, 44
    propagation of, 37, 39, 40, 44
Freesia hybrids, 233
French Roman hyacinth, 205
French zonals, 90
Fuchsia hybrids, 233
fungi, 22, 59, 268
    anthracnose, 276, *277*
    botrytis, 276, *277*
    cures for, 276-279
    damping off, 276, *277*, 308
    fungicides for, 278, 284
    powdery mildew, *277*, 278
    spread by insects, 278
    types of, 276-279

Gardenia jasminoides, 233
Garner, W. W., 46
genetics, 90-91
geraniums:
    geographic origins of, 87-88
    hybridization of, 87
German ivy (*Senecio mikanioides*), 194
germination, *see* seed propagation
gesneriads, 73-86
    Achimenes flava, 80
    cuttings of, 80, 81
    feeding of, 79, 80, 83, 84
    flowering season of, 80, 81, 82, 83, 84, 85
    geographic origins of, 81, 82, 84
    humidity for, 79, 80, 83, 85
    Hypocyrta nummularia, 80-81
    H. wettsteinii, 80
    Kohleria 'Amabilis' (*Isoloma ceciliae*), 81
    K. strigosa, 81
    light for, 74, 78, 79, 83
    Nautilocalyx lynchii, 81
    outdoor cultivation of, 82, 83
    Petrocosmea kerii, 81-82
    potting of, 80
    propagation of, 80, 81, 84, 85, 86, 296
    pruning of, 81, 83
    Ramonda myconii, 82
    Rechsteineria cardinalis, 82
    R. leuchotricha, 83
    R. various, 82-83